DAVID FOSKETT
PATRICIA PASKINS
STEVE THORPE
JOHN CAMPBELL

PRACTICAL COOKERY

FOR THE LEVEL 1 DIPLOMA

D1581278

HODDER
EDUCATION

Orders: please contact Bookpoint Ltd, 130 Milton Park, Abingdon, Oxon OX14 4SB. Telephone: (44) 01235 827720. Fax: (44) 01235 400454. Lines are open from 9.00 to 5.00, Monday to Saturday, with a 24-hour message answering service. You can also order through our website www.hoddereducation.co.uk

If you have any comments to make about this, or any of our other titles, please send them to educationenquiries@hodder.co.uk

British Library Cataloguing in Publication Data

A catalogue record for this title is available from the British Library

ISBN: 978 1 444 18749 6

First edition published as *Foundation Practical Cookery*, 2009.

This edition published 2013.

Impression number   10 9 8 7 6 5 4 3 2 1

Year   2013, 2014, 2015, 2016, 2017

Copyright © 2013 David Foskett, Patricia Paskins, Steve Thorpe, John Campbell

Hachette UK's policy is to use papers that are natural, renewable and recyclable products and made from wood grown in sustainable forests. The logging and manufacturing processes are expected to conform to the environmental regulations of the country of origin.

Typeset by Aptara, Inc.

Printed in Italy for Hodder Education, an Hachette UK Company, 338 Euston Road, London NW1 3BH.

Contents

How to use this book

Practical Cookery for the Level 1 Diploma has been written to cover everything you need for the Level 1 Diploma in Introduction to Professional Cookery. The book is divided into 12 chapters, each covering one of the 12 units that make up the Diploma qualification.

You will find the following features in the book:

Ingredients lists for making smaller and larger quantities.

All the preparation you need to do.

Step-by-step photos of how key dishes are made.

Professional tips from the workplace, connecting theory to real life.

Safety boxes, with the food safety and H&S tips you can't afford to miss.

Deep frying and shallow frying

Recipe 3 Fish cakes

Ingredients	4 portions	10 portions
Cooked white fish and/or salmon	200 g	500 g
Potato, mashed	200 g	500 g
Eggs, beaten	1	2
Flour	25 g	60 g
Fresh white breadcrumbs	50 g	125 g

Get ready to cook

1 Prepare, clean, wash and thoroughly dry the fish, then poach it.
2 Prepare the mashed potato.
3 Beat the eggs.

Cooking

1 Combine the fish and potatoes. Taste and correct the seasoning.

2 Using a little flour, form the mixture into a long roll on a clean work surface.

3 Divide the mixture into two or four pieces per portion.

4 Mould each piece into a ball.

Practical Cookery for the Level 1 Diploma

(218)

Deep frying and shallow frying

- Eggs
- Fruit
- Flour-based products (sweet and savoury)
- Ready-made products.

Frying mediums

The same fats and oils are used as in deep frying.

If shallow-fried food needs to be cooked in butter, you should use clarified butter, which has a higher burning point than unclarified butter, so it will not burn as easily. To clarify butter, melt it and then carefully strain off the fat, leaving behind the clear liquid.

Points to consider when shallow frying

- When shallow frying continuously over a busy period, prepare and cook the food in a systematic way.
- Cleaning the pans after every use, even in batch cooking, will ensure the best presentation.
- Food should be dry to ensure that it fries correctly and that oil/fat is not spat out of the pan towards the chef.
- Food items should be placed in the pan presentation side down first so that turning once will help enhance presentation of the finished dish.

Temperature and time control are particularly important as all shallow-fried foods should have an appetising golden-brown colour on both sides. The temperature should initially be hot; the heat should then be reduced and the food turned when necessary.

Methods

There are four methods of shallow frying:

- **To shallow fry** (meunière), cook the food in a small amount of fat or oil in a frying pan or sauté pan. Fry the presentation side of the food first (the side that will be seen when it is on the

Professional tip

Some of the frying medium (oil or butter) will be absorbed by the food, which will change its nutritional content (in other words, will make it more fatty). Protect items from absorbing the fat in which they are cooked by applying a coating.

(!) Health and safety

Add food to the pan carefully, away from you, to avoid being splashed by hot fat. Always keep your sleeves rolled down to prevent splashing fat from burning your forearm.

In the recipes, the main methods of cookery are shown by icons. So if you want to practise shallow frying, look for that icon. They look like this:

Boiling

Baking

Steaming

Roasting

Poaching

Shallow frying

Stewing or casseroling

Deep frying

Grilling

Braising

Using the QR codes

There are free videos and recipes on the website. Look out for the QR codes throughout the book. They look like this.

To use the QR codes to view the videos you will need a QR code reader for your smartphone/tablet. There are many free readers available, depending on the smartphone/tablet you are using. We have supplied some suggestions below, but this is not an exhaustive list and you should only download software compatible with your device and operating system. We do not endorse any of the third-party products listed below and downloading them is at your own risk.

- for iPhone/iPad, Qrafter – http://itunes.apple.com/app/qrafter-qr-code-reader-generator/id416098700
- for Android, QR Droid – https://market.android.com/details?id=la.droid.qr&hl=en
- for Blackberry, QR Scanner Pro – http://appworld.blackberry.com/webstore/content/13962
- for Windows/Symbian, Upcode – http://www.upc.fi/en/upcode/download/

Once you have downloaded a QR code reader, simply open the reader app and use it to take a photo of the code. The video will then load on your smartphone/tablet.

If you cannot read the QR code or you are using a computer, the web link next to the code will take you directly to the same video.

The terms and conditions which govern these free online resources may be seen at http://bit.ly/yfVC0P

Acknowledgements

We are most grateful to Booker Group plc, in particular Ron Hickey, Niall Brannigan and Stuart Hyslop, for their support in the development of the book, including the provision of much of the food shown in the photographs.

We are also very grateful to Watts Farms for providing some of the fruit and vegetables used in the photographs.

Steve Thorpe thanks his colleagues at City College for sharing and discussing.

We would also like to thank the publishing team at Hodder, particularly Gemma Parsons for her market research and guidance and Debbie Noble for her editorial excellence and support.

Photography

Most of the photos in this book are by Andrew Callaghan of Callaghan Studios. The photography work could not have been done without the generous help of the authors and their colleagues and students at the University of West London (UWL). The publishers would particularly like to acknowledge the following for their work.

John Campbell, Olly Rouse and Gary Farrelly organised the cookery. They were assisted in the kitchen by:

- Sapphira Greenyer
- Ryan Hester
- Omar Khan
- James Knowles
- Tarkan Nevzat
- Elizabeth Rose.

The authors and publishers are grateful to everyone involved for their hard work.

Picture credits

Every effort has been made to trace the copyright holders of material reproduced here. The authors and publishers would like to thank the following for permission to reproduce copyright illustrations.

Page 3 top © omicron – Fotolia, bottom © Bananastock/Photolibrary Group Ltd/Getty Images; page 4 © Stockbyte/Getty Images Ltd; page 5 top © Silke Wolff – Fotolia.com, bottom © Monkey Business – Fotolia.com; page 7 Compass; page 21 Booker Group; page 24 © AVAVA – Fotolia; page 25 left © clearviewstock – Fotolia, right © James Steidl – Fotolia; page 26 top, the photo by Eric Erbe; digital colorization by Christopher Pooley/material produced by ARS, is in the public

Foreword

One of the first books that I used as a student was *Practical Cookery*, and I use my copy to help write recipes, even today! At the heart of it all is a strong partnership with industry, that ensures the book reflects modern practice and will help you prepare for your career, just as it did with mine. So it is with great excitement that I write the foreword for this exciting new *Practical Cookery* Level 1 title by David Foskett and his dedicated team for students passionate about the industry. The book combines essential elements, carefully selected recipes, and professional photographs that clearly illustrate step-by-step procedures as well as useful shots of the finished product, topped off with expertise from these professional chefs.

My career as a professional chef started at the age of 16 when I began my formal training at Scarborough Technical College and won the Student of the Year award three years running, after which Anthony Worrall Thompson gave me the fantastic opportunity to work in London in the kitchens of 190 Queensgate, followed by dell'Ugo. I then continued to work in London and France in Michelin star rated restaurants and at the age of 21, I opened the Hotel and Bistro du Vin in Winchester as Head Chef, where I changed the menu every day!

Since my days at Scarborough, I have been able to open restaurants, write a number of my own cookery books, and also venture into television, something which I very much enjoy as part of my job. Despite the industry giving me so many great opportunities, food has remained at the heart of it! I would not have been able to achieve all of this without a firm understanding of the basics. Basic skills and recipes are fundamental because they provide the framework for a successful career in professional cookery. *Practical Cookery* provides an invaluable foundation of professional skills and knowledge, balancing the traditional with the modern and I am sure this new *Practical Cookery* title will be of invaluable use to you in your training.

James Martin

Booker Group PLC
Choice up, price down, better service

Booker Wholesale

The UK's leading food and drink wholesaler, supplying to over 338,000 independent chefs and caterers in the food industry.

We offer a huge range of foods from the best fresh meat and produce through to a large variety of dry goods and ingredients. Customers can also choose from our exclusive own brands to provide a choice of products and price points that suits each chefs' business. Customers can also order via the web and we deliver free of charge.

We provide excellent quality for outstanding value; with everyday low prices that are locked down throughout the season so customers can trust the cost price will not increase.

The price you see is the price you pay!

Ritter-Courivaud

The leading food distributors to the UK's fine dining sector since 1929.

Our vast product range includes top quality lines from around the world, from caviar and affinés cheese, to fresh mushrooms, truffles and charcuterie including an extensive range of Sardinian salciccia and a vast variety of patisserie ingredients for the discerning patissier.

We are committed to sourcing the finest and most original products to provide our chefs with everything they need to build and sustain a successful and profitable business.

Chef Direct

The new force in UK foodservice, created to cater for the specific needs of multi-site foodservice operators looking for more choice. Customers will benefit from Booker's scale, as the UK's largest food wholesaler, combined with our award-winning logistics capability.

Chef Direct offers restaurant and catering chains a customised solution, combining great product choice with good prices and excellent service. Customers can access an unparalleled range of both own-label and branded products, plus bespoke product ranging to meet any business's specific operational needs.

Just visit **www.booker.co.uk** to find your nearest branch, more information on all our services, or to quickly and simply order online!

The catering and hospitality industry

This chapter covers Unit 101, Investigate the catering and hospitality industry.

By the end of this chapter you should be able to:

- Explain the meaning of hospitality
- Explain the meaning of catering
- Describe the hospitality and catering industry structure and sectors
- List the different types of hospitality and catering operations
- Identify the different establishments within the commercial and service sectors
- Describe the main features of the hospitality and catering establishments

- Identify the staffing structures for the different types of catering establishments
- List the main job roles in catering establishments
- List the types of qualifications available in the hospitality industry and catering sector
- Identify the training and experience available in the hospitality and catering sector
- List the employment rights and responsibilities
- Identify associations related to professional cookery.

Hospitality and catering

What does hospitality mean?

Hospitality means to be hospitable, to look after people by providing services such as food, drink and accommodation. This could be, for example, bedrooms and meeting rooms in hotels. In some cases hospitality will also cover entertainment.

What does catering mean?

Catering means the provision of food and drink.

The hospitality and catering industry structure, sectors and operations

The hospitality industry is one of the largest industries in the UK. It is one of the largest employers (employing nearly two million people) and continues to grow. Therefore there are lots of opportunities to work in hospitality and catering and it provides excellent opportunities for employment, education and training. Every operation is different and creates different opportunities and challenges.

The industry can be divided into two sectors: the **commercial** sector and **public service** sector.

The commercial sector

In the commercial sector providing hospitality and catering is the main purpose of the organisation.

The commercial sector is made up of the following different types of establishments:

Table 1.1 Types of commercial establishment

Establishment	Operations
Hotels, lodges and guest houses	Accommodation and catering
Restaurants	Catering
Cafés and fast food outlets	Catering
Pubs, bars and nightclubs	Catering
Casinos and gambling	Catering
Visitor attractions and tourist services (e.g. museums, theme parks and cinemas)	Catering
Hostels	Accommodation and sometimes catering
Travel (e.g. airlines, railways and cruise ships)	Catering and sometimes accommodation
Events (e.g. sports tournaments and weddings)	Catering
Corporate hospitality	Catering
Contract	Catering and sometimes accommodation

The public service sector

The public service sector is also known as the cost sector or the food services sector. In this sector the provision of hospitality is not the main purpose of the company. Often the hospitality is provided by a different company. For example, a bank, whose main purpose is financial services, may have their catering and hospitality provided by a contractor.

Whether the catering is provided by a contractor or is an in-house service, it will still be required to operate at a profit or a surplus.

The public sector refers to the following types of establishments:

Table 1.2 Types of public service sector establishment

Establishments	Operations within the sector
Hospitals and residential care homes (nursing homes)	Catering and accommodation
Prisons	Catering and accommodation
Armed forces	Catering and accommodation
School meals	Catering (the provision of food mainly, limited beverages)
College refectory	Catering
Industrial catering	Catering and, in some cases, accommodation

Features of establishments within the commercial and public service sectors

Hotels

The main purpose of a hotel is to provide accommodation. Some hotels also provide meeting space, spa and leisure facilities, and function facilities. All hotels will provide food and drink, except perhaps budget hotels.

Hotels include:
- Guest houses – bed and breakfast accommodation
- Budget hotels (e.g. Travel Lodge, Premier Inn). These hotels sell bedrooms at cheaper rates than many other hotels.
- One star
- Two star
- Three star
- Four star
- Luxury hotels (e.g. five star)
- Large hotel chains (e.g. Hilton, Intercontinental, Radisson Edwardian, Mandarin Oriental, Sheraton)

▲ Hotel

Most hotels operate 24 hours a day, 365 days a year, with the exception of seasonal hotels that close during quieter periods. Hotels in holiday resorts, for example, often only open from May to October and close in the winter.

The ways in which hotels operate differs from location to location and according to the hotel's style of star rating. Hotels have to match their products and services to their customers' expectations. Different pricing policies are set depending on the types of customers the hotel is serving and the furniture and fittings in hotels differ again according to the star rating. For example, a luxury hotel will be lavish and more expensive than a business hotel, which will be functional and often streamlined. All hotels need to provide a safe, comfortable, pleasurable, secure and clean environment that is value for money.

There are many opportunities for employment in hotels. Hotels require chefs, waiters, receptionists, restaurant supervisors, general managers and housekeepers. They also have information technology specialists, a marketing manager, accounts managers, event and banqueting staff, general managers and maintenance engineers to name a few roles.

Restaurants

There are over 65,000 restaurants in the UK, offering a range of styles and cuisines, including European, Chinese, Japanese, Indian, Mexican, Lebanese and Caribbean to name a few.

Restaurants will fall into one of the following categories:
- Fast food
- Brasserie
- Bistro
- Fine dining
- Cafés
- Coffee shops

▲ Restaurant

Opening times vary according to location, style of operation and demand. Many restaurants close on a Monday; some only offer dinner. In city centres many open for lunch and dinner late into the night.

Location is an important factor when choosing to open a restaurant. For example, when opening a fine dining restaurant it has to be in an area that will attract the right type of customers, where people have the money to spend on luxury goods.

The design, furniture and fittings of restaurants vary enormously and will reflect the type of customer the restaurant is aimed at. Many chain restaurants will have the same design and furniture in all of their restaurants, to promote and protect their brand. In fine dining restaurants it is all about comfort and luxury; in fast food restaurants the seats are small and usually less comfortable so that people do not stay too long.

Pricing in restaurants also varies according to the style, type of operation, location and the type of customer they are trying to attract. Some people expect to pay high prices and will not go to restaurants if the price is too low as they perceive price to reflect quality.

First courses

Salad of endive with Roquefort, chives and walnuts
Oak smoked salmon with lime and horseradish dressing, served with blini
Half dozen Fines de Claire oysters
Ham hock ravioli with white beans, trompettes and parsley

Main courses

Pot roast free-range chicken, tagliatelle of asparagus and morels
Dover sole pan fried with brown butter and capers
John Dory with chives and ginger crust, aromatic broth
Roast rib of Aberdeen Angus beef with Yorkshire pudding and roast potatoes
Saffron risotto cake with stuffed tomato, grilled vegetables and Parmesan

Desserts

Aniseed parfait with ginger bread and spiced port figs
Crisp apple tart with clotted cream and Calvados
Honey roast pear with caramel sauce and cardamom custard
Apricot and chocolate soufflé

▲ This is a menu from a fine dining establishment

Jobs in restaurants include chefs, waiters, receptionists and managers. Skills and expertise needed by staff will vary: some establishments will require semi-skilled people (for example large volume catering and fast food); in fine dining restaurants highly skilled chefs and waiters are needed.

Cafés and fast food outlets

There are a range of different types of cafés and fast food outlets.

Examples of popular fast food outlets include McDonalds, Burger King and Subway. Fast food chains such as McDonalds open seven days a week, often late into the evening. Some are open 24 hours a day in busy town and city centres and may also have drive-ins.

A fast food restaurant will be in any area where there are large numbers of people passing by and need food quickly. For instance, chip shops and fast food takeaways do well near colleges, schools, universities and in local community shopping areas.

Fast food outlets have managers, shift supervisors and a range of operational staff, porters and cleaners.

Cafés include popular chains such as Starbucks and Costa, as well as independent cafés, taxi cab cafés and transport cafés. Small cafés are usually run by individuals who purchase the food, cook and serve at the counter. They may have some assistance.

▲ Fast food outlet

Pubs and bars

Public houses, commonly known as pubs, provide alcoholic drinks and must today serve some sort of food such as bar snacks. Some provide a full restaurant service; these are known as gastro pubs.

Bars serving alcoholic drinks are found in a range of operations. In order to sell alcoholic drinks you have to apply for a Personal Licence from the local council. The business requires a Premises Licence.

▲ Gastro pub

The contract catering food service sector

Contract catering companies may be delivering their service within the commercial sector or the public service sector – they operate in hotels, restaurants, schools, colleges, hospitals and airlines. In addition to food and drink provision, they provide a range of services including security, facilities services such as reception, maintenance, pest control and retail. Examples of companies that offer contract services are ISS, Aramark, Compass, Initial and Sodexo.

Jobs in contract catering include chefs, cooks, food service staff, receptionists, managers and operations directors. Most contract catering units have a flexible approach to staffing; many will not work on the traditional **partie** system but chefs and assistants will divide the work up.

Hospitals and residential homes

In this sector people are carefully looked after by well-trained nurses and care assistants. People are provided with security and personal care, warmth, comfort, good accommodation and meals.

In hospitals food is an important part of the healing process, helping to build a patient's strength so they recover to full health. Dieticians are employed and play an important role in making sure patients receive the right nutrition to nurse them back to health and advising them on healthy diets once they leave hospital. Catering in hospitals operates 365 days a year, from approximately 6am to 8pm.

The same is also true in nursing and care homes. Patients and residents get a choice at breakfast, lunch and dinner.

Hospitals also cater for staff and visitors. Some NHS hospitals have high street branded coffee shops for patients and visitors. They may also provide hospitality for meetings and small conferences.

Jobs in hospitals and care homes include chefs, cooks, kitchen assistants, food service staff, catering managers and hotel services managers. Hospitals have a team of skilled and semi-skilled chefs who do a range of jobs. The

▲ Hospital catering

catering manager will work with the head chef to make sure patients and staff are served with good nutritional food.

College and university refectories

College and university refectories may be operated by the in-house hospitality services or by a contractor. These operations serve breakfast, lunch and dinner. They will also cover private functions. Many college and university restaurants have been upgraded and refurbished to create very pleasant eating environments which match the standards of many high street restaurants.

In college refectories pricing has to be low to suit the students, who are price sensitive.

Jobs in these establishments include chefs, cooks, food service staff, managers and supervisors. They differ from one college and one university to another.

School meals

Schools are required to serve fresh, nutritious food and follow strict nutritional guidelines. Many of the dining rooms in schools are used for a dual purpose – doubling up as an assembly hall or sports hall.

Jobs in schools include cooks, assistant cooks and area managers. School kitchens usually have a head cook or kitchen manager, and a number of kitchen assistants depending on the style of operation and the number of meals served.

Prison services

This is a major operation which provides inmates and staff with food and drink, serving breakfast, lunch and dinner. Inmates also work in the kitchens under supervision, and in many prisons are able to take professional cookery qualifications.

Catering jobs in prisons include chefs (who are usually prison officers). Most prisons will have a head chef and a small number of kitchen staff employed by the prison.

Armed forces

It is important to provide the army, navy, air force and the marines with wholesome, nutritional food, to satisfy appetites and to maintain morale. Apart from providing food and drink in the barracks,

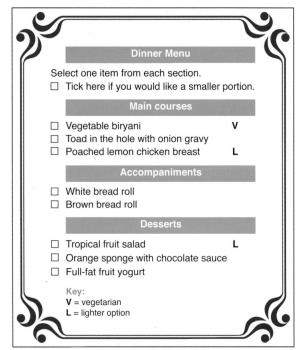

Dinner Menu

Select one item from each section.
☐ Tick here if you would like a smaller portion.

Main courses
☐ Vegetable biryani   V
☐ Toad in the hole with onion gravy
☐ Poached lemon chicken breast   L

Accompaniments
☐ White bread roll
☐ Brown bread roll

Desserts
☐ Tropical fruit salad   L
☐ Orange sponge with chocolate sauce
☐ Full-fat fruit yogurt

Key:
V = vegetarian
L = lighter option

▲ This is an example of a basic menu used in a hospital

Thursday

Pasta spirals with sausage
Vegetable casserole
Jacket potato with tuna

★ ★ ★

Potato wedges
Sweetcorn
Garden salad

★ ★ ★

Raisin sponge pudding with custard
Fruit salad pot

▲ This is an example of a menu for school meals

armed forces chefs work on location in the field and on board ship. Standards are maintained wherever the troops are deployed, which can often be a major logistical operation. The armed forces train chefs and food service staff to a high level.

▲ Army dining facility

Jobs include all grades of chefs, who are different ranks of the armed forces. They may also employ civilian instructors. There will also be different ranks of food service staff. They operate a range of different staffing structures depending on the unit, for example the officers' mess operation will be very different from the field kitchen in a war zone.

Industrial catering

This is a wide sector, feeding people at work in offices, factories and commercial establishments. Industrial catering provides food and drink and in some cases may also provide accommodation. It includes self-service restaurants, fine dining, brasseries, coffee shops, food to go and snack bars. It will also cover functions and events.

Furnishings and fittings can replicate the high street, offering excellent eating environments. Private corporate dining rooms in some of the large organisations serve food and drink of the highest quality.

Jobs will include a wide variety of roles, including chefs, cooks, waiters, food service staff, managers, supervisors, receptionists, butlers.

Activity

1 What does corporate hospitality mean?
2 What does industrial catering mean?
3 The catering industry has two main sectors: one is the commercial sector. What is the name of the other sector?
4 A hotel is one establishment that provides accommodation. Name two other establishments that provide accommodation.
5 Gastro pubs provide catering. Name two other establishments that provide catering.

KEY WORDS

Hospitality – to be hospitable, to look after people by providing services such as food, drink and accommodation.

Catering – the provision of food and drink.

Commercial sector – providing hospitality and catering is the main purpose of the organisation.

Public service sector – the provision of hospitality is not the main purpose of the company.

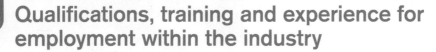

Qualifications, training and experience for employment within the industry

The hospitality industry offers a variety of jobs. There are a large number of jobs which are part-time; many of these are taken up by young people (usually students). Much of this employment is on a casual basis and people work when they are required to by the organisation – when they are busy, especially when they need extra staff for functions and special events.

Staffing structures

All establishments and organisations have a staffing structure. Within this structure people are given job roles and a job description, which provides details of what they are required to contribute to the achievement of the aims and objectives of the establishment or organisation. In small organisations some employees will be required to cover more than one job role. For example, in a small hotel an employee may have to service the rooms, cover reception and serve in the dining room. In larger organisations the job roles will be more specific and often very detailed.

There are three categories of staff in the industry.

Operational staff

These are often the staff who work in practical areas – in kitchens, bars, reception and rooms. They have practical skills in food preparation, serving, customer care and servicing and cleaning the bedrooms and public areas. These staff perform the everyday functions which customers rely on, for example the provision of food, drink and accommodation.

Operational staff include commis chefs, chef de cuisine, cook, waiter, wine waiter, room attendant and kitchen assistants.

Supervisory staff

Staff at supervisory level normally have experience of at working at an operational level. They oversee and supervise the work of the operational staff and are concerned with the day-to-day issues and problems that may occur. Operational staff report to the supervisor.

Supervisory staff include sectional chef (chef de partie), sous chef and head waiter.

Management staff

Managers monitor and develop overall quality standards, making sure that all staff deliver to the required standard expected by customers. Managers are also responsible for making sure that the organisation is compliant with legislative requirements (for example health and safety policies and employment law).

Senior managers are involved in planning the future – assessing future trends, fashions and markets. They will also have responsibility for budgeting and finance.

Management staff include head chef, head cook, catering manager, restaurant manager and bar manager.

The following diagram shows an example of a staffing structure for a kitchen of a medium-sized, 200-room hotel, with dining room and banqueting facilities for 300 people.

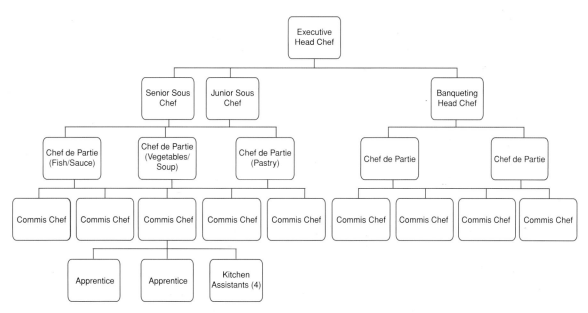

▲ Staffing structure for a medium-sized hotel kitchen

The second diagram is an example of a kitchen organisation structure of a 50–80 seater brasserie, which is open for 5 lunches and 6 dinners.

Job roles in the different catering establishments

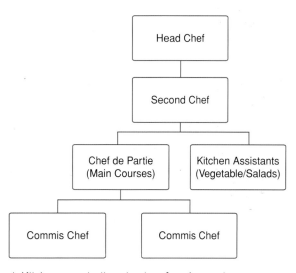

▲ Kitchen organisation structure for a brasserie

- **Executive chef** – a manager who oversees the whole kitchen operation. This may include the planning and organisation of the kitchen, purchasing, budgeting and forecasting.
- **Head chef** – has a similar role to an executive chef. Head chefs run a major kitchen operation; an executive chef usually manages several operations.
- **Senior sous chef** – deputises for the head chef or executive chef and has a range of similar responsibilities, usually managing several operations. They are supported by a junior sous chef.
- **Chef de partie** – responsible for a specific section (for example, pastry). They supervise commis chefs in their section.
- **Commis chef** – this is an operational role. Commis chefs prepare and cook food under the supervision of the chef de partie.

Training and experience: how to develop your employment prospects

To develop your career you must constantly take advantage of the learning opportunities that are available. In the hospitality industry people are educated and trained by chefs from around the world who are creative and innovative, and who can teach you about a range of food and styles of cooking, using new ingredients, developing new styles and new ways of presenting food.

Training can be provided in a number of ways:

College-based learning

Some people choose to attend full-time college courses in hospitality and catering. Students are taught by teachers who are well qualified and have good industrial experience. Students often study other skills such as communication, numeracy and IT at the same time as their hospitality and catering course.

Some people choose to do an apprenticeship and attend college on a day-release basis – learning at work and in college. Partnership arrangements often exist between the college and employers.

> **Professional tip**
>
> Communication, numeracy and information technology are important skills which employers value. Take an interest in these to help you to progress your career.

Work-based learning

This is often called learning on the job and takes various forms. Many large employers have their own training programmes, which cover a range of subjects, such as food safety, health and safety, customer care, employment law and finance. These courses range from one day to three days, but some can be done in units over one year or more. Some of these courses at work are managed by training providers.

E-learning

More and more courses are incorporating technology and using the internet, allowing students to work at their own pace. There are many resources available to enhance your learning, including video. E-learning courses are often interactive.

Work placements

Many college courses send students out on placement; much of this is for short periods and is usually unpaid. This is a real opportunity for learning, finding out about the organisation, how systems and procedures work and how you think they can be improved in an organisation.

> **Professional tip**
>
> When on a work placement always show interest, be polite and well mannered at all times. Keep a diary, write down what you have learnt, ask questions and take in all the knowledge that is available.

Qualifications

Colleges offer a range of qualifications for those who are working, or want to work, in the hospitality and catering industry. Qualifications provide you with the skills and knowledge you need to be proficient and to allow you to apply for the jobs in the industry.

There are a range of qualifications available:

VRQs

Vocational Related Qualifications (VRQs) are full-time courses delivered in a college. Courses available include Diplomas in Professional Cookery at Levels 1, 2 and 3. Level 1 is an introduction to professional cookery; Level 2 develops your skills and knowledge; and Level 3 is a more advanced qualification. These qualifications do not require you to be working, but it is advisable to gain some experience in the industry, perhaps through part-time work. VRQs are assessed by written and practical assessment.

NVQs

Work-based qualifications are called National Vocational Qualifications (NVQs). These are delivered and assessed in the workplace, but some colleges do offer these qualifications to full-time students. NVQs in Food Preparation and Cooking are available at Levels 1, 2 and 3 and are assessed by observation in the workplace and by a portfolio. As you progress through the different levels your skills develop and your understanding becomes wider and more in-depth.

Food safety and health and safety

There is a range of short courses in Food Safety, Health and Safety and Customer Care which many people take. The purpose of these qualifications is to increase knowledge and skills in these important areas. Food Safety at Level 2, for example, is a one-day course which is a requirement by many employers before working in a professional kitchen.

Higher education

For those people who want to progress their careers, there are opportunities to take higher level courses that combine practical applied learning with theory. These courses include a range of business skills such as marketing, finance, management and human resource management. A chef starting out at Level 1 can progress onto a Bachelors degree or even a Masters degree.

> **Professional tip**
> Try to gain as many qualifications and as much experience as you can so that you will be attractive to future employers.

Employment rights and responsibilities

Everyone in employment has rights and responsibilities.

Employers must provide an employee with:
- a detailed job description
- a contract of employment that gives details of working hours, the amount of annual leave the employee will have and the notice period
- a safe and working environment, which complies with the relevant health and safety, food safety and employment laws
- at least the minimum wage.

Employees must:
- work to their contract and their job description
- follow the organisation's policies, systems and procedures
- follow health and safety and food safety law and make sure they work safely and securely.

Health and safety
For more information on health and safety visit www.hse.gov.uk.

Associations related to professional cookery

As a chef you can join a number of professional associations where you can meet other chefs and suppliers, and which will help you to develop your knowledge.

National associations

Some examples of national associations include:

- The Academy of Culinary Arts
- Craft Guild of Chefs
- Master of Great Britain
- The British Culinary Federation
- The Institute of Hospitality
- Springboard UK – promotes careers in the industry
- British Hospitality Association – represents employers and lobbies government on issues relating to hospitality and tourism
- People 1st – the Sector Skills Council for the industry. This organisation researches trends in the industry, advises on qualifications and gains feedback on training and education from employers.

> **Professional tip**
>
> When you are qualified, try to join a professional association. This will introduce you to other professionals and may help you to develop your career.

Local associations

Many of the national associations listed have local branches where meeting are held. For example, Springboard UK has a number of local branches, and People 1st gathers information on employment trends and training needs at a local level.

There may also be other associations specific to your local area.

Activity

1 Give two examples of operational staff.
2 Give two examples of types of training and experience available in the hospitality and catering sector.
3 Give two examples of types of qualification available in the hospitality and catering sector.
4 When you are offered a job you have a right to be:
   - given a contract
   - provided with details of the contracted working hours
   - given details of annual leave

   List three more employment rights.
5 Give two examples of associations you may like to join when you become a qualified chef.

KEY WORDS

Operational staff – staff who work in practical areas.

Supervisory staff – staff who oversee and supervise the work of the operational staff and are concerned with day-to-day issues and problems that may occur.

Management staff – staff who monitor and develop overall quality standards, making sure that all staff deliver to the required standard expected by customers. Managers are also responsible for compliance with legislative requirements. Senior managers are also responsible for budgeting, finance and planning for the future.

E-learning – learning using online resources.

VRQ – vocational related qualification. Full-time courses delivered in college and assessed by written and practical assessment.

NVQ – national vocational qualification. Qualifications that are delivered and assessed in the workplace and assessed by observation in the workplace and by a portfolio.

Test yourself

1   What is the difference between **hospitality** and **catering**?
2   Give three examples of establishments in the commercial sector.
3   Give three examples of establishments in the public service sector.
4   List three differences between a fine dining restaurant and a fast food outlet.
5   Describe three features of catering in a hospital.
6   Give an example of a management job in the industry.
7   Give two examples of types of operational jobs in the industry.
8   What is meant by work-based learning?
9   What type of qualification is a full-time course delivered in a college that does not require you to be working in the industry?
10   Give three examples of responsibilities of an employee.

2 Food safety

This chapter covers Unit 202, Food safety in catering.

By the end of this chapter you should be able to:

- Outline the importance of food safety procedures, risk assessment, safe food handling and behaviour
- Describe how to report food safety hazards
- Outline the legal responsibilities of food handlers and food business operators
- Explain the importance of personal hygiene in food safety and describe effective personal hygiene practices
- Explain how to keep the work area and equipment clean, tidy and safe

- State how work flow, work surfaces and equipment can reduce contamination risks and aid cleaning
- Outline the importance of pest control
- State the sources and risks to food safety from contamination and cross-contamination
- Explain how to deal with food spoilage
- Describe safe food handling practices and procedures
- Explain the importance of temperature controls
- Describe stock control procedures.

Food safety and personal responsibility

Everyone has the right to be served safe food that will not cause them illness or harm. **Food safety** means putting in place all of the measures needed to make sure that food and drinks are suitable, safe and fit to eat.

Food safety procedures and safe food handling

Good standards of food safety are essential to comply with the law and avoid legal action, to build a successful business with a good reputation and to provide clean and safe premises for employees and customers.

Food handlers can help to achieve high standards of food safety by following best practice and by being aware that they can contaminate food and cause food poisoning by their actions if their personal hygiene is not of the highest standard.

Good food safety standards can be achieved by:

- Protecting food from contamination from the time it is delivered right through to serving the food – 'farm to fork'
- Putting measures in place to prevent the multiplication of bacteria
- Destroying bacteria already present in food, on equipment and surfaces
- Working in a clean, hygienic and organised way; this includes having good standards of personal hygiene and observing correct handwashing procedures
- Observing the correct temperatures for storage, preparation, cooking and holding of food
- Reporting anything that could contaminate food or prevent good food safety practice, including reporting any unacceptable behaviour or illness
- Carrying out food safety training and being part of the risk assessment processes.

Why are we so concerned about food safety?

Eating contaminated food can result in **food poisoning**, causing harm, illness and in some cases even death. The number of reported cases of food poisoning each year remains unacceptably high and, as a large number of food poisoning cases are never reported, no one knows the actual number.

Food poisoning is usually caused by eating food that has become contaminated with bacteria or the toxins they may produce. Sometimes it can be caused by eating foods such as poisonous mushrooms or chemicals that may have got into food or by organisms such as viruses.

The main symptoms of food poisoning are:

- Nausea
- Vomiting
- Diarrhoea
- Dehydration
- Sometimes fever and headache.

> **Professional tip**
>
> The most usual time taken between eating contaminated food and developing these symptoms is 12–36 hours, but it can be as little as one hour or as long as several days.

Food safety hazards

Food safety hazards can be categorised into the following four groups:

- **Chemical** – chemicals such as cleaning fluids, disinfectants, machine oil, insecticides, pesticides and rodenticides can accidentally get into food and make the consumer feel ill.
- **Physical** – items such as glass, nuts, bolts and oil from machinery, mercury from thermometers, flaking paint or tile grouting, pen tops, threads from worn clothing, buttons, blue plasters, hair or insects can get into foods.
- **Biological** – pathogenic bacteria, viruses, yeasts, moulds, spoilage bacteria and enzymes may be present in food. **Pathogenic bacteria** may multiply to dangerous levels but remain undetectable. If they get into the human body they can cause illness.
- **Allergenic** – the immune system in some people can react to certain foods. Allergies are usually associated with nuts, dairy products, wheat-based products (affecting those with a gluten allergy), eggs and shellfish. Some people may also have an allergy to some vegetables, plants and mushrooms. Reactions include swelling, itching, rashes and breathlessness. It may even cause **anaphylactic shock**.

Risk assessment

Those working in the kitchen may be the first to become aware of possible hazards. These must be reported immediately to the supervisor, head chef or line manager.

It is important to assess these hazards and put measures in place to reduce the risk of them occurring. Under the Food Hygiene Regulations 2006 all businesses must have a food safety management system and keep the necessary records to support it.

Hazard Analysis Critical Control Point (HACCP)

This is a food safety management system which requires those running a food business to analyse any hazards that could lead to food poisoning or cause other food-related problems by identifying the critical control points or stages in any food process where hazards could occur.

Once the hazards have been identified measures are put in place to control them and keep the food safe.

The HACCP system has seven stages:

1 Identify hazards – what could go wrong?
2 Identify Critical Control Points (CCPs). These are the important stages where things could go wrong.
3 Set critical limits for each CCP – for example, temperature requirements on delivery of fresh chicken.
4 Monitor CCPs and put checks in place to stop problems happening.
5 Corrective action – what will be done if something goes wrong?
6 Verification – check that the HACCP plan is working.
7 Documentation – record all of the above.

The system must be updated regularly, especially when new items are introduced to the menu or systems change (for example, a new piece of cooking equipment is used). New controls must be put in place to include them.

Keeping the records that support this system is very important for due diligence. This is proving that you have completed the necessary procedures to ensure food safety. Records may include staff training records, fridge and freezer temperature records, records of reported staff illness, lists of suppliers, calibration of temperature probes and many more relevant records.

Safer Food Better Business

The Food Standards Agency launched this system for smaller or limited businesses. It is based on the principles of HACCP but in an easy to understand format. It has pre-printed pages and charts to enter the relevant information such as temperatures of individual dishes. It concentrates mainly on the four Cs: **c**ross-contamination, **c**leaning, **c**hilling and **c**ooking. The management section includes a diary with opening/closing checks, and pages for relevant records such as staff training and supplier details.

A copy of Safer Food Better Business is available from www.food.gov.uk.

Legal responsibilities

The law and food business operators

All food businesses must be registered with the local authority, must cooperate with the Environmental Health Officer/Environmental Health Practitioner (EHO/EHP) and put proper food safety practices in place. An EHO/EHP is employed by local authorities to oversee the standards of food safety in their area. They can enter any food premises at any reasonable time to inspect them. They can advise, serve notices for improvement and in extreme cases inform the courts to take legal action resulting in fines or even the closure of food premises and imprisonment.

Scores on the Doors

This was introduced to help raise food safety standards. After an EHO/EHP inspection, a star rating certificate for compliance with food safety is given to a business. The stars range from five down to zero. Five stars would be awarded for excellent standards and zero stars for poor standards. The certificate can then to be placed on the door or window of premises or can be seen on local authority and food standards agency websites.

The law and food handlers

Individual food handlers also have legal responsibilities. It is a legal requirement that they:

- Receive food safety training relevant to the work they are doing so that they understand the principles of food safety and how to avoid food poisoning
- Work in a way that does not endanger or contaminate food and not serve food they know is contaminated
- Report anything that may have an effect on food safety such as a fridge running at the wrong temperature and cooperate with food safety measures the employer puts in place
- Report any illness, especially if stomach related, to a supervisor before starting work. After suffering such an illness they must not return to work until 48 hours after the last symptom.

Professional tip

For further information about food safety matters speak to your line manager, the EHO/EHP, or look at your local authority food safety websites. Also try the Food Standards Agency www.food.gov.uk, the Chartered Institute of Environmental Health (CIEH) www.cieh.org and www.highfield.co.uk.

KEY WORDS

Food safety – putting measures in place to ensure food is safe to eat and will not cause illness.

Hazard – anything with the potential to cause harm.

Hazard analysis – identifying all the possible hazards and putting in measures to prevent them causing harm.

Critical Control Point – a point at which something could go wrong and a control measure could be put in place to keep the hazard under control.

EHO/EHP – employed by local authorities to ensure that the required standards of food safety are met.

Legal requirement – something that must be done by law.

Due diligence – proving that you have completed the necessary procedures to ensure food safety.

Activity

1. What are three advantages of a business having good standards of food safety?
2. What is food poisoning and what are the main symptoms?
3. Suggest three possible food safety hazards in a kitchen.
4. What must a food handler do if they arrive at work feeling unwell?
5. Suggest some of the ways that a food handler can help to achieve high standards of food safety.

Personal hygiene

It is very important for all food handlers to take care with personal hygiene and to adopt good practices when working with food to avoid contaminating the food with pathogenic bacteria such as staphylococcus, which can cause food poisoning.

Food handlers must:

- Arrive at work clean (bath or shower daily) and with clean hair
- Wear appropriate protective clothing
- Keep nails short, clean and not bitten − definitely no nail varnish or false nails
- Not wear jewellery and watches when handling food; these items can trap bacteria and could cause physical contamination by falling into food
- Not wear cosmetics and strong perfumes
- Not smoke in food preparation areas
- Not eat food or sweets and chewing gum when handling food as this may also transfer bacteria to food.

Protective clothing

Protective clothing is worn in the kitchen to protect food from contamination as well as protecting the wearer from heat, burns and splashes. Some people allergic to certain food items, chemicals, plastics or cleaning materials can suffer a skin reaction called contact dermatitis. Good kitchen clothing can also protect the wearer from an allergic reaction.

Kitchen protective clothing usually consists of chef's jacket, trousers, apron and safety shoes. Hair must also be contained in a suitable hat or hair net. Kitchen clothing should only be used in the kitchen and should completely cover any personal clothing. At break times food handlers must not smoke wearing kitchen clothing.

All items of clothing should fit well, be in good repair and suitable for the tasks being completed; pockets should be on the inside. Materials that are comfortable and durable and can be laundered at high temperatures, such as cotton are the most usual.

> **Professional tip**
> Kitchen clothing itself could contaminate food. If it gets dirty or stained change it for clean clothing.

See Chapter 6 Personal Workplace Skills for more information.

Hand washing

Contamination from hands can happen very easily and could result in harmful bacteria being passed on to food. Great care must be taken with hand washing to avoid this; thorough hand washing is essential:

- Use a basin provided just for hand washing
- Wet hands under warm running water
- Apply liquid soap

- Rub hands together between fingers and thumbs
- Remember fingertips, nails and wrists (if a nailbrush is used make sure it is clean and disinfected)
- Rinse off under the running water
- Dry hands on a paper towel and use the paper towel to turn off the tap then dispose of it into a foot-operated waste bin.

Hands should be washed:
- When you enter the kitchen, before starting work and handling any food
- After a break
- After using the toilet
- After smoking or eating
- Between different tasks, but especially after handling raw and before handling cooked/high risk food
- If you touch hair, nose or mouth/face
- After coughing/sneezing and nose blowing
- After you apply or change a dressing on a cut or burn
- After using cleaning materials, cleaning preparation areas, equipment or contaminated surfaces
- After handling kitchen waste, external food packaging, money or flowers.

Personal illnesses

Report any illness to the supervisor as soon as possible and before handling any food. This is a legal requirement and would include:
- Diarrhoea and/or vomiting, nausea and stomach pain; this may well be food poisoning
- Infected (septic) cuts, burns or spots
- Eye or ear infections
- Cold or flu symptoms including sore throat
- Skin problems such as dermatitis.

Also report illness you had when away from work and family members or friends you have contact with who have the above symptoms, especially where they are stomach related.

Cuts and wounds

Any infected (septic) cuts and wounds should be reported to a supervisor. Wash, dry then cover any cuts, burns or grazes with a brightly coloured waterproof dressing, then wash hands.

KEY WORDS

Personal hygiene – keeping yourself clean and hygienic to avoid contaminating food.

Contamination – anything in food that should not be there. Contaminated food could cause harm or may just be unpleasant.

Pathogenic bacteria – micro-organisms that could multiply in food and cause food poisoning.

Septic – cuts, burns and so on infected with pathogenic bacteria. They are often wet with a white or yellow appearance.

Safety shoes – strong, enclosed shoes with reinforced toecaps to protect the feet from heavy or sharp objects and hot liquids.

1 Suggest five personal hygiene rules you would include in a kitchen poster for staff information.
2 Why should jewellery and watches not be worn in the kitchen?
3 What is the correct procedure to follow if you cut your finger while working?
4 What are the main reasons for wearing protective clothing in the kitchen?
5 Why should kitchen clothing not be worn outside of the kitchen?

Keeping work areas clean and hygienic

It is a legal requirement that food areas are kept clean and hygienic and that food premises are designed with good food safety in mind.

Controlling cross-contamination

Cross-contamination is when bacteria or other contaminants are transferred from contaminated food (often raw food) to ready-to-eat food. It is a cause of food poisoning and care must be taken to avoid it. Causes of cross-contamination include:

- Foods touching, for example, raw and cooked meat
- Raw meat or poultry dripping onto high-risk foods
- Soil from dirty vegetables coming into contact with high-risk foods
- Dirty cloths or dirty equipment
- Equipment used for raw then cooked food without proper cleaning/disinfection such as chopping boards or knives
- Hands touching raw food then cooked food, or not washing hands thoroughly between tasks and after breaks.

Having separate areas for different foods, storage, processes and service will help to reduce the risk of contamination and assist efficient working and effective cleaning. A **linear workflow** in food production areas should also be in place:

1 Delivery
2 Storage
3 Preparation
4 Cooking
5 Hot holding
6 Serving.

▲ Cross-contamination video, http://bit.ly/YPgGWB

This means there will be no crossover of activities that could result in cross-contamination.

'Dirty areas' that involve preparation or storage of raw foods or cleaning of items such as dirty vegetables need to be kept separate from the 'clean areas' where cold preparations, finishing and serving takes place.

Separate areas for raw and high-risk foods are always recommended and if this is not possible keep them well away from each other, making sure that working areas are thoroughly cleaned and disinfected between tasks.

Work area and equipment

Kitchen surfaces and equipment should be installed to allow for efficient cleaning and disinfection. Equipment and surfaces need to be smooth, impervious (not absorb liquids) and must of course be **non-corrosive**, non-toxic and must not crack, chip or flake. Many kitchens have a 'no glass' policy to prevent the possibility of broken glass getting into food. The table below provides examples of the types of materials and requirements of work areas.

Table 2.1 Requirements of work areas

Lighting	Must allow for tasks being completed safely and without eye strain and so cleaning can be carried out efficiently.
Ventilation	Using canopies over essential areas prevents excessive heat, condensation, circulation of air-borne contaminants, grease vapours, odours and gives a more comfortable working environment.
Floors	Need to be hard wearing and in good condition; they must be impervious, non-slip and easy to keep clean. Edges between floor and walls should be coved (curved) to prevent dirt collecting in corners.
Walls	Need to be non-porous, smooth, easy to clean and light in colour. Suitable wall coverings are plastic cladding and stainless steel sheeting.
Ceilings	Ceiling finishes must resist build up of condensation, which could encourage mould. They should be of a non-flaking material and be washable. Non-porous ceiling panels and tiles are often used; non-flaking paints are also useful.
Drainage	Drainage must be adequate for the work being completed without causing flooding. If channels, grease traps and gullies are used they should allow for frequent cleaning.
Windows/doors	These provide possibilities for pests to enter the building so should fit well into the frames with no gaps. They should be fitted with screening, strip-curtains and doors should have metal kick plates.

Colour-coded equipment

Worktops and chopping boards will come into contact with the food you prepare so need special attention. Make sure that chopping boards are in good condition, cracks and splits could hold onto bacteria and this could be transferred to food. Colour-coded chopping boards are a good way to keep different types of food separate.

> **Professional tip**
>
> As well as colour-coded chopping boards some kitchens also provide colour-coded knives, cloths, cleaning equipment, storage trays, bowls and even staff uniforms to help prevent cross-contamination.

Kitchen cloths

Kitchen cloths are a perfect growing area for bacteria. Different cloths for different areas will help to reduce cross-contamination and it is especially important to use different cloths for raw food and cooked food preparation. Use of disposable cloths or kitchen towels is the most hygienic way to clean food areas.

▲ Colour-coded chopping boards

Use tea towels with great care as they can easily spread bacteria. Do not use them as an all-purpose cloth, and do not keep them on the shoulder (the cloth touches the neck and hair and these can be sources of bacteria).

Maintenance

All food premises, fittings and equipment must be kept in good repair to ensure food safety. Cracked surfaces or chipped equipment could support the multiplication of bacteria and a fridge running at the wrong temperature may allow bacteria to multiply in food. If you notice anything is damaged, broken or faulty report it to a supervisor immediately. You may have specific reporting forms to do this.

Cleaning and disinfection

Clean food areas play an essential part in the production of safe food and it is a requirement to plan, record and check all cleaning as part of a planned cleaning schedule.

As a food handler it is your responsibility, along with those working with you, to keep food areas clean and hygienic at all times. Clean as you go and do not allow waste to build up; clean up any spills straight away.

Some kitchen areas such as floors and walls will need planned and thorough cleaning but some items, especially in high risk areas and where high risk foods are handled, need both cleaning and disinfection. These are:

- **All food contact surfaces**, such as chopping boards, bowls, spoons, whisks
- **All hand contact surfaces**, such as fridge handles and door handles
- **Cleaning materials and equipment**, such as mops, buckets, cloths, hand wash basins.

Cleaning products

Detergents – designed to remove grease and dirt and hold them in suspension in water; they do not kill bacteria. Detergent works best with hot water.

Disinfectant – designed to destroy bacteria if used properly. Disinfectants must be left on a cleaned grease-free surface for the required amount of time to be effective and works best with cool water.

Sanitiser – cleans and disinfects and usually comes in spray form. It is very useful for work surfaces and equipment especially between tasks and also for hand contact surfaces such as fridge handles.

Steriliser – can be used after cleaning to make a surface or piece of equipment bacteria free.

Cleaning and disinfection of kitchen equipment

Clean and sanitise worktops and chopping boards before working on them and do this again after use, paying particular attention when they have been used for raw foods.

Small equipment, such as knives, chopping boards, bowls, spoons, tongs, as well as serving cutlery and crockery could be the cause of cross-contamination. Wash them well, especially when used for a variety of food and for raw foods.

This small equipment can be cleaned and disinfected very effectively by putting it through a dishwasher. Loose debris is scraped or sprayed off, the machine washes at approximately 55°C using a detergent then rinses at 82°C, which disinfects and allows items to air dry quickly.

If a dishwasher cannot be used a double sink method may be in place. Loose debris is removed, the items are washed thoroughly with detergent and hot water then rinsed in a second sink in very hot water (82°C if possible) and allowed to air dry.

Large equipment such as large mixing machines and ovens cannot be moved so need to be cleaned where they are. This is called 'clean in place' and each item will have a specific method outlined on the cleaning schedule. Sometimes steam cleaning methods are used that also disinfect the items.

Cleaning of kitchen surfaces

For kitchen surfaces one of the following processes is recommended:

Table 2.2 Kitchen surface cleaning processes

Six stage	Four stage
1 Remove debris and loose particles	1 Remove debris and loose particles
2 Main clean to remove soiling grease	2 Main clean using hot water and sanitiser
3 Rinse using clean hot water and cloth to remove detergent	3 Rinse using clean hot water and cloth if recommended on instructions
4 Apply disinfectant. Leave for contact time recommended on the container.	4 Allow to air dry or use kitchen paper
5 Rinse off the disinfectant if recommended	
6 Allow to air dry or use kitchen paper	

Safe use and storage of chemicals and materials

When using any cleaning or disinfection chemicals it is important to use with care. The 2002 Control of Substances Hazardous to Health (COSHH) Regulations state that employees must be kept safe from chemical harm by appropriate training, risk assessment, planning and provision of personal protective equipment (PPE) where it is needed.

Always follow instructions for chemical use, how they should be diluted or mixed and how they should be disposed of. Kitchen areas will display safety data sheets with information on chemicals, how they are to be used and how to deal with spillages and accidents. Make sure you are familiar with this information.

Most chemicals such as detergent or disinfectant only stay active for an hour or two so long soaking of cloths and mops is not recommended. Wash/disinfect the items, squeeze out then allow them to air dry.

Do not store cleaning chemicals in food preparation and cooking areas; use separate, lockable storage and restrict who has access to it. All chemicals must be stored in their original containers with the instruction label visible.

Make sure that items such as cloths and paper towel, and fibres from mops do not get into open food. When using sprays such as sanitiser spray take care not to spray it on the skin or eyes and do not spray over open food.

If cleaning materials are spilled warn others, put up a wet floor sign, wear rubber gloves and a mask if needed, soak up the excess with kitchen paper then clean the area. If cleaning materials are spilled onto the skin wash off with cold water and dry. If there is a skin reaction or chemicals are splashed in the eyes, seek first aid immediately and report the incident.

Waste disposal

Kitchen waste should be placed in waste bins with lids (preferably foot-operated and lined with a strong bin liner). They need to be kept in good condition, and away from direct sunlight. Bins should be emptied regularly to avoid cross-contamination and odour and never left unemptied in the kitchen overnight as this could result in the multiplication of bacteria and attracting pests.

▲ Sanitising a surface

Staff in kitchens need to become familiar with the separation of different waste items ready for collection and recyling. This may include bottles, cans, waste food, paper and plastic items.

Pests and pest control

Pests in food premises can be a serious source of contamination and disease; having them near food cannot be allowed and is against the law. Pests in food premises can also lead to:

- Legal action
- Loss of profit
- Closure of the business
- Loss of reputation
- Poor staff morale
- Damage to equipment and wastage of food.

Pests can be attracted to food premises because there is food, warmth, shelter, water and possible nesting materials; all reasonable measures must be put in place to keep them out.

Any suspicion of pests being present must be reported to the supervisor or manager immediately. Pest problems are best dealt with by a recognised pest contractor; they can also complete audits and give advice.

Pests include rats and mice; flies and wasps; cockroaches; ants; weevils; birds; domestic pets and wild cats. Signs of pest invasion include sightings of droppings; unpleasant smells; smear marks; damaged or gnawed packaging and food spillages; pupae, larvae, eggs or cases; and holes in skirting boards, door and window frames or gnawed wires.

Pests can be kept out or dealt with in a number of ways:

- Block entry – make sure there are no holes around pipework; remove any gaps and cavities where they could get in; seal all drain covers.
- Damage to the building or fixtures and fittings must be repaired quickly.

- Use window/door screening/netting.
- Check deliveries/packaging for pests.
- Place baits and traps in relevant places.
- Use electronic fly killer.
- Seal containers and do not leave food out in the open.
- Avoid build up of waste in the kitchen.
- Do not keep outside waste too close to kitchen and ensure containers are emptied regularly and the area is clean and tidy.
- Arrange for professional and organised pest management control, surveys and reports.

> **Professional tip**
>
> The only pests you can deal with yourself are flying insects with an electronic fly killer. For all other pests professional help is needed.

▲ Housefly and German cockroach

KEY WORDS

Cross-contamination – when contaminants are moved from one place to another, for example, bacteria from raw food being transferred to cooked food.

High-risk areas – areas that could be sources of contamination, for example raw meat or dirty vegetable preparation areas.

Low-risk areas – where clean processes are carried out.

Disinfection – bringing any pathogenic bacteria present to a safe level.

Corrosive – action that breaks a material down, such as rusting.

Cleaning schedule – a planned programme of cleaning areas and equipment.

Sanitise – cleaning and disinfecting together with one product.

COSHH – Control of Substances Hazardous to Health; this is legislation to ensure safe use of chemicals.

Pest – a creature that could enter food premises, cause damage and contaminate food.

Activity

1. Make a poster or checklist for new kitchen staff highlighting ten ways that they can avoid cross-contamination in a kitchen. Include some illustrations.
2. Suggest six kitchen areas or items that should be both **cleaned** and **disinfected**.
3. If you entered the kitchen in the morning and saw small black pellets, chewed packaging and spilled flour, what would you think the problem was and what would you do about it?
4. If you had a number of small kitchen items you wanted to clean and disinfect, what are the rinse temperatures you would need to achieve to disinfect? How could you do this easily?
5. Which colour-coded chopping board would you use to cut each of the following:
   - a raw salmon
   - b cooked chicken
   - c bread
   - d cucumber
   - e uncooked carrots
   - f raw fillet beef
   - g cooked savoury flan.

Keeping food safe

Sources and risks to food safety

Food poisoning can be an unpleasant illness for anyone but in some groups of people who are referred to as 'high risk' it can be very serious or even fatal.

These high risk groups include:

- Babies and the very young
- Elderly people
- Pregnant women
- Those who are already unwell or recovering from an illness (that is, those with a weakened immune system).

There are a range of sources of contamination and cross-contamination.

Microbial risks – pathogenic bacteria

Bacteria are very small, so small that you would need to use a microscope to see them; you would not be able to taste them or smell them on food. This is why pathogens (the bacteria associated with food poisoning) are so dangerous – you cannot tell if they are in food or not. When bacteria have food, warmth, moisture and time, they can multiply every 10–20 minutes by dividing in half.

In this example, from one careless action with a dirty cloth 6,000 pathogens have multiplied to 3 million in 2 hours 40 minutes.

1 million pathogens per gram of food is enough to cause food poisoning.

Pathogenic bacteria may act in different ways to cause food poisoning. They can multiply in food then infect the person eating it. Some bacteria can produce **toxins** (poisons) as they multiply or die. Toxins can survive boiling temperatures for half an hour or more. Some can produce **spores** to protect themselves from very high or low temperatures or from chemicals such as disinfectant. Normal cooking procedures do not destroy spores.

Some common food poisoning bacteria include:

Salmonella – used to be the most common cause of food poisoning but modern methods

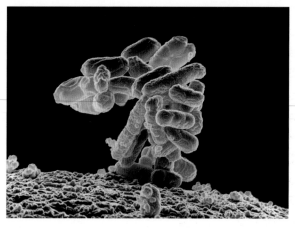

▲ Bacteria multiplying by dividing in two

Time		Number of pathogens on the chicken
9.40	A chicken has been cooked to 75°C and left in the kitchen, uncovered, to cool. No bacteria survived.	0
10.00	A chef uses a dirty cloth to transfer the chicken to a plate.	6,000
10.20		12,000
10.40		24,000
11.00		48,000
11.20		96,000
11.40		192,000
12.00		384,000
12.20		768,000
12.40		1.5 million
1.00		3 million

▲ Hazard timeline

have reduced it in chickens and in eggs, so food poisoning from this source has reduced. The main source of salmonella is the human and animal gut and excreta, but it can also be found in pests such as rodents, insects and birds and in raw meat and poultry, eggs and shellfish. Salmonella poisoning can also be passed on through human carriers.

Staphylococcus aureus – the main source of this organism is the human body (it may be present on skin, hair and scalp, nose, throat, etc.). Cuts, spots, burns and boils will also be a source of this organism. When staphylococcus multiplies in food a toxin (poison) is produced which can be very difficult to kill. To avoid food poisoning from this organism food handlers need to maintain very high standards of personal hygiene and report any illness they may have to their supervisor before handling food.

Clostridium perfringens – often present in human and animal faeces and raw meat, poultry and vegetables (also insects, soil, dust and sewage). A number of food poisoning incidents from this organism have occurred when large quantities of meat are brought up to cooking temperatures slowly then allowed to cool slowly for later use or re-heating. Clostridium perfringens can produce spores during this heating/cooling. Spores are very resistant to any further cooking and allow bacteria to survive in conditions that would usually kill them.

Bacillus cereus – can produce both spores and toxins so can be a dangerous pathogen. It is often associated with cooking rice in large quantities, cooling it too slowly and then reheating. The reheating temperatures would not be enough to destroy spores and toxins. It has also been linked with other cereal crops, spices, soil and vegetables.

Clostridium botulinum – rare, but symptoms can be very serious, even fatal. Sources tend to be intestines of fish, vegetables and soil.

E coli – present in the intestines (and excreta) of animals and humans, raw meat and can be present on raw vegetables. Poisoning from this source can be very dangerous because it can lead to kidney failure.

Food-borne diseases

Other organisms are said to cause **food-borne illness**. These do not multiply in food but use food to get into the human gut where they then multiply and cause a range of illnesses, some of them serious. They include:

Campylobacter – this now causes more food-related illness than any other organism. It is found in raw poultry and meat, sewage, animals, insects and birds.

Listeria – this organism is of concern because it can multiply (slowly) at fridge temperatures (i.e. below 5°C). It has been linked with such chilled products as unpasteurised cheeses, paté and prepared salads as well as cook/chill meals.

Typhoid – can be very serious and is caused by a type of salmonella. It is often linked with poor drainage and sewage systems, untreated water and carriers.

Bacillary dysentery – caused by an organism called shigella and can come from sewage, manure, infected people and contaminated food and water.

Norovirus – like all viruses this will not multiply on food but may live for a short time on surfaces, utensils and food and use these to get into the body. The most usual way this is spread is airborne, person to person, water or sewage.

Other sources and risks to food safety include chemical, physical and allergenic risks. For more information on these see page 15.

Food spoilage

This is food that has spoiled or 'gone off'. Unlike contamination with bacteria it can usually be detected by sight, smell, taste or texture. Signs of spoilage include mould; slimy, over-wet or over-dry food; sour smell or taste; discoloured and wrinkled food; or other texture changes.

It is caused by natural breakdown of the food by spoilage organisms such as spoilage bacteria, enzymes, moulds and yeasts which, in some cases, may not be harmful themselves but cause the food to deteriorate. Spoilage may also be caused by poor storage, poor handling or by contamination of the food.

Food spoilage can account for a significant amount of unnecessary waste in a business and if food stock is being managed and stored properly it should not happen.

Any food that has spoiled or is out of date must be reported to the supervisor/line manager then disposed of appropriately and marked 'not for human consumption'. It should be separated from general waste and be disposed of away from food storage areas.

See details later in this chapter on stock rotation and how this can help reduce food spoilage.

Safe food handling practices and procedures

Temperature control

Temperature plays a very important role in food safety. The temperatures between 5°C and 63°C are referred to as the **danger zone** because this is the temperature range where it is possible for bacteria to multiply, with most rapid activity at around 37°C. When cooking food take it through the danger zone quickly. Most food should be cooked to 75°C to kill bacteria. When cooling food, cool it quickly (within 90 minutes) so it is not in the danger zone longer than necessary.

Electronic temperature probes can be used to measure the temperature in the centre of both hot and cold food. They are also good for recording the temperature of deliveries and checking of food temperatures in fridges. Make sure the probe is clean and disinfected before

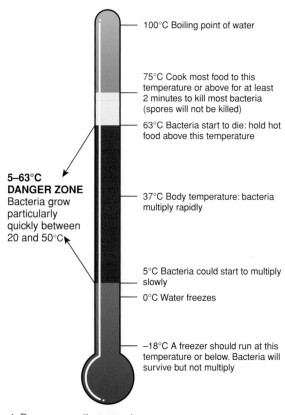

100°C Boiling point of water

75°C Cook most food to this temperature or above for at least 2 minutes to kill most bacteria (spores will not be killed)

63°C Bacteria start to die: hold hot food above this temperature

5–63°C DANGER ZONE Bacteria grow particularly quickly between 20 and 50°C

37°C Body temperature: bacteria multiply rapidly

5°C Bacteria could start to multiply slowly

0°C Water freezes

−18°C A freezer should run at this temperature or below. Bacteria will survive but not multiply

▲ Danger zone thermometer

Practical Cookery for the Level 1 Diploma

use (disposable disinfectant wipes are useful for this). Place the probe into the centre of the food making sure it is not touching bone or the cooking container.

The running temperature of refrigerators, freezers and chill cabinets should be checked and recorded at least once a day. Refrigerators and chill cabinets should be below 5°C and freezers below −18°C.

Systems are now available to log temperatures of all fridges, freezers and display cabinets in a business. Temperatures are recorded and sent to a central computer several times a day. These can then be printed or stored electronically as part of due diligence record keeping. Units not running at correct temperatures will be highlighted.

Preparation

Monitor the time that food spends at kitchen temperatures and keep this to a minimum. When preparing large amounts do so in batches, keeping the majority of the food refrigerated until it is needed. It is important that the core (centre) temperature of food does not go above 8°C.

If you need to defrost frozen food, place it in a deep tray, cover with film and label with what the item is and the date when defrosting was started. This is best done in a specific thawing cabinet. Alternatively, place at the bottom of the fridge where thawing liquid cannot drip onto anything else. Defrost food completely (no ice crystals on any part); once thawed the item should remain at refrigerator temperatures then be cooked thoroughly within 12 hours.

Cooking

Cooking food to a core temperature of **75°C** for **two** minutes will kill most bacteria and these temperatures are important, especially where large amounts are being cooked or the consumers are in the high-risk categories (see page 26).

However, some dishes on hotel and restaurant menus may be cooked to a lower temperature than this according to individual dish and customer requirements. Lower temperatures − but no lower than 63°C − can be used when a whole piece of meat such as a steak is cooked. Always cook to the higher recommended temperature where meat has been boned/rolled or minced or where food is part of a made up dish such as fishcakes or fish pie. The cooking temperature needs to be appropriate to ensure most bacteria are killed.

> **Professional tip**
> Sometimes where customers choose dishes cooked to temperatures lower than those recommended a warning is put on the menu stating that customers eat these at their own risk.

Chilling

If food is being cooled/chilled to serve cold or for reheating at a later time, it must be cooled to **8°C** within **90 minutes**. This will help prevent multiplication of any bacteria that may be present and avoids any possible problem with spores. The best way to do this is in a blast chiller.

Reheating

If reheating previously cooked food, reheat to 75°C+ (the recommendation is 82°C in Scotland). The temperature in the centre of the food must be maintained for at least two minutes and re-heating must only be done once.

Holding for service, serving and transporting

Cooked food being held for service, served or transported must be kept above **63°C** for hot food or below **5°C** for cold food.

Stock control procedures

Food deliveries

For food to remain in best condition and be safe to eat correct storage is essential. Only approved suppliers who can assure that food is delivered in the best condition should be used. Food must be delivered in suitable packaging, within the required use by or best before dates and at the correct temperature (see below).

All deliveries should be checked against the delivery note then moved to the appropriate storage area as soon as possible and chilled/frozen food within 15 minutes of delivery. Use a food probe to check the temperature of food deliveries: chilled food should be below 5°C; frozen foods should be at or below −18°C. Many suppliers will now provide a print-out of temperatures at which food was delivered.

Dry goods should be in undamaged packaging, well within best before dates, be completely dry and in perfect condition on delivery.

Storage

Remove food items from outer boxes before placing the products in fridge, freezer or dry store. Food should be stored with correct labelling so it is clear what the commodity is. Table 2.3 gives storage instructions and temperatures for different commodities.

Date marking and stock rotation

Adopt a 'first in – first out' (FIFO) policy to use older stock first and observe storage dates (best before) on packaged food.

- **Use-by dates** are given for perishable foods that need refrigeration (this must be observed by law).
- **Best before dates** are provided for other items not needing refrigerated storage.

KEY WORDS

Pathogenic bacteria – bacteria that could cause illness.

Toxin – a poison produced by some bacteria.

Spore – a state some bacteria can achieve to survive high temperatures and disinfection.

Food spoilage – food deteriorating, usually detected by taste, smell, appearance, texture, colour and so on.

Danger zone – the temperature range where bacterial multiplication could take place: 5°C–63°C.

FIFO – first in-first out, referring to using older food stocks before new deliveries.

Use-by date – these are on perishable foods that need refrigeration and must be observed by law.

Best before date – for non-perishable foods that do not need refrigeration. It is best practice not to use after this date.

Table 2.3 Storage instructions and temperatures

Food type	Storage temperature	Storage instructions
Refrigerated items in a multi-use fridge	Fridge running at below 5°C	All food must be covered and labelled with name of the item and the date. Always store raw food at the bottom of the fridge with other items above. Keep high-risk foods well away from raw foods. Never overload the fridge; to operate properly cold air must be allowed to circulate between items. Wrap strong smelling foods very well as the smell (and taste) can transfer to other foods, e.g. milk. Record the temperature at which the fridge is operating. Do this at least once a day and keep the fridge temperatures with other kitchen records.
Frozen foods	Freezer running at −18°C or below.	Separate raw foods from ready-to-eat foods and never allow food to be re-frozen once it has de-frosted. Any food that is to be frozen must be well wrapped or placed in a suitable container with a lid (items may also be vacuum packed). Make sure that all food is labelled and dated before freezing.
Raw meat and poultry	Fridges should be running at temperatures between 0°C and 2°C	Wherever possible store in fridges just for meat and poultry to avoid drip contamination. If not already packaged, place on trays, cover well with cling film and label. If it is necessary to store meat/poultry in a multi-use fridge make sure it is covered, labelled and placed at the bottom of the fridge running below 5°C and is well away from other items.
Dry goods (including items such as rice, dried pasta, sugar, flour, grains)	A cool, well-ventilated dry store area	Should be kept in clean, covered containers on wheels or in smaller sealed containers on shelves to stop pests getting into them. Storage should be in a cool, well-ventilated dry store area and well-managed stock rotation is essential. Retain packaging information as this may include essential **allergy advice**.
Fish	Fridge running at 1–2°C	A specific fish fridge is preferable. Remove fresh fish from ice containers and place on trays, cover well with cling film and label. If it is necessary to store fish in a multi-use fridge make sure it is well covered, labelled and placed at the bottom of the fridge running below 5°C well away from other items. Remember that odours from fish can get into other items such as milk or eggs.
Dairy Products/eggs	Milk and cream, eggs and cheese should be stored below 5°C. Sterilised or UHT milk can be kept in the dry store. Eggs should be stored at a constant temperature and a fridge is the best place to store them.	Milk and cream, eggs and cheese should be stored in their original containers. For sterilised or UHT milk follow the storage instructions on the label.
Fruit, vegetables and salad items	Dependent on type; refrigerated items should be stored at around 8°C to avoid any chill damage.	Storage conditions will vary according to type, e.g. sacks of potatoes, root vegetables and some fruit can be stored in a cool, well-ventilated store room but salad items, green vegetables, soft fruit and tropical fruit would be better in refrigerated storage.
Canned products	Dry store area	Cans are usually stored in the dry store area and once again rotation of stock is essential. Canned food will carry best before dates and it is not advisable to use after this date. 'Blown' cans must never be used and do not use badly dented or rusty cans. Once opened, transfer any unused canned food to a clean bowl, cover and label it and store in the fridge for up to two days.
Cooked foods	Below 5°C	These include a wide range of foods, e.g. pies, paté, cream cakes, desserts and savoury flans. They will usually be 'high risk' foods so correct storage is essential. For specific storage instructions see the labelling on the individual items, but generally, keep items below 5°C. Store carefully, wrapped and labelled and well away from and above raw foods to avoid any cross-contamination.

Activity

1 What are the main differences between pathogenic bacteria and viruses?
2 What are the four requirements needed for bacteria to multiply? If they have these requirements, how quickly can they divide?
3 What is the temperature range referred to as the danger zone? Why should food be kept out of this zone as much as possible? Suggest three good working practices that will prevent food from being in this zone too long.
4 Show on the diagram below where you would position these different chilled foods in a multi-use fridge: raw chicken, cooked ham, cream, salmon fillets, cooked vegetable quiche, eggs, cheese, cooked pasties, paté, fresh pasta, rump steak, milk, raw sausages, butter, frozen chicken drumsticks that need to be defrosted.
5 There is already some cream cheese in the fridge with a use-by date of today, crème fraiche with a use-by date of tomorrow and some yoghurt with a use-by date of yesterday. What should be done with these items? At what temperature should the fridge be running?

Test yourself

1 What is food poisoning?
2 List five personal hygiene practices you could include on a personal hygiene checklist for kitchen staff.
3 What do the letters HACCP stand for and how is this used?
4 If you wanted help or advice about food safety, where could you find it?
5 What signs would make you suspect there was a rodent pest problem in a kitchen? What would you do about it?
6 Which people would be included in the 'high risk' group for food poisoning and why are they high risk?
7 How is food spoilage different from food contaminated with pathogenic bacteria? Which do you think may be most dangerous and why?
8 What are the temperatures between 5°C and 63°C called? Why are these temperatures important?
9 How can you check the temperature of food?
10 Describe the procedures you should follow when receiving a food delivery.

Health and safety

This chapter covers Unit 103, Health and safety awareness for catering and hospitality.

By the end of this chapter you should be able to:

- Define health and safety and state the factors that affect health and safety in the workplace
- Identify the benefits of good health and safety standards and state the cost of poor health and safety standards
- Define the most commonly used terms in health and safety
- Identify the responsibilities of employers and employees under current legislation and list the consequences of non-compliance with this legislation
- List the causes of slips, trips and falls at work and state ways they could be minimised
- Identify the main injuries from manual handling and state ways to reduce the risk of injury from lifting, carrying and handling
- Identify ways machinery and equipment can cause injury and list the control measures to avoid accidents from these

- State types of hazardous substances and list the control measures to prevent exposure and to protect employees
- Indicate the main causes of fires and explosions and how elements of the fire triangle can be used to extinguish a fire
- Identify the dangers associated with electricity and the measures to prevent these dangers
- List the primary reasons for working safely
- State the functions of PPE, including employers' and employees' responsibilities regarding provision, use, care and maintenance of PPE
- State how the main types of safety signs can be identified
- Identify hazards and incidents that require reporting.

Health and safety practices in the catering and hospitality workplace

Health and safety are very important in the hospitality industry. You need to understand the principles of health and safety and how to apply them when you are working.

Health is when a person feels physically and mentally well, is not suffering from illness or disease and is able to complete their work well without their home or leisure time being affected by their work.

Safety means that there is an absence of risks. You should feel and are safe and secure in your workplace, where you should expect to be able to complete your work without it causing you any injury, harm or illness.

Factors affecting health and safety in the workplace

The reasons why accidents can happen in kitchens and other hospitality areas can be divided into the categories below.

Occupational factors

Kitchen and restaurant equipment can potentially be very dangerous. You will need to consider the safe use of knives and other sharp tools, mixing and cutting machinery, open gas jets or flames, steam, smoke (from smoking equipment), very hot surfaces such as solid top stoves and a wide range of other items.

The food you work with and the process you complete can also be hazardous. For example, those working frequently with flour can suffer from inhaling the dust (a mask could be worn); some can develop an allergy to items such as yeast or nuts; frequent handling of items such as fish or some vegetables can cause skin irritation (use of gloves or masks may be needed). Occasionally sharp fish or meat bones may cause cuts.

You will be dealing with chemicals for cleaning, disinfection, grease removal and a range of other processes. It is important to handle these with care and follow instructions to prevent skin and possible inhalation problems. Use the required Personal Protective Equipment (PPE) such as gloves. Long sleeves will help to prevent skin contact and masks reduce inhalation problems.

Environmental factors

The environment you work in could have hazards too, and employers are legally bound to provide suitable working conditions and facilities.

Facilities include changing and rest rooms with storage for personal belongings, toilets and hand washing basins, first aid equipment, drinking water and PPE that is kept in good condition with somewhere to store it.

Accidents and ill health can occur when working in very high temperatures, where you can become over hot, dehydrated, dizzy and feel sick.

Poor lighting can make working conditions difficult and poor vision could lead to accidents.

Prolonged high noise levels can result in ear damage and high levels of noise could lead to accidents when called instructions or warnings are not heard.

Human factors

Those working in a kitchen may be inexperienced or may not have had proper training for the tasks they are completing; this can lead to accidents or injury. Anyone without the skills or experience needed must be supervised until full training is given.

Someone who is not concentrating fully on what they are doing or is just being careless can cause injury to themselves or to someone else. A lack of concentration and poor performance can be because of someone's mental or physical state. For example, they may have a physical condition such as a back injury, be suffering from stress, feel overworked, or have personal concerns, all of which may result in them losing concentration and performing poorly. Anyone at work under the influence of alcohol, drugs or other substances may lose concentration and the ability to complete their job well; they should not be working and certainly should not be operating machinery.

 Health and safety

Work in an organised, clean and tidy way. This will help to reduce the risk of accidents and injury.

 Health and safety

If you are aware of anything in your workplace that could be a health and safety problem either put it right yourself, such as a wet floor, or report it to a supervisor, such as a faulty cable on a mixer.

The benefits of good health and safety procedures in the workplace

Prevents legal action

By law all employers must have proper health and safety measures and procedures in place. Failure to do this may result in legal action, which can lead to high fines and, in extreme cases, even imprisonment. Employees also must comply with health and safety legislation and cooperate with the health and safety procedures set up by their employers.

To reduce the possibility of accidents and illness

Health and safety regulations and practices are in place to protect employees from work-related accidents or illness. Everyone needs to feel safe at work. If employers are health and safety focused and comply with legislation, and employees cooperate with the measures put in place by employers, accidents and injury at work can be avoided.

To preserve and promote a good reputation

First-rate employers will want to have a good reputation for their standards of health and safety. It will help to achieve well-motivated employees who can work efficiently without unnecessary accidents and injury. Businesses with good health and safety procedures are likely to have high standards in other areas too, making them an employer that people will want to work for. Poor health and safety standards can result in accidents, injury or even death. Accidents, injuries and deaths may be well-publicised locally and in the press, leading to a loss of reputation as well as possible legal action, loss of business or even being closed down.

Costs

There can be very high costs as a result of a business not having good health and safety procedures in place. Poor standards could include reduced performance from employees, resulting in less income and profit. Accidents, injury and illness could occur resulting in personal suffering, stress, enforced changes in lifestyle, long-term illness or disability and also loss of income. Anyone suffering in this way has a right to take legal action and claim compensation from the employer who has been negligent. An employer may also need to cover pay while an employee is sick. In some cases death has occurred as a result of poor health and safety in workplaces.

Being negligent about health and safety can also lead to costs from prosecution, fines, legal costs and being prevented from trading, as well as the bad publicity from reports of accidents and incidents due to health and safety issues.

KEY WORDS

Negligent – not taking care or ignoring something.

Compensation – a payment that may be made because of accident or injury.

Hazard – something with the potential to cause harm.

Environmental – your surroundings or location.

Occupational – work related.

Activity

1 Kitchen equipment can be dangerous and could cause harm if not used properly. List five items or areas that could be dangerous, the harm that could be caused and how it could be avoided.
2 What facilities should an employer provide for kitchen staff?
3 What are three advantages of employers having good health and safety standards?
4 Why must a person under the influence of alcohol or drugs not work in a kitchen?

Frequently used health and safety terms

Workplace – the location where most of your work is completed; it could also include a different site, off-site functions or work vehicles.

Accident – an unplanned incident which may cause injury.

EHO/EHP – Environmental Health Officer (now often called Environmental Health Practitioner). This person is employed by the local authority to enforce health and safety (and food safety) standards in their area, but also to offer help, advice and training on these matters.

Hazard – something that could possibly cause harm.

Control measure – something put in place to make a hazard as safe as possible.

PPE – Personal Protective Equipment (and clothing). This is equipment or clothing to protect you from hazards at work. In a kitchen it may include a full chef's uniform but also items such as disposable gloves, masks and safety shoes. For more information on PPE see below.

PAT – Portable Appliance Testing. This usually involves a qualified electrician testing the electrical equipment in an area such as a kitchen to ensure it is safe to use.

Electric shock – when a current of electricity passes through the body.

Evacuation route – the route designated for leaving the building quickly.

Occupational health – care of employees' health while at work.

Manual handling – lifting of heavy or awkward items.

Noise – often unwanted sound that can be loud.

Report – recording something, often in writing. An incident or accident would need to be reported.

Harassment – behaviour, including bullying, that makes someone feel threatened or uncomfortable.

Risk assessment – identifying hazards and risks in a workplace.

Responsibilities of employers and employees for health and safety

It is essential that working safely becomes part of the culture of every workplace to prevent accidents and injuries, to maintain health and to increase productivity. Working safely can increase productivity because there will be fewer interruptions to deal with minor injuries, collisions, falls, faulty equipment and a wide range of other safety-related issues.

Employers have a responsibility to provide a safe workplace which will not cause employees illness or harm. It means that the premises themselves are safe, with good lighting and ventilation and that equipment has been tested for safety and is maintained correctly. There must be measures and training in place to deal with chemicals without causing harm. Risk assessments must have been completed and employees should receive a health and safety policy statement, which outlines the employer's commitment to health and safety and the measures in place to keep the workplace safe and comply with the law. Safety equipment and clothing must be provided and staff should receive ongoing health and safety training.

> **Professional tip**
>
> The 1974 Health and Safety at Work Act lays down the requirements for health and safety in the workplace.

Employees have responsibilities too. They must work in a safe way so they do not endanger themselves or others working with them. They must cooperate with the health and safety measures the employer has put in place and wear the safety clothing and equipment provided. They should also report anything they notice which poses a health and safety risk or is potentially dangerous.

Consequences of non-compliance

Compliance with the requirements for health and safety in the workplace is overseen by Environmental Health Officers (Environmental Health Practitioners) who are employed by the local authority. They can enter premises at any reasonable time to conduct their investigations.

The EHO (EHP) may give verbal or written advice or could issue:

- an **improvement notice**, which means the business is given a set amount of time to improve on certain issues highlighted
- a **prohibition notice**, which means the business is unsafe to operate and can be closed down.

Non-compliance with health and safety requirements can result in fines, prosecution and closure of the business, and in extreme cases imprisonment for up to two years.

If employees do not comply with health and safety requirements they may be given verbal and written warnings from their employer, they could lose their job and could even be prosecuted.

Activity

1 What is occupational health?
2 What action may be taken if a kitchen employee continuously ignores the health and safety rules put in place by their employer?
3 What are three of the responsibilities an employee has for health and safety at work?
4 What is a health and safety policy statement? Why is it important to you at work?
5 Why might a prohibition notice be issued?

KEY WORDS

Productivity – the amount of work that can be completed in a certain time.

Improvement notice – a business is given a set amount of time to improve on certain issues highlighted.

Prohibition notice – a business is unsafe to operate and can be closed down.

Hazards in the workplace

A **hazard** is something with potential to cause harm.

A **risk** is the likelihood of someone being harmed by the hazard.

In a kitchen and other hospitality areas there are a number of reasons why hazards may be present and these can lead to accidents occurring. The most common accidents occurring in hospitality areas are caused by:

- Slips, trips and falls
- Handling of heavy or awkward items
- Injuries from machinery and equipment
- Exposure to harmful substances.

Slips, trips and falls

Slips, trips and falls are the most frequent cause of accident and injury, not just because of the incident itself. The person could fall onto something very hot like a deep fryer or solid top stove, could spill something they are carrying onto themselves such as a pan of hot soup, or could fall onto a sharp object such as a knife. They could also hit their head on a table or piece of equipment as they fall or could fall onto moving machinery.

Health and safety

Health and Safety Executive (HSE) statistics show that slips and trips are the single most common cause of injuries at work, accounting for over a third of all major work injuries. They cost employers over £512 million a year in lost production. For more information visit the Health and Safety Executive website: www.hse.gov.uk.

Table 3.1 shows some of the causes of slips, trips and falls and how they could be avoided.

Table 3.1 Causes of slips, trips and falls

Cause of accident	Example	Ways to reduce the risk
Bad design and structure of the building	Uneven floors or narrow, steep stairways	Improved design of buildings or improvement to specific areas to make them safe.
Poor signage	Not pointing out hazardous areas such as where floors can become slippery or where there is a step down.	Clear and visible signage in the appropriate places. Staff must be made aware of and understand what these signs mean.
Bad housekeeping standards	Untidy, badly kept areas; boxes or debris on floors and walkways.	Good housekeeping standards: keep areas clean and tidy and easier to work in.
Poor lighting	Lighting not sufficient for tasks being completed so there are dim or dark areas; poor vision can lead to hazards not being seen.	Lighting systems need to be sufficient for the tasks being carried out and well maintained so they work properly. They must also be kept clean – dirty, greasy light fittings will not give off as much light.

(continued)

Table 3.1 (continued)

Cause of accident	Example	Ways to reduce the risk
Poor ventilation	For example extraction units not working, making work areas very hot and uncomfortable and causing workers to feel unwell. Condensation can make areas steamy or wet, also leading to accidents.	Ventilation needs to be sufficient, well-maintained and in good working order. Un-cleaned ventilation systems will not work properly.
Dangerous working practices	For example allowing electrical flexes to trail across a floor or not cleaning spills of water or oil from a floor, resulting in slips and falls.	Everyone must work to the same high health and safety standards and rules. Staff must be trained in good practice and put that good practice in place.
Distraction or lack of attention	Such as not looking where you are going or not taking care with stairs, especially when you cannot see your feet (for example when carrying trays, large saucepans or boxes).	Always give the tasks you are completing and where you are walking your full attention.
Trying to work too quickly	Working in hospitality can often put you under pressure, especially at busy times making you work faster. Warnings about wet floors may be forgotten and people can bump into each other, which can be especially dangerous where hot, heavy or sharp items are involved.	Although there may be a temptation to rush at busy times, the work may actually get completed more slowly if there is a collision or fall. Try to develop efficient working systems instead.
Not following the rules for health and safety	For example, not using the systems of work or ways of moving around the area that have been set up to ensure health and safety; not keeping walkways free of hazards so slips and falls may happen.	Always follow procedures, advice and training given. Employers and their employees both have a legal responsibility for health and safety at work.
Not wearing or using the correct PPE (personal protective equipment)	For example not wearing non-slip safety shoes in the kitchen; not wearing aprons properly so the apron or the ties may be tripped over.	Always wear or use the correct PPE to keep yourself safe and wear/use it properly. Wear aprons so they cannot be tripped over.
Not in the right physical or mental state for working	Such as an illness, injury or personal problems. If these are occupying your mind you could be working with less care and accidents could happen.	Speak with your supervisor or line manager to discuss a solution. If there is an occupational health department they may be able to offer advice.

Manual handling

When working in hospitality it is very likely that you will need to lift or move objects that may be heavy, large, or of an awkward or unusual shape. In addition to this the items may be at varying temperatures, from freezing to boiling, and some items could be damp or greasy. All of these could possibly cause injury if not handled properly.

The main injuries that can occur from manual handling are:

- Back and spinal injuries
- Muscular injuries
- Fractures
- Sprains
- Cuts, bruises and burns.

Avoiding injury from lifting and carrying

- First, consider the item or load. Think about its weight, size, temperature and shape. Is it possible to make the load smaller, for example, unloading large cans of tomatoes from their outer cases?

- Consider the distance you need to move the item and whether the distance could be minimised.
- Ask for help – the task is often easier with two people.
- Is there any lifting equipment available for you to use?
- Consider using a trolley but again do not lift anything onto the trolley that is too heavy for you. Do not load the trolley too high because you will not be able to see what is in front of you and the load may become unstable and fall off.
- Consider the environment – are there any uneven floors, stairs, high or low temperatures or low lighting? These will all make a difference.
- Avoid handling wet or greasy loads and do not try to move items when floors are wet or slippery.
- Wear the correct PPE, for example, a padded jacket and gloves when working in walk-in fridges and freezers.
- Do not unload, carry or store heavy items, sharp items or hot items above your shoulder height.
- Do not lift and carry heavy, hot or awkward items if you feel unwell.
- If you are lifting, unloading or moving heavy items as a regular part of your job you should receive manual handling training.

Correct lifting technique

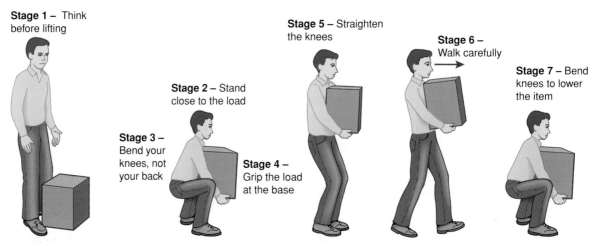

Stage 1 – Think before lifting

Stage 2 – Stand close to the load

Stage 3 – Bend your knees, not your back

Stage 4 – Grip the load at the base

Stage 5 – Straighten the knees

Stage 6 – Walk carefully

Stage 7 – Bend knees to lower the item

▲ Correct lifting technique

Assess the load – can it be made smaller? Can lifting or carrying equipment be used? Consider the weight and shape and where you need to move it to.

Stand close to the load, with feet apart and your weight evenly spread; chin tucked in, shoulders level.

Bend the knees, keeping the back straight and grip the load at the base or with handles keeping it close to your body.

Bring the load up to waist height and straighten the knees.

Walk carefully, making sure that you can see where you are going.

Lower the item in place again with bent knees and straight back.

Machinery and equipment

There is a variety of machinery and equipment you may use in hospitality areas. If they are not used properly they have the potential to cause harm.

Some of the possible hazards are:

- **Not using the machinery properly** – Machinery is designed to be used in certain ways without causing any injury to the operator. However, if it is used wrongly, not assembled correctly or the required safety procedures are not in place, accidents and injuries may be the result. Always make sure you have had full training before using any piece of equipment or machine. If you are still unsure ask for further training before using it.

- **The equipment is faulty and not working properly** – All equipment must be in good working condition and regularly maintained to do the job for which it is intended without causing any injury. Report any faulty or dangerous equipment to a supervisor immediately and warn others not to use it.

- **Entanglement or entrapment** – This is getting trapped or tangled in machine parts. It could be long hair, strings from an apron, or jewellery or watches caught in the moving parts of a mixing machine. Injuries can be caused by putting a hand or spatula into a machine to free trapped food. Most machines now have guards in place to prevent this. To avoid accidents always wear the correct PPE, make sure that hair is fully enclosed in a hat and do not wear jewellery, watches or anything else that could get caught in machinery.

- **Impact** – Impact is something hitting or falling on you, such as heavy equipment falling onto you from a high shelf (do not store heavy items high up), a heavily loaded trolley running into you (do not leave unattended) or a shelf collapsing onto you. Good maintenance should prevent this.

- **Ejection** could be a dough hook not attached properly and flying off the machine when switched on (proper guards in place should prevent this), or machine parts flying off and hitting you (good maintenance is needed).

Hazardous substances

In hospitality areas there are a number of substances you may use that could be hazardous to health if not used properly. They include cleaning chemicals such as detergents, disinfectants, sanitisers, degreasers and descalers, fuel gels and spirits and cooking liquids and gases. Harm could be caused by the substance entering the body through the skin, eyes, by swallowing, or inhaling through the nose. Anyone using chemicals in their job must be trained in their correct use and provided with suitable protective equipment or clothing such as gloves or goggles.

The Control of Substances Hazardous to Health (COSHH) Regulations were consolidated in 2002 and are the main legislation dealing with hazardous substances. They state that any substances or chemicals that could be hazardous to health must be:

- Stored, handled and disposed of according to COSHH regulations
- Identified on the packaging or container
- Identified in writing and given a risk rating so safety precautions can be put in place
- Labelled appropriately as toxic, harmful, irritant, corrosive, explosive and oxidising (see page 42).

Corrosive

Flammable

Harmful

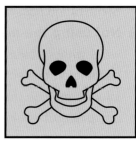
Toxic

▲ Labels for hazardous chemicals

When using chemicals:

- Make sure they are stored in a lockable cupboard away from the kitchen and not in direct sunlight
- Store in the original container, with the label in place and the top or lid firmly in place
- Read instructions carefully and dilute exactly as directed
- Never mix different chemicals
- If splashed on skin rinse with cold water and know the first aid procedures
- Dispose of chemicals in the way recommended on the container.

KEY WORDS

Hazard – something with potential to cause harm.

Risk – the likelihood of someone being harmed by the hazard.

Debris – rubbish, waste and unwanted items.

Condensation – moisture and water droplets produced by steam.

Extraction (kitchen) – removal of stale air, steam and condensation.

Impact – being hit by something or colliding with it.

Ejection – something being thrown out at high speed.

Fire and explosion

Fire and possible explosions are always risks that need to be considered in hospitality premises. They may be caused by gas jets or open flames, overheated oils and other hot liquid substances, and by fuel gels. They could also be caused by electrical faults or faulty equipment, gas leaks or gas build-up and chemicals, but also by carelessness and misuse of equipment. Smoking can always be a cause of fire and is not allowed in most buildings, but also do not smoke outside near gas canisters, waste oil or items such as paper and cardboard.

The Regulatory Reform (Fire Safety) Order which came into force in 2006 applies to England and Wales (Scotland and Northern Ireland have similar laws). These laws put the responsibility for fire safety onto the employer or business owner. They must conduct a risk assessment of the premises and business, identify the risks and put measures in place to make them as safe as possible. This may include:

- Having fire alarms and testing them regularly to make sure they are working
- Making sure that escape routes are clearly marked and there are no obstacles in the way
- Ensuring that fire detection systems are in place
- Providing suitable equipment for extinguishing fires.

Three elements are needed for fire – heat, oxygen and fuel. If one of these is taken away the fire will not start or continue. Extinguishing fires relies on removing one of these elements, such as restricting the supply of oxygen (a foam extinguisher acts in this way), or removing the heat (a water extinguisher cools the burning material down).

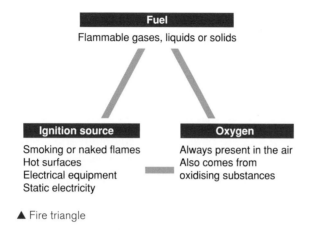

Fuel
Flammable gases, liquids or solids

Ignition source
Smoking or naked flames
Hot surfaces
Electrical equipment
Static electricity

Oxygen
Always present in the air
Also comes from
oxidising substances

▲ Fire triangle

Training in procedures to follow in case of fire or other emergency is essential for all staff. There must be a fire and evacuation plan in place. Staff must know how to follow the plan and evacuate the building safely, assisting customers and visitors where appropriate.

Fire extinguishers are a very important part of fire safety and there are different types for use on various kinds of fire. Only use an extinguisher if it is safe for you to do so and if you have been trained in its use.

KNOW YOUR FIRE EXTINGUISHER COLOUR CODE

WATER	DRY POWDER	FOAM	CO₂ CARBON DIOXIDE	VAPOURISING LIQUIDS

| Unsafe all voltages. Wood, paper, textiles, etc. | Safe all voltages Flammable liquids | Unsafe all voltages Flammable liquids | Safe all voltages Flammable liquids | Safe all voltages Flammable liquids |

▲ Types of fire extinguisher and their uses

If a fire breaks out in your work area:

● Raise the alarm and warn others verbally
● Turn off gas supplies using a central cut off point if possible
● Never put yourself in danger; only tackle small fires and only if you have been trained to do so
● Leave by the appointed escape route and go to the assembly point. Remain there and do not re-enter the building until told that you can do so.

Risk assessment – an examination of anything in the workplace that could possibly harm people.

Toxic – poisonous and harmful.

Fuel gels – flammable gels often used to heat food service equipment.

Obstacle – a hazard or something in the way.

Evacuate – leave the building.

Assembly point – the place where people should stand when they have been evacuated from a building.

Electricity and the possible dangers

Hospitality establishments use a range of electrical equipment and it must be used with care to avoid accidents and injury. Under the Electricity at Work Regulations (1989) all electrical equipment must be tested for safety annually (this is called PAT testing – see page 36 for more information) by a qualified electrician. They will also check that cables and flexes are in good working order and are not damaged and that the correct fuses are being used. Circuit breakers must also be regularly checked.

If you notice any damaged or faulty electrical equipment do not use it, warn others and report it to a supervisor or manager. If a person comes into direct contact with an electrical current electric shock can occur, which can be serious or even fatal. Faulty electrical equipment can also cause fire and may result in burns. If someone you are working with has an electric shock:

- Switch off the electricity
- Raise the alarm
- Call for medical help or first aid.

If it is not possible to switch the electricity off, free the person from it, protecting yourself using something like a thick dry oven cloth or something made from wood or rubber – the electricity will not conduct through these. Do not touch the person directly or the electricity will be transmitted to you.

Activity

1 If you were asked to put away a large delivery of frozen foods, what are four safety precautions you should take?

2 What is the most frequent cause of accidents and injury in the hospitality industry? Suggest four ways that these could be avoided.

3 If you need to use a large mixing machine for the first time, what do you need to consider?

4 For a fire to start, heat is needed. What are the other two elements that need to be present?

5 Suggest two problems with electrical equipment that you would need to report to a supervisor or manager.

Circuit breaker – a safety device that breaks the flow of electricity in emergency or in case of electrical overload.

Irritant – can cause a reaction or irritation of the skin.

Corrosive – breaks things down or wears them away, for example attacks metals.

Oxidising – reacts in the presence of oxygen.

Health and safety procedures

It is important to follow health and safety procedures to:

- Prevent accidents and injuries
- Maintain health
- Increase productivity.

Activity

Insert the missing words from the list below into the gaps in the text.

health   prosecution   standards   employees

reputation   accidents   law   productivity

Maintaining high .... of health and safety at work is of the greatest importance. It will help to prevent .... and injury as well as maintaining the ...... and wellbeing of .... Good health and safety procedures mean that you will also comply with the ... and avoid risk of ...., as well as increasing .... and building a good ....

Personal Protective Equipment (PPE)

Personal Protective Equipment and clothing is designed to protect employees as they work. Typical PPE may consist of a full chef's uniform, which protects the body from heat, spills and sharp objects; and reinforced safety shoes to protect feet from hot, heavy or sharp items. PPE may be provided for special tasks such as a padded jacket and gloves for working in a freezer, or goggles and mask when using strong oven cleaning chemicals and strong rubber gloves when cleaning pots and pans.

Employers have a responsibility to provide the correct PPE for their employees. The PPE that employers provide must be kept in good, clean condition and replaced as necessary. There must be somewhere provided such as a locker for an employee to store their PPE; changing facilities must also be available.

The employee must use the appropriate PPE provided and look after it properly. They must report any defects with the PPE to the employer.

Safety signs

Health and safety signs point out health and safety messages using shape, colour, symbols, pictures and words but should not replace other methods of controlling risks. The signs are divided into four general categories:

Yellow signs/warning signs

These warn of various dangers such as wet floors, hot surfaces or corrosive materials. Probably the most frequently used yellow sign is the tent-shaped wet floor sign.

▲ Yellow sign

Blue signs/mandatory signs

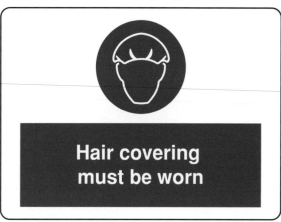

Hair covering must be worn

▲ Blue sign

These inform about precautions that must be taken such as how to progress safely through certain areas or the PPE that must be used.

Red signs/prohibition or fire fighting signs

Red signs inform of what must not be done in a particular area, for example, no entry or no smoking. Red signs are also used for fire fighting equipment such as hose reels.

No smoking on site

▲ Red sign

Green signs/safe signs

First aid

Fire exit

▲ Green sign

Green signs are used to guide people to fire escapes and emergency exits. Green is also used to point out where first aid equipment is kept or where first aid rooms are.

Reporting hazards and incidents

It is sometimes necessary for employees to report matters they think may affect health and safety. These would usually be reported to a supervisor or line manager and would include:

- Damage or misuse of the building or equipment
- Ill health, including dermatitis or infectious diseases
- Environmental problems, including excessive noise or heat
- Abuse from others, such as bullying, physical or mental abuse.

It is important to report and record any accident or injury you may have at work, no matter how small. The system most workplaces use for this is individual paper accident report forms which are then stored in a file. Sometimes an electronic system may be used.

KEY WORDS

Mandatory – something that you must do or must use.

Prohibition – something you must not do, not use or an area you must not go into.

Dermatitis – a skin problem causing inflammation of the skin, making it red, scaly and itchy.

Contact dermatitis – occurs in some people when their skin reacts to certain chemicals or foods they work with. It can be controlled by avoiding direct contact between the substances or food and the skin, for example by wearing gloves.

Test yourself

1 Suggest four effects there could be on staff working in a kitchen with poor lighting and ventilation.
2 If someone slips, trips or falls in a kitchen what are four additional injuries that could occur?
3 What do the letters COSHH stand for? What is COSHH designed to do?
4 What are four ways that an accidental fire could start in a kitchen?
5 What happens when someone has an electric shock? If you saw someone having an electric shock what should you do? What must you not do?
6 When using machinery, what could cause someone to get entangled or entrapped in it?
7 What is meant by each of the following terms?
    – PAT testing
    – EHO/EHP
    – Evacuation route
    – Risk assessment
    – Productivity
8 What are four responsibilities of employees under health and safety requirements?
9 Give an example of each of these health and safety signs. What information is each giving?
    – Yellow sign
    – Blue sign
    – Red Sign
    – Green sign
10 What are three health and safety related matters you should report to a supervisor or line manager?

Healthier foods and special diets

This chapter covers Unit 104, Introduction to healthier foods and special diets.

By the end of the chapter you should be able to:

- State the benefits of healthier ingredients
- Identify the types of ingredients that contribute to a healthier diet
- Describe the consequences of not having healthier ingredients
- Describe why it is important for catering establishments to offer healthier choices
- Identify sources of current government nutritional guidelines and outline current nutritional guidelines

- Describe the changes that can be made to dishes to make them healthier choices according to current nutritional guidelines
- Identify groups of people who have special dietary needs
- Identify dietary/nutritional requirements of vulnerable groups
- Identify the dietary/nutritional requirements of those who need special diets.

Healthier diets

The importance and benefits of a healthy diet

There are no bad foods, only bad diets. No single food provides all of the nutrients essential to keep us healthy. We need to eat a variety of foods to give us all the nutrients we need for a healthy diet. A balanced diet also makes our mealtimes more interesting.

A healthier diet and good nutrition can increase life expectancy, reduce the risk of illness (for example, heart attack, diabetes, cancers and stroke), give people increased energy levels and improve their quality of life. Improving our diets will reduce the cost to the National Health Service, as fewer people have conditions or illnesses related to poor nutrition that need to be treated.

Types of ingredients that contribute to a healthier diet

The best way to stay fit and healthy is to eat a diet high in fruit, vegetables, wholegrains and plant-based foods like beans and lentils, but low in fat, sugar and salt. This will ensure you receive all of the nutrients detailed above in the correct quantities.

Nutritionists give very simple advice on eating a healthy diet. This includes:

- **Choose, where possible, wholefoods** such as wholemeal flour, wholemeal bread and pasta and brown rice, which have a high fibre content and are less refined.
- **Eat a variety of fruit and vegetables**. They contain valuable vitamins, minerals, fibre and folic acid, which help to protect us from illness. They also contain antioxidants which help to protect the body's cells from damage. Ideally you should aim to eat at least five portions of fruit and vegetables a day.
- **Eat pulses**, for example peas, beans and lentils.
- **Eat lean meat and low fat dairy products**. High consumption of red meat may increase chances of colorectal cancer and possible cancers of the pancreas, breasts, prostate and kidney.

- **Concentrate on building your diet on starchy foods**. Starchy foods include cereals such as wheat, rye, oats, barley, rice and some vegetables such as potatoes, sweet potatoes and yams.
- **Eat more oily fish rich in Omega 3 oils**. Omega 3 fatty acids in oily fish may reduce the growth of cancer cells in animals. Fish is rich in vitamins and a source of protein.
- **Avoid saturated fats**. Use polyunsaturated fats and monounsaturated fats, e.g. sunflower oil, olive oil. Some reports suggest that a high fat diet may increase the possibilities of cancers.

- **Avoid high levels of sugar**.
- **Consume less salt** – eat a maximum of 6g a day
- **Drink plenty of water**.
- **Take regular exercise**.
- **Always have breakfast**.

Professional tip

Poultry has not been linked to any type of cancer, so it is a good alternative to red meat.

Nutrients

Nutrients in foods help our bodies to do everyday things like moving, growing and seeing. They also help our bodies to heal themselves if they are injured, and a balanced diet can help to prevent illness and disease.

The main nutrients are:

- Carbohydrates
- Protein
- Fats
- Vitamins
- Minerals
- Water.

Carbohydrates

We need carbohydrates for energy. There are three main types or carbohydrate:

- Sugars
- Starches
- Fibre.

▲ Foods high in carbohydrates

Sugars

Sugars are the simple form of carbohydrate. There are several types of sugar:

- Glucose – found in the blood of animals and in fruit and honey
- Fructose – found in fruit, honey and cane sugar

- Sucrose – found in beet and cane sugar
- Lactose – found in milk
- Maltose – found in cereal grains and used in beer making.

Starches

Starches are present in many foods, such as:

- Pasta
- Cereals
- Cakes, biscuits and bread
- Whole grains, such as rice, barley, tapioca
- Powdered grains, such as flour, cornflour, ground rice, arrowroot
- Vegetables
- Unripe fruit, such as bananas, apples, cooking pears.

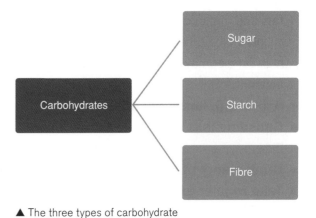

▲ The three types of carbohydrate

Fibre

Unlike other carbohydrates, dietary fibre cannot be digested and does not provide energy to the body. However, dietary fibre is essential for a balanced diet because it:

- Helps to remove waste and toxins from the body, and maintain bowel action
- Helps to control the digestion and processing of nutrients
- Adds bulk to the diet, helping us to stop feeling hungry; it is used in many slimming foods.

Fibre is found in:

- Fruits and vegetables
- Wholemeal and granary bread
- Wholegrain cereals
- Wholemeal pasta
- Wholegrain rice
- Pulses (peas and beans) and lentils.

Activity

Plan a high carbohydrate menu with a high water and vitamin content for a team of road runners to eat the night before they run a marathon.

Proteins

We need protein so that our bodies can grow and repair themselves. The lifespan of the cells in our bodies varies from a week to a few months. As the cells die they need to be replaced. We need protein for our cells to repair and for new ones to grow.

We also use protein for energy. Any protein that is not used up in repairing and growing cells is converted into carbohydrate or fat.

Animal protein is found in meat, game, poultry, fish, eggs, milk and cheese. Vegetable protein is found in vegetable seeds, pulses, peas, beans, nuts and wheat, and in special vegetarian products such as Quorn.

Fats

Fats are naturally present in many foods and are an essential part of our diet.

- Fats provide the body with energy.
- Fats form an insulating layer under the skin, and this helps to protect the vital organs and to keep the body warm.
- Fat is also needed to build cell membranes in the body.

Animal fats are butter, dripping (beef), suet, lard (pork), cheese, cream, bacon, meat fat and oily fish. Vegetables fats are margarine, cooking oils, nut oils and soya bean oils.

▲ Foods high in protein

Too much fat is bad for us. It can lead to:

- Being overweight (obesity)
- High levels of cholesterol, which can clog the heart's blood vessels (arteries)
- Heart disease
- Bad breath (halitosis)
- Type 2 diabetes.

There are two types of fats:

1 Saturated fat
2 Unsaturated fat.

A diet high in saturated fat is thought to increase the risk of heart disease. In an average Western diet, the saturated fat mainly comes from:

- Meat and meat products
- Milk, cheese, cream and butter
- Other oils and fats (e.g. olive oil)
- Biscuits and cakes
- Saturated fats are also present in eggs, fish and poultry.

Use low-fat dairy products to provide calcium without excess saturated fats.

Vitamins

Vitamins are chemicals that are vital for life. They are found in small amounts in many foods. If your diet is deficient in any vitamins, you can

▲ Foods rich in vitamins

become ill or unhealthy. Vitamins help with many of our bodily functions, such as growth and protection from disease.

The table below shows the most important vitamins, how they are used in the body and what foods they can be found in.

Table 4.1 Important vitamins

Vitamin	How it is used in the body	Ingredients containing it (these are just some examples)
Vitamin A	Helps children to grow Helps the body resist infection	Fatty foods Dark green vegetables Eggs
Vitamin D	Controls how the body uses calcium Essential for healthy bones and teeth	Oily fish Dairy produce Egg yolks
Vitamin B	Helps convert carbohydrates into energy Helps children to grow Good for the nervous system	Yeast Liver and kidney Oats
Vitamin C	Helps cuts to heal Helps children to grow Prevents gum infections	Potatoes Green vegetables Fruit

Minerals

There are 19 minerals in total, most of which our bodies need, in very small quantities, to function properly.

- We need minerals to build our bones and teeth.
- Minerals help us to carry out bodily functions.
- Minerals help to control the levels of fluids in our bodies.

We will now look at a few of the most important minerals for our bodies.

Table 4.2 Important minerals

Mineral	How it is used in the body	Ingredients containing it (these are just some examples)
Calcium	Builds bones and teeth Helps muscles to work Helps blood to clot	Milk Green vegetables Wholemeal bread
Iron	Helps keep blood healthy	Lean meat and offal Wholemeal flour Fish
Phosphorus	Builds bones and teeth Good for the brain	Cheese Eggs Fish
Sodium	Regulates water in the body Helps muscles and nerves to work	Salt
Iodine	Helps the thyroid gland to work (affecting growth and weight)	Seafood
Potassium	Regulates water in the body Helps muscles and nerves to work	Leafy vegetables Citrus fruit Bananas

Water

Water is vital to life. Without it we cannot survive for very long. We lose water from our bodies through urine and sweat, and we need to replace it regularly to prevent dehydration. It is recommended that we drink eight glasses of water a day.

Our organs require water to function properly:

- Water regulates our body temperature – when we sweat the water evaporates from our skin and cools us down.
- Water helps to remove waste products from our bodies – if these waste products are not removed they can release poisons, which can damage our organs or make us ill.
- We need water to help our bodies absorb nutrients, vitamins and minerals, and to help our digestive system.
- Water acts as a lubricant, helping our eyes and joints to work and stay healthy.

> **Professional tip**
> Always offer water in a restaurant. Tap water is more environmentally friendly than bottled water.

Sources of water are drinks of all kinds; foods such as fruits, vegetables, meat, eggs; and fibre.

Consequences of not having healthier ingredients

We have looked at the importance of good nutrition in the diet. It is also important to examine the effects if there is a lack of one or more of the nutrients in your diet. Not using healthier ingredients can lead to a low immune system, obesity, skin problems, lack of energy, higher risk of ill health and reduced bowel function.

> **Activity**
>
> Take any dessert or pastry recipe and modify it, reducing the sugar or using a sugar substitute.

Why is it important for catering establishments to offer healthier choices?

Chefs today need to understand ingredients as customers are becoming more aware of the need for good nutrition and therefore there is an increased demand for healthier foods. Increasing the choice of healthier food could lead to increased sales; if they do not offer a wider choice of healthier options they could see a decrease in sales.

The government continues to emphasise the need to eat more healthily, especially with the introduction of nutritionally balanced school meals and by encouraging caterers to sign up to nutritional labelling.

Current government guidelines

The government has produced a number of papers on health and nutrition. Further information on current government nutritional guidelines can be found on the following websites:

- The Food Standards Agency: www.food.gov.uk
- The British Nutrition Foundation: www.nutrition.org.uk
- Department of Health: www.dh.gov.uk
- School Food Trust: www.schoolfoodtrust.org.uk
- Department for Environment, Food and Rural Affairs: www.defra.gov.uk

Changes that can be made to dishes to make them healthier

It is very easy to adapt recipes to make them healthier. Always look for alternative healthier ingredients.

- **Substitute healthier ingredients**
- **Add extra vegetables** (when garnishing dishes, think about fresh vegetables to increase the fibre, vitamins and minerals)
- **Reduce added fat and use low fat cooking methods** (for example, use olive oil or sunflower oil instead of butter and animal fats; use yoghurt or crème fraîche in place of cream)
- **Reduce sugar**
- **Reduce salt** (herbs and spices can be used in place of salt).

Activity

1   Why should a caterer offer healthy alternatives on the menu? What would the consequences be if an establishment did not have alternative healthy ingredients available?
2   Suggest ways in which the following menu can be made healthy:
   - Avocado and prawn salad in a creamy mayonnaise
   - Stir fry beef and vegetables.

KEY WORDS

Balanced diet – a balanced diet contains sufficient amounts of fibre and the various nutrients (carbohydrates, fats, proteins, vitamins, and minerals) to ensure good health. Food should also provide the appropriate amount of energy and adequate amounts of water.

Nutrient – a chemical providing nourishment and purpose in the diet.

Obesity – a medical condition in which excess body fat has accumulated to the extent that it may have an adverse effect on health, leading to reduced life expectancy and/or increased health problems.

Cholesterol – a substance produced by the body which can clog the arteries to the heart. Not all cholesterol is bad; some types of cholesterol are important for the nervous system and other body functions.

Antioxidant – molecules that help prevent cancer cells forming in the body.

Immune system – a system of the body that fights against disease.

Special diets

There are various reasons why people may follow a particular type of diet.

Vulnerable groups with special dietary requirements

There are certain groups of people in the population who have special nutritional needs.

Pregnant and breast-feeding women

Pregnant and breast-feeding women should avoid foods that have a high risk of food poisoning, such as soft mould-ripened cheese, pâté, raw eggs, undercooked meat, poultry and fish. They should also avoid liver and alcohol.

Expectant mothers require a well-balanced high nutritional diet, which is high in vitamins and minerals to include folic acid and vitamin B_9, which are found in leafy green vegetables like spinach, orange juice and enriched grains. This reduces the risk of a baby being born with a serious neural tube defect like spinal bifida. They should not, however, increase vitamin A in their diet, as too much could harm the baby.

Breast-feeding women need high levels of nutrition to support the baby and their own wellbeing.

▲ This young child has special dietary needs – and so does her pregnant mother

Children and teenagers

As children grow their nutritional requirements change. Children need a varied and balanced diet rich in protein, carbohydrate, vitamins and minerals.

Children are growing and developing very quickly, which means they have high nutrient needs. Their diet requires plenty of foods which provide not just the energy they need to be active, but also foods which deliver vitamins and minerals too.

Very young children, who are weaned, can eat the same types of foods as adults but because their tummies are relatively small, it is easy for them to quickly fill up. Pre-school children should have small, regular, frequent meals and regular snacks containing nutrient-dense foods, for example milk and egg.

Children over the age of five can eat the same meals as the rest of the family, including more starchy foods and plenty of fruit and vegetables, but their portion sizes should be smaller and with low amounts of saturated fat.

Teenagers need to have a good, nutritionally balanced diet. Girls need to make sure that they are getting enough iron in their diet to help with the effects of puberty.

The elderly

As we get older our bodies start to slow down and our appetite will get smaller. However, elderly people still need a nutritionally balanced diet to stay healthy.

The elderly often require small nutritional meals throughout the day. Elderly people are at increased risk from nutrient deficiencies and should ensure an adequate intake of calcium, vitamin D, folic acid, vitamin E, C and B_{12}, B_6,

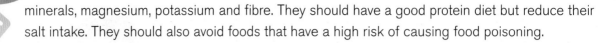

minerals, magnesium, potassium and fibre. They should have a good protein diet but reduce their salt intake. They should also avoid foods that have a high risk of causing food poisoning.

People who are ill

People who are ill, at home or in hospital, need balanced meals with plenty of the nutrients to help them recover. Good nutritional food is part of the healing process. Food should also be easy to eat and digest.

Special diets

Vegetarians

Most vegetarians choose to eat this way because they believe it is healthier, or because they do not agree with eating animals rather than for a medical reason. They avoid foods that would cause an animal to be killed.

Vegetarians have a lower risk of heart disease, stroke, diabetes, gallstones, kidney stones and colon cancer than people who eat meat. They are also less likely to be overweight or have raised cholesterol levels.

Vegans

Vegans do not eat meat, fish, dairy products, eggs, or any other animal product.

Cultural/religious diets

Different cultures and religions often have their own ways of cooking and different types of cuisine. Our culture and/or religion may affect what we choose to eat and our taste preferences.

Dietary practices have always been incorporated into the religious practices of people around the world. People who follow some religions abstain, or are forbidden, from consuming certain foods and drinks; others restrict foods and drinks during their holy days; while still others associate dietary and food preparation practices with rituals of the faith. For example:

- Christians celebrate Christmas, Easter and Shrove Tuesday with special foods. During Lent, some Christians fast.
- Muslims are only permitted to eat meat from a Halal butcher and they fast during Ramadan.
- Strict Hindus are vegetarian and do not eat meat.
- Sikhs do not have strict rules about food but many are vegetarian.
- Buddhists are vegetarians.
- Jews have strict dietary laws. Shellfish, pork and birds of prey are forbidden. Jews may only eat meat purchased from a Kosher butcher.

Diabetics

Diabetes is a medical condition where the body cannot produce insulin, does not produce energy from the insulin or the insulin produced does not work. Insulin is the chemical hormone that controls the level of sugar in the blood. There are a large number of people in society with diabetes and it is on the increase partly due to the high levels of sugar in the diet. Diabetes can be fatal if not treated.

Each diabetic will have different dietary requirements; as a result, there is no one diabetic diet that will work for everyone and people should pick a diet that matches their individual needs. Finding the balance between the amount of carbohydrates and fat is important. It is necessary for diabetics to cut down on the amount of fat, particularly saturated (animal) fat, choose monounsaturated fats, such as olive oil and rapeseed oil. Diabetics should eat regular meals based on starchy carbohydrate foods such as bread, pasta, chapattis, potatoes, yam, noodles, rice and cereals. They should also include plenty of fresh fruits and vegetables in their diet.

Allergies and intolerances

Food allergies are a type of intolerance where the body's immune system sees certain foods as harmful and this causes an allergic reaction. Food allergies can cause anaphylactic shock (which makes the throat and mouth swell so that it is difficult to swallow or breathe); they can also cause nausea, vomiting and unconsciousness. Some allergic reactions can be fatal.

Almost any food may cause an allergic reaction in certain people, so it is important that caterers tell customers what is in the dishes on their menu. However, there are a number of foods which are now known to be causes of common allergies, including:

- Milk – lactose
- Dairy products – yoghurt, cheese, butter
- Fish
- Shellfish – mussels, clams, lobster, prawns, shrimps
- Eggs
- Nuts (particularly peanuts, cashew nuts, pecans, Brazil nuts, walnuts)
- Certain types of vegetables
- Certain seeds – pumpkin, sesame
- Soya beans – tofu, textured vegetable protein
- Lupin – chemical found in plants, peanuts, peas, lentils, beans
- Sulphates – chemical found in wine and certain foods; SO_2 – sulphur dioxide is used as a preservative
- Gluten – from wheat products: bread, cakes, biscuits.

The most common allergies of all are nuts and shellfish.

People who suffer from an allergy are required to carry an epipen, which contains an antidote that counteracts the effect of an anaphylactic shock. The person injects the pen themselves as soon as they need emergency treatment.

Some people are intolerant to gluten, which for them damages the small intestine and causes a condition called coeliac disease.

> **Professional tip**
>
> Make sure that all the staff are fully aware of food allergies and they know all the ingredients that make up a recipe.

Activity

1 What is the difference between a vegetarian and a vegan diet?
2 List some examples of festival foods from any religion you are familiar with.
3 List reasons why you think diabetes is on the increase.

KEY WORDS

Diabetes – a medical condition where the body cannot regulate the glucose levels in the body.

Allergy – when a person's immune system reacts to certain types of food.

Intolerance – the body reacts to certain types of food but does not involve the immune system, and produces less dramatic symptoms.

Test yourself

1 State the benefits of a healthy diet.
2 List four types of ingredients that contribute to a healthy diet.
3 What is the purpose of fibre in the diet?
4 What valuable nutrient is contained in oily fish?
5 Give an example of an unsaturated fat.
6 How might a chef reduce the amount of salt that he or she uses in a recipe?
7 What is the difference between a food allergy and a food intolerance?
8 Name two alternative ingredients to fresh cream.
9 For a chosen religion, describe how religious beliefs have an effect on the diet.
10 What are the differences between the dietary needs of a pre-school child and a teenager?

5 Kitchen equipment

This chapter covers Unit 105, Introduction to kitchen equipment.

By the end of this chapter you should be able to:

- State factors involved in selecting equipment and utensils for use
- State how to use equipment and utensils correctly and safety
- Identify hazards associated with using, cleaning and storing equipment and utensils
- State how to carry out routine care and storage of equipment and utensils
- Identify the different types of knives and cutting equipment and uses
- State the importance of correct and safe use of knives and cutting equipment
- Describe how to clean, maintain and store knives and cutting equipment
- Identify relevant age restrictions specific to the use of cutting equipment.

In this chapter you will learn about the various types of equipment, large and small, used in the hospitality and catering industry. Every piece of equipment has a purpose and has been specially designed for that particular purpose. For example, whisks have been designed for whisking and scales for weighing. One of the essential skills of being a chef is to be able to identify and use the correct equipment for the task, to avoid mistakes and accidents.

Large and small items of equipment and utensils

How to choose equipment

Think carefully about what the equipment is going to be used for and for how long. There is a wide variety of equipment on the market and you must learn to assess its durability and usefulness. Consider the material equipment is made from: stainless steel, for example, is very durable and is a good choice if you are looking for long-lasting and hard-wearing equipment.

Also consider how easy equipment is to clean. Equipment that is more difficult to clean is less likely to be cleaned properly; harsh abrasives may have to be used, which may result in damage to the equipment.

When choosing equipment it is also important to know the size of the equipment you will need to do the job. If you are producing a large quantity of food at one time, for example, you will need larger pans than if you are cooking smaller quantities or fewer meals.

Using equipment correctly and safely

Kitchen equipment can be divided into two categories:

1 **Large equipment** – for example, ovens, hobs, grills, steamers and fryers. This also includes large mechanical equipment such as refrigerators and dishwashers.
2 **Small equipment and utensils** – for example, spoons, whisks and ladles. This also includes small mechanical equipment such as peelers, mincers and mixers.

You need to know how to use a range of large and small equipment and utensils correctly and safely and be able to identify any hazards associated with using, cleaning and storing them.

Large equipment

Conventional ovens

There is a large variety of conventional ovens available, which are fuelled by either gas or electricity. Some have grills built in.

> **Health and safety**
>
> With gas ovens, it is very important to light the gas once it is turned on. Gas ovens and ranges must be fitted with a flame failure device. This switches off the gas if the flame blows out, to prevent explosion.

Convection ovens (fan-assisted ovens)

These ovens have a built-in fan, which circulates hot air around the oven. This increases the temperature in all parts of the oven, making it more efficient and meaning that cooking temperatures can be lowered. For example, something that would have to be cooked at 200°C in a conventional oven might cook at 180°C in a convection oven. Convection ovens are very good for baking and roasting.

Cleaning conventional and convection ovens: allow the equipment to cool before scrubbing it down and wiping it clean. Apply a little oil to the surface of solid tops to keep the surface in good condition.

> **Health and safety**
>
> When cleaning, always use protective clothing and allow the equipment to cool down first to avoid accidental burns. When using a chemical oven cleaner, always wear a safety mask and thick rubber gloves.

Combination ovens

Combination ovens can be used as an oven or steamer or both. Steam is injected into the oven when you are baking and roasting, to increase the moisture content (humidity) of the oven. The ovens are fuelled by gas or electricity. They are fully automatic, having built-in computers that can be pre-programmed to cook food for exactly the right amount of time and are also able to keep food at the correct temperature. Latest versions monitor internal temperatures of the food, allowing the chef to achieve exact core temperature and deliver precise cooking textures. A computer system also records how often the oven is used and the temperatures used.

Cleaning combination ovens: many modern models are self-cleaning, but they need to be checked regularly to make sure the cleaning programme is efficient.

> **Professional tip**
>
> Combination technology is changing all the time. Modern ovens are energy efficient and time and labour saving.

Health and safety

Take care when removing trays from the oven. When using a combination oven as a steamer, make sure you release the steam gently before opening the door.

Microwave ovens

Microwave ovens use high-frequency power. The energy waves disturb the molecules in food and move them, causing friction and heating the food. Microwave ovens can cook food more quickly than conventional ovens. They are often used for reheating food.

Cleaning microwave ovens: clean up spillages immediately with hot, mild detergent water. This prevents bacteria growing and reduces the risk of contaminating other foods.

 Health and safety

If the door seal is damaged, do not use and report to your employer or manager immediately. Microwave ovens should be inspected regularly.

Metal should never be used in a microwave unless it has a metal reflector. Using metal in a microwave without a metal reflector causes sparks and small explosions in the oven.

Solid top hobs

These are also known as solid top stoves and are made of solid metal with a burner. They have a single flat surface, meaning saucepans can be moved around easily during cooking. The middle of the hob has intense heat; the side is not so hot and is used to simmer. Solid top hobs may be gas or electric. Gas-operated hobs have removable rings in the centre, which can be removed to expose the flame and allow the chef to place the saucepan directly onto the flame. This intense heat allows the food to cook quicker or liquid to reduce quickly.

Cleaning solid top hobs: remove all food debris, clean with hot detergent water, dry and lightly oil.

 Health and safety

Solid top hobs have a pilot light and a flame-failure device which switches off the gas for safety. However, they still require regular safety checks by a qualified gas fitter.

Open range hobs

These are stoves where the flame is exposed; the saucepans are placed on metal bars over the flame. It is more difficult to move the saucepans around on this type of hob than on solid top hobs. To simmer, the flame has to be reduced using a switch that controls each flame.

Cleaning open range hobs: remove the metal bars, wash in hot detergent water and dry. Clean the stove surface with hot detergent water after removing any food debris; a light abrasive may be required for any baked on food. Dry and replace metal bars.

> **! Health and safety**
>
> Similarly to solid top hobs, these stoves are fitted with a flame-failure device, but require regular safety checks by a qualified gas fitter.

Induction hobs

The burners on induction hobs are called induction coils. The coil will heat up only when a pan with a metal base (such as a stainless steel pan) is in direct contact with the hob. When the pan is removed from the hob it turns off straight away and cools down quickly. The hob will feel slightly warm after it is turned off. Water boils rapidly on an induction hob and overall food cooks more quickly than on other types of hobs.

Cleaning induction hobs: induction hobs are very easy to clean and usually require only a wipe down with mild detergent water.

> **! Health and safety**
>
> Induction hobs are much safer than conventional hobs because they stay relatively cool even when cooking. There is very little chance of burning from direct contact with the hob.

Steamers

- **Atmospheric steamer** – operates at normal atmospheric pressure (the same pressure as outside the steamer), creating steam at just above 100°C. These are often normal saucepans with a metal basket in them.
- **Pressure steamers** – a good way to cook delicate food and foods cooked in a pouch. Some pressure steamers cook at high pressure and some at low pressure. In low-pressure steamers the temperature of the steam is 70°C and so food is cooked slowly. In high-pressure steamers the temperature of the steam is 120°C and so food is cooked faster.
- **Dual steamers** – these can switch between low and high pressure. At low pressure they cook in the same way as pressure steamers. At high pressure the food is cooked more quickly than atmospheric steamers and pressure steamers.

All steamers are available in a variety of sizes. In addition, combination ovens can be used to combine steaming and conventional oven cooking to get the benefits of both.

Cleaning steamers: steamers have to be cleaned regularly. The inside of the steamer, trays and runners should be washed in hot detergent water, then rinsed and dried. Door controls should be lightly greased occasionally and the door left slightly open to allow air to circulate when the steamer is not in use. If water is held in the steamer then it must be changed regularly. The water chamber should be drained and cleaned before fresh water is added.

Health and safety

The main safety hazard associated with steamers is scalding. Take care when opening steamer doors: open the door slowly to allow the steam to escape gradually from the oven, then carefully remove the food items.

Before use, check that the steamer is clean and safe to use. Any faults must be reported immediately.

Deep fat fryers

A deep fat fryer has a container with enough oil in it to cover the food. The oil is heated to very hot temperatures. A cool zone, which is a chamber at the base of the cooking pan, collects odd bits of food such as breadcrumbs or batter from fish when it is being fried. Some fryers are computerised; these can be programmed to heat the oil to the correct temperature and cook the food for the right amount of time.

Cleaning a deep fat fryer: when frying, remove all the food debris immediately and keep the oil as clean as possible. You will need to remove the oil to clean the fryer. Make sure the fryer is switched off and the oil is cool before removing it and put suitable containers in place to drain the oil into. Replace with clean oil.

Health and safety

Deep fat fryers are possibly the most dangerous piece of equipment in the kitchen. Many kitchen fires have been started through careless use of the deep fat fryer. Take care not to splash the oil when placing items of food in the fryer as this can cause serious burns and eye injuries. Avoid placing wet food into the fryer. Never throw food items in the deep fat fryer from a height. Place the food in carefully. When changing the oil, always allow it to cool first.

Salamander

A salamander (also known as an overhead grill) is heated from above by gas or electricity. Most salamanders have more than one set of heating elements or jets, and it is not always necessary to have them all fully turned on.

Cleaning salamanders: salamanders have a tray to catch grease and food debris. This needs to be emptied and thoroughly cleaned with hot detergent water. Soda is very useful for removing grease.

> **! Health and safety**
>
> Take care when placing food under and removing food from the salamander. Wear appropriate protective clothing when cleaning a salamander.

Under-fired (under-heated) grills

The heat source for these is underneath the grill. Under-fired grills are used to cook food quickly, so they need to reach a high temperature. This type of grill makes criss-cross marks on the food, known as **quadrillage**.

Cleaning under-fired grills: when the bars are cool, they should be removed and washed in hot water containing a grease solvent (detergent). They should then be rinsed, dried and replaced in the grill. If firebricks are used for lining the grill, take care with these as they break easily.

> **! Health and safety**
>
> Take care when placing food on the grill, moving it around on the grill and removing it – always use tongs. Be extra careful when brushing the food with oil and do not allow the oil to drip on the flame.

▲ Quadrillage

Contact grills

These are sometimes called double-sided grills or infragrills. They have two heating surfaces, which face each other. The food is placed on one surface and is then covered by the second. These grills are electrically heated and cook certain foods, such a toast in a toaster, very quickly.

Cleaning contact grills: turn off the electricity when cleaning and avoid using water. Lightly scrape clean.

> **! Health and safety**
>
> Always allow the grills and griddles to cool down before cleaning to prevent burns. Take great care when placing the food on or in the grill.

Bain-marie

Bain-marie means 'water bath'. These are open wells of water for keeping food hot. They are available in many designs, some of which are built into hot cupboards and some into serving controls. They are heated by steam, gas or electricity. Water baths are also used for gentle cooking of foods in a vacuum bag.

Cleaning bain-maries: turn off the heat after use. Drain the water away and clean the bain-marie inside and out with hot detergent water. Then rinse it and dry it. If it has a drain-off tap, this should be closed.

 Health and safety

It is important to never allow the bain-marie to run dry when the heat is turned on. Check the temperature regularly: never allow it to differ from the recipe and safety requirements.

Hot cupboards

Commonly referred to as a hotplate, a hot cupboard is used for heating plates and serving dishes, and for keeping food hot. You must make sure that the temperature in the hot cupboard is kept at around 63–70°C so that the food is not too hot or too cold. Hot cupboards may be heated by gas, steam or electricity.

Cleaning hot cupboards: hot cupboards must be emptied and cleaned after each service.

 Health and safety

Take care when taking plates, dishes and food in and out of hot cupboards to avoid burns and scalds.

Proving cabinets

Proving cabinets are used for proving yeast products, such as bread dough. They provide a warm and moist atmosphere that allows the yeast to grow, causing the dough to rise (prove). The most suitable temperature for this is 37°C. Proving cabinets have a drain to collect the excess water as the moist air cools.

Refrigerators and chill rooms

Refrigerators and chill rooms keep food chilled at between 1°C and 5°C. These cold conditions slow down the growth of bacteria and spoilage enzymes that make food go 'off'. They are used to store a whole range of products.

Cleaning refrigerators and chill rooms: chill rooms and refrigerators must be tidied once a day and cleaned out once a week. Clean with hot water and suitable cleaning chemicals – diluted bicarbonate of soda is most suitable.

Health and safety

The way that food is stored in chill rooms and refrigerators is very important. There must not be cross-contamination between different foods, as this spreads bacteria. All food must be covered and labelled with its use by date.

The internal temperature of chill rooms and refrigerators must be checked at least twice a day.

Freezers

Freezers are used to store food between −18°C and −20°C. Food in the freezer does not last indefinitely, but the low temperature slows down the growth of bacteria and means that the food will last longer.

Cleaning freezers: most freezers today are frost-free, which means that they do not need to be defrosted. Tidy the freezer at least once a week. Clean it out every three to six months using a mild cleaning fluid, mild detergent or diluted bicarbonate of soda.

Health and safety

As in chill rooms, all food stored in a freezer must be covered and date labelled.

Activity

1 When a combination oven is set to introduce steam into the cooking process, what safety precautions should you take when placing food into and removing it from the oven?
2 When lifting a heavy drum of cooking oil from the floor to fill a fryer, you should bend your knees and keep your back straight. What other safety precautions should you observe?
3 How should you clean an open range hob?
4 Describe what a bain-marie is used for.
5 Describe how a microwave cooks food.

Small equipment and utensils

Each piece of small equipment has a specific use in the kitchen. Small equipment and utensils are made from a variety of materials, including non-stick coated metal, iron, steel and heat-proof plastic. Small equipment must be looked after, cleaned and stored safely and hygienically.

Cooking pans

Baking sheets are made in various sizes from black wrought steel. They are used for baking and pastry work.

Baking tins (sometimes called cake tins) are used for baking cakes, bread and sponges. The mixture is placed in the tin before cooking.

Griddle pans have raised ribs to mark the food. The griddle lines (quadrillage) give the food a chargrilled effect. Modern griddle pans have a non-stick surface.

Non-stick frying pans are coated with a material such as Teflon, which prevents the food from sticking to them. They are usually used for shallow frying.

Roasting trays are metal trays, usually made of stainless steel. They have deep sides and are used for roasting food such as meat and vegetables.

Saucepans come in various sizes and are made in a variety of materials. Some are made solely of stainless steel; others contain a mixture of metals, such as stainless steel with an aluminium layer and a thick copper coil. Saucepans are used for a variety of cooking methods, including boiling, poaching and stewing.

Sauté pans are shallow, straight-sided pans made from stainless steel or a mixture of metals. They are used for shallow frying when a sauce is made after the food is fried. They may also be used for poaching, especially for shallow-poached fish.

Woks are shallow, rounded frying pans use for stir-frying and oriental cookery. They are made from material that can conduct heat quickly. Thick copper-core stainless steel is the most effective.

 Health and safety

Incorrect pan storage can result in pans falling from the shelves, causing injury and damage to the equipment. Store pans upside down on clean racks. Check that handles are not loose.

Items stored at a great height may cause people to stretch, causing back strain. Minimise the risk by storing pans at a lower level, so people to not need to stretch for them.

Utensils

Bowls come in various sizes and can be stainless steel or plastic. They are used for a variety of purposes, including mixing, blending and storing food.

Colanders are available in a variety of sizes and usually made from stainless steel. for draining liquids.

Conical strainers are usually stainless steel with large mesh. They are used for general straining and passing of liquids, soups and sauces.

Cooling racks are made from stainless steel mesh and are usually rectangular Baked items are placed on cooling racks to cool. The mesh allows air to circulate, enabling the items to cool quickly.

Cutlet bats are made from metal and used to bat out meat, making it thinner.

Flan rings are used to make flan cases and flans. The flan ring is lined with pastry to make the pastry case, and then filled with the flan mixture or tart filling.

Fish slices are made from stainless steel. They are used for lifting and sliding food on and off trays to serving dishes.

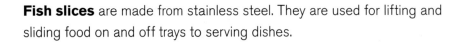

Food mixers are labour-saving electrical devices used for many different tasks in the kitchen. They have a range of attachments for different jobs such as mincing, cutting, blending and mixing.

Ladles come in various sizes. They are large, scoop-shaped spoons used to add liquids to cooking pots, and to serve sauces and stews.

Liquidisers and blenders are pieces of mechanical equipment used to blend solid food into liquids. They can be made from glass, plastic or stainless steel.

Mashers can be manual or electric and are used for mashing vegetables.

Measuring jugs are available in a variety of sizes. They can be made from stainless steel, glass or plastic. They are used for measuring liquids.

Moulds come in many shapes and sizes. They are used for shaping and moulding food for presentation, for example, tartlets, mousses, custards and blancmange. Moulds can be very difficult to clean – you must make sure that all food debris is removed and that the mould is cleaned properly to prevent cross-contamination.

Rolling pins are used for rolling pastry manually. Today they are usually made from plastic.

Scales are used to weigh ingredients.

Sieves are made from plastic with a nylon or metal mesh. They are available in various sizes. They are a type of strainer and can be used to sieve dry ingredients such as flour or for purées.

Skimming spoons are made from stainless steel and have holes in them. They are used for skimming and draining. Skimming is removing fat and other unwanted substances from the top liquids, such as stocks and soups.

Spiders are made from stainless steel. They are used for removing food from containers, saucepans, water, etc. They are also used to remove food from a deep fat fryer.

Spoons come in a variety of sizes for serving and moving food to and from containers. They are made from stainless steel.

Whisks are wired and used for whisking and beating air into products, for example, whisking egg whites. Heavier wired whisks are available for whisking sauces.

Care, cleanliness and storage

Thoroughly wash all equipment, pans and utensils with hot detergent and water after use. Rinse with hot water and then dry thoroughly. Incomplete cleaning and drying can lead to build up of mould, food contamination and cross-contamination.

Health and safety

Always make sure that the safety guards are in place before using mechanical equipment. Report any faulty equipment to your line manager or supervisor. Always make sure that mechanical equipment is regularly serviced and maintained in good working order.

Cutting boards

These are used for chopping and slicing food on. The most popular boards are made from polyethylene or plastic. Different boards should be used for different foods, to avoid cross-contamination. The accepted UK system is shown here.

Cutting boards must be stored correctly in a safe and hygienic way, preferably on a rack allowing circulation of air so that after they have been thoroughly cleaned they are allowed to dry and other types of boards or equipment cannot contaminate them. Incorrect storage of boards may lead to cross-contamination and food poisoning.

COLOUR CODED CUTTING BOARDS
eliminate the risk of bacterial cross contamination during food preparation

RED — RAW MEAT
BLUE — RAW FISH
YELLOW — COOKED MEAT
GREEN — SALAD & FRUIT
BROWN — VEGETABLES
WHITE — BAKERY & DAIRY

▲ The UK system of colour coding

Knives and cutting equipment

Knives

The professional chef will use a whole range of knives in the kitchen; each type of knife is used for a specific job and skill. It is important that knives are used safely and efficiently.

Boning knives are short-bladed knives used for boning meat. The blade is strong and rigid, with a pointed end. The inflexible blade allows the chef to get close to the bones and cut away the meat.

Butcher's saws are commonly used in butchery to saw through bones.

Carving knives and forks – a French carving knife has a long, thin blade and is known as a tranchard. A carving fork is two-pronged. It is strong enough to support meats for carving, and to lift them to and from containers.

Chopping knives are used for a variety of jobs, such as chopping, cutting, slicing and shredding vegetables, meat and fruit.

Filleting knives are used for filleting fish (removing the flesh from the bones). They have a very flexible blade, which allows the chef to move the knife easily around the bone structure of fish.

Meat cleavers are also known as choppers and are usually used for chopping bones.

Paring knives (also known as **office knives**) are small, multi-purpose vegetable knives. They are used for topping and tailing vegetables, and for peeling certain fruits and vegetables.

Palette knives are flat for lifting and scraping, turning and spreading. They are also useful for a variety of tasks in the pastry section.

Serrated-edge carving knives are used for slicing foods. They have a long, thick serrated blade, which is used in a sawing action. These knives are not sharpened in the kitchen but have to be sent to a specialist company to be sharpened.

Turning knives have a small curved blade. They are used for shaping vegetables in a variety of ways.

Other cutting equipment

Corers are used to remove the fibrous core from fruits such as apples, pineapples and pears. They have a rounded blade, which you push down into the centre of the fruit to cut through the fruit around the core. The core stays tightly inside the corer and is removed from the fruit when you pull it out.

Food processors are electrical machines used for many jobs in the kitchen. They usually come with a range of blades for cutting, puréeing, slicing, grating and mixing.

Graters are made from stainless steel. They come in various sizes and are used to shred and grate food such as cheese, the zest of citrus fruits and vegetables. Graters usually have a choice of grating edges: fine, medium or large.

Gravity-feed slicers have very sharp cutting blades and must be operated with a safety guard. They are used for slicing meat so that every slice is the same thickness.

> ! **Health and safety**
>
> There is an age restriction for the use of gravity feed slicing machines; you must be over 18 to use them.
>
> It is advisable to have a separate slicing machine for raw and cooked food. This is recommended by food safety officers.

Kitchen scissors are used for a number of purposes in the kitchen. Fish scissors are used for cutting fins from fish. Poultry scissors are used to portion poultry.

Mandolins are specialist pieces of equipment used for slicing vegetables. The blade is made from stainless steel and is adjustable to different widths, for thick or thin slices of food. They are usually used to slice vegetables such as potatoes, courgettes, cucumbers and carrots. The blade is particularly sharp, so you should be very careful when using one. Modern mandolins have an in-built safety guard.

Mincers are stand alone or attachments that fit to a mixer. They have a circular cutting blade which forces the food through a plate with different size holes depending on the requirements of the size of mince required.

Peelers are used for peeling certain vegetables and fruit.

Sharpening equipment

A **carborundum** is used for sharpening knives.

Steels are used for sharpening knives. They are cylindrical pieces of steel with a handle at one end. To sharpen a knife, run the knife at an angle along the steel edge.

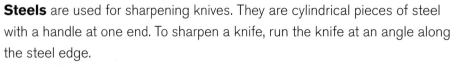

Whet stones are also used for sharpening knives.

Safe use of knives

Knives are essential tools for all chefs, but they can cause serious injury to the user or to someone else if used incorrectly or carelessly. Knives that are looked after and treated with care will give good service and will be less likely to cause injury.

By following a few simple rules you should be able to avoid serious injury from knives and keep accidental cuts to an absolute minimum. Use your knives correctly at all times.

- Hold a cook's knife with your finger around the handle (thumb and index fingers on opposite sides) and well clear of the blade edge. This will sometimes vary, depending on the size and design of the knife, and the task you are carrying out.
- Grasp the knife firmly for full control.
- Always make sure that the fingers and thumb of the hand not holding the knife are well tucked in to avoid cutting them.
- If carrying a knife in the kitchen, hold it to the side of your body, with the blade pointing downwards and backwards.
- Never run while holding a knife.
- When handing a knife to someone else, offer them the handle while you hold the top (blunt edge) of the blade.
- Keep the blade away from you when cleaning or drying knives, and never run your finger along the blade edge.
- Do not have more than one knife at a time on a chopping board. When not using a knife, place it at the side of the board with the blade pointing in. Never carry knives around on top of chopping boards because they could slide off.
- Do not let knives overhang the edge of the work surface; they could be knocked off or fall and cause injury. Never try to catch a falling knife; stand back until it reaches the floor.
- Never leave a knife on a surface with the blade pointing outwards. You or someone else could put their hand down on the blade of the knife.
- Never place knives in washing-up water; the blade will not be visible so someone can put their hands in the water and cut themselves.
- Keep the handle of the knife clean and dry. If the handle is greasy or wet it could slip in your hands during use.
- Keep knives visible, i.e. not under vegetable peelings or a dishcloth.

Maintenance and care of knives – sharpening

Knives that are kept sharp are safer than blunt knives, provided that they are handled with care. This is because a sharp knife will cut efficiently and cleanly without needing too much pressure to cut through the food. A blunt knife is less easy to control; it will need more pressure and force and is likely to slip sideways, possibly causing injury as well as poorly prepared food.

Keep knives sharp by sharpening them frequently with a steel or other sharpening tool. Make sure that you are shown how to do this safely.

If a knife has become very blunt it may need to be re-ground by someone who specialises in doing this. An electric or manually operated grinding wheel is used to replace the lost 'edge' on the knife. Arrangements can be made for mobile units to visit your premises to re-grind knives, or they can be sent away to be re-ground.

Some chefs use a sharpening stone.

Cleaning

A knife can very easily transfer harmful bacteria from one place to another, becoming a 'vehicle' of contamination. Follow a few simple rules to avoid this:

- Wash and dry knives thoroughly between tasks.
- Do not use the same cloth to clean knives between tasks, especially when you are preparing raw or high-risk foods.
- If you have used a knife on raw meat or poultry, be sure to disinfect it before use it for another task. Detergents remove the grease, but disinfectants kill harmful bacteria.
- When you have finished working with a knife, wash it thoroughly with hot detergent water, then rinse it, dry it and put it away. Bacteria will multiply on dirty or wet knives.

> **Professional tip**
>
> Take great care of your knives; always keep them clean. There are a variety of knives on the market – some have handles made of easy to clean material.

Storage

Store knives carefully, preferably in a box or carrying case with compartments to keep the knives separate and easy to find. Do not just throw knives loosely into a drawer or locker.

Age restrictions specific to the use of cutting equipment

There is an age restriction for the use of potentially dangerous equipment in the kitchen such as gravity feed slicing machines; you must be over 18 to use them.

> ### Activity
>
> 1 It is important to use knives and cutting equipment correctly to prevent accidents and injury to yourself and others. Give four other reasons why it is important to use knives and cutting equipment correctly.
> 2 Identify the following knives and state what they are used for:
>
>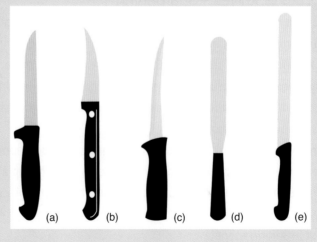
>
> (a) (b) (c) (d) (e)

Test yourself

1 Name a piece of equipment that saves energy.
2 Describe the various processes that a combination oven can be used for.
3 What is the purpose of a cool zone in a deep fat fryer?
4 Why should you not use blunt knives?
5 How can a professional knife be sharpened?
6 What is the legal age when a person can use a gravity feed slicing machine?
7 What piece of equipment would you use to purée a soup?
8 What would you use a mandolin for?
9 How would you clean a deep fat fryer?
10 What are the health and safety points you need to consider when using a bain-marie?

This chapter covers Unit 106, Introduction to personal workplace skills.

By the end of this chapter you should be able to:

- Identify the correct uniform for work, state the reasons for wearing the uniform correctly and describe the correct care and maintenance of uniform

- State the importance of maintaining personal hygiene and a professional personal appearance and identify poor hygiene and practices in relation to personal appearance and behaviour

- State the importance of punctuality and attendance, the effect that punctuality and attendance have on work colleagues and the procedures to follow if absent or late

- State the reasons for planning of tasks and the importance of working within set time frames

- Identify the communication skills used in teams and state the importance of communicating within and between teams

- Describe the importance of knowing your own limitations and asking for advice and assistance and state who to ask for advice and assistance

- State what makes a good team

- State the importance of effective communication with customers and describe the correct methods of dealing with customer requests

- State the possible barriers to communication.

This chapter concentrates on the personal skills required by employers, which are a very important part of working life. These skills include attendance at work, punctuality, presenting a positive, professional image, good time management, effective communication and teamwork.

▲ A well presented professional chef

Personal appearance

As a chef you must always look clean and professional. You need to practice a high level of personal hygiene. The protective clothing you wear at work must be clean, hygienic and in good repair.

The chef's uniform

Wearing clean, hygienic kitchen clothing is a legal requirement when you work with food. Your uniform will protect you from hot liquids and other dangers you may come into contact with in the kitchen. You will need a clean uniform every day and must change it if it gets dirty or stained. Clean clothing is important to prevent the transfer of bacteria from dirty clothing to food.

A clean uniform also promotes a professional image; it gives a visible sign of cleanliness and good hygiene standards. It will show a positive impression to customers and visitors, giving them confidence in the establishment.

Chef's jacket

These jackets are designed as hygienic work wear, as well as to protect the chef in the kitchen. They are usually made from lightweight and comfortable fabrics such as cotton, a coated cotton or polyester-cotton. White is still the preferred colour because dirt and stains will be visible and white withstands hot laundry well.

Your jacket should fit well and not be too tight. You should be able to move easily so that if, for example, hot liquid is spilled on it, you can pull it away from your skin easily to prevent burning.

It is safer to wear jackets with long sleeves as these protect your arms from splashed hot liquids or fats to reduce the risk of burns and scalds; they will also protect from possible contact dermatitis (see Chapter 2).

Remember to change your chefs' jacket daily and more frequently if dirty or stained.

▲ Chef's jacket and trousers

Chef's trousers

These were traditionally blue/white check but now a variety of colours and designs are available. Like jackets, cotton, cotton mixtures or coated cotton are the preferred fabrics. They should be loose fitting so that they are comfortable and can be pulled away from the skin easily to prevent burning if hot liquid is spilled on them.

Chef's apron

Aprons also come in a variety of fabrics and styles – they can be a full 'bib' apron or tie at the waist. Your apron should come to just below your knees and be wide enough to wrap around the body; the ties are crossed over then tied at the front. This offers maximum protection from spilt hot liquids and oil and the ties at the front mean it can be removed quickly if necessary.

Sometimes different colours of apron are used for different purposes. For example, butchers' aprons are blue and white striped. They can also be used to separate different kitchen tasks such as raw preparation and cooked food. Remember to change your apron regularly especially if dirty or stained.

Chef's or cook's hat

The tall chef's hat (toque) is a traditional item and often shows the status of a chef. Skullcaps are now used in many modern kitchens because they are more comfortable, cheaper and easier to wash. A wide variety of colours are available so chef status or sections being worked in can be shown by different-coloured skullcaps.

   The main purpose of a hat is to prevent loose hair getting into the food. Where the hair is longer than collar length a hairnet should be worn under the hat. Disposable hats are now available and come in a variety of styles.

▲ Chef's hat

Neckties

Traditionally, kitchens have been very hot places and chefs have worn a necktie to mop perspiration from their brow. With improved ventilation systems they are no longer essential and with some modern styles of chef's jackets neckties are not appropriate. They are available in a wide range of colours so, like the hats, can denote status or section.

Safety shoes

There are many different varieties of safety shoes. They must be sturdy, with reinforced toecaps that protect the feet from falling heavy or sharp objects and from hot liquids. Shoes should be the correct size, comfortable and offer good support because chefs spend a long time on their feet; they must also be kept clean. Open-toed shoes or trainers must not be worn in the kitchen; they would not protect the feet from hot, heavy or sharp items.

▲ Safety shoes

Kitchen cloths

Increasingly kitchens are not using the traditional chef's cloths but use disposable kitchen paper or roll for cleaning tasks. This is much more hygienic and cross-contamination is less likely to occur. Special thick oven cloths would be used for handling hot saucepans and trays. Where chefs do use the traditional cloth it must be clean and dry; if dirty or stained, replace it.

 Health and safety
Never use a damp or wet cloth to hold hot items; the heat conducts more quickly and can cause burns.

 Health and safety
If using a kitchen cloth, do not keep it on the shoulder (the cloth touches neck and hair and these can be sources of bacteria).

KEY WORDS

Toque – a traditional tall chef's hat.
Chef's skullcap – a close-fitting hat.
Status – someone's seniority or position.

Care and maintenance of your uniform

Kitchen uniform needs proper care and must be repaired or replaced when necessary. It must be well laundered and ironed, kept in good condition and repair carried out as necessary. Shoes too must be kept in good repair, cleaned and polished.

 Health and safety

Make sure your uniform is in good repair. The ends of sleeves can fray and hanging threads could get into food, catch on machinery or catch on fire over gas jets.

The importance of personal hygiene and appearance

A smart, clean, professional image is as important when working in a kitchen as it is for front of house staff. Increasingly chefs are visible to customers and may spend some of their time in the restaurant areas.

Personal hygiene is extremely important when handling food because bacteria can be transferred easily from humans to food (see Chapter 2 for more information).

A daily shower or bath is essential to remove body odour, sweat, dirt and bacteria. Change your underwear daily and use antiperspirant deodorants.

Hands and nails

- Keep nails short and clean.
- Wash your hands well and regularly with liquid soap/hand-wash. This is especially important after visiting the toilet, before entering the kitchen and between tasks. (For further detail on hand washing see Chapter 2.)
- Dry your hands thoroughly using disposable towels; an antibacterial gel could then be applied.
- When handling high-risk foods, wear disposable gloves and change these gloves for each task.
- Always cover any cuts with blue waterproof dressing (plaster) then wash hands thoroughly.

 Health and safety

High-risk foods are 'ready to eat' foods that usually will not have any further cooking so it is very important to avoid any possible contamination of them.

 Health and safety

Blue dressings are used because they are easy to detect if they fall into food. They can also be identified by metal detectors used by food manufacturers because they contain a narrow metal strip.

Jewellery and cosmetics

- Do not wear jewellery or watches in the kitchen. These items trap bacteria that could contaminate food, the items themselves may fall into food and could also become caught in machinery and cause injury.
- Avoid the use of perfumes and aftershaves when working with food and cosmetics should only be used vary sparingly.

> **Health and safety**
>
> Strong smelling items such as perfumes, aftershave and even strong smelling deodorants can taint the food being handled so should not be used by food handlers. In a hot kitchen cosmetics can flake and could fall into food, they also stop the cooling processes of the skin working properly.

For more information also see the personal hygiene section in Chapter 2.

Hair

Hair can be both a physical and bacterial contaminant if it gets into food. It can also be the cause of customer complaints and possible loss of custom.

- Hair must be washed regularly and kept clean and tidy.
- Your hair must be short or tied back neatly. Wear a suitable kitchen hat that stops hair from getting into food. If hair is longer than collar length, wear a net under the hat.
- Men should be clean shaven or wear a beard net.

> **Professional tip**
>
> It is not a legal requirement for chefs to wear a hat but it is strongly recommended that they do so.

Dental hygiene

It is important to look after your teeth and mouth as part of good grooming as well as to maintain good health.

- Clean your teeth at least twice a day and use a mouthwash.
- Visit your dentist regularly.
- Do not touch your mouth when handling food.

Feet

Chefs and others working in the hospitality industry are likely to be on their feet for much of the day so it is essential to take care of feet. Make sure they are dried thoroughly after a bath or shower and keep toenails neatly cut. Wear clean, well fitting, absorbent socks and proper, well fitting kitchen shoes (see above).

Poor hygiene and practices: what to avoid

Generally you should not eat or drink in food production areas during working times, unless tasting food to ensure quality and check seasoning. Drinking water is permitted and encouraged – some establishments provide water coolers for staff use.

Never wear your uniform outside the kitchen premises as bacteria can be carried from the outside on your uniform into the kitchen where it can then get into food.

Do not chew gum while in uniform and in the kitchen. It looks very unprofessional and will prevent you from tasting the food properly.

Smoking is not allowed in public areas. It is very unhygienic as the fingers touch the lips and can transfer bacteria on to food. If chefs smoke during their break period outside, they must not be in uniform and must wash their hands thoroughly on their return to the kitchen.

Make sure you wash your hands regularly and thoroughly. Irregular and incorrect hand washing can cause cross-contamination.

Activity

1 A good chef's uniform looks smart and professional. What are the other reasons for wearing it?
2 What explanation would you give to others in your kitchen about the importance of wearing a chef's hat? What type of chef's hat would you recommend?
3 Why is it important to wear safety shoes in a kitchen and not trainers?
4 Why should chefs not wear their kitchen uniform when going outside for a break?
5 Why are so many kitchens now using disposable kitchen paper rather than cloths?

Time management, punctuality and attendance

Punctuality and attendance

Working as a chef is very time dependant. Food needs to be prepared, cooked and served on time without long delays. It is therefore important to be a punctual and reliable employee to meet customer and employer expectations. You will be part of a team who support each other and regular absence from work or lateness will have a detrimental effect on the whole team. It is courteous to both your colleagues and employer to be punctual and not let the team down.

Employers expect you to do the job you are employed and paid to do within your contract of employment. People who are regularly late or absent from work are in danger of losing their job. Occasional genuine sickness may be unavoidable and a good employer will treat this with understanding.

A good employee is reliable, dependable and works well as part of the team. Employers are always looking for good employees, so with the right attitude and skills you will progress well as a chef. Being reliable and dependable often means that you will need to be flexible, show willingness and develop a 'can do', 'will do' attitude. You might be asked to change your shift to cover for someone else – try to do this even if it means that you will have to rearrange your social life.

Procedures to follow if you are absent or late

If you need to be absent from work for a genuine reason, give your manager plenty of notice so that temporary cover can be arranged. If you are sick, then you must inform your line manager immediately using an operational procedure that has been explained to you (this may be either by phone, text or e-mail).

The importance of working within set time frames

Careful and efficient time management is critical in the hospitality and catering industry. Chefs often work to tight, non-flexible schedules. Lunch and dinner need to be served at the times the customer wants them. Therefore, you may need to work to tight deadlines and targets both as an individual chef and as a team. This often means prioritising jobs and knowing how long certain tasks take so that they can be fairly distributed among the team in order to get the work done in time and to the standard required by the organisation and by the customers.

Some chefs produce a time plan for the work they need to complete. Planning may involve allocating time for each task, prioritising importance and integrating tasks, for example making a sauce while the meat is cooking.

KEY WORDS

Contract of employment – a formal agreement document between employer and employee.
Time management – planning your work so you use the available time well.
Reliable – trustworthy and consistent.
Dependable – responsible and loyal.
Prioritising – putting the most important tasks first.
Operational procedure – the standards set by an employer for the way things must be done.

Activity

1 If your bus or train to work was late and you knew you were going to be 30 minutes late for work what should you do?
2 What are the qualities that make you a good employee?
3 Why do chefs need to manage their time well?
4 What are the advantages to you of being a good employee and team member?

Teamwork

Being able to work well as part of a team is essential in the hospitality industry. A successful hospitality business may have many teams including in reception, bars, food service, kitchens, maintenance, housekeeping, porters and so on. All of these departments need to work together as a wider team to ensure an efficient workflow and to meet employer and customer expectations.

Effective communication within your own team and between the different teams is very important for a successful business and will help to develop a good team spirit and form positive working relationships. Talking to one another, exchanging ideas, prioritising tasks and helping and supporting each other are all part of effective teamwork.

Communication skills

Speaking

Always speak clearly, with good pronunciation and sufficient volume. Check whether the person can hear and understand what you are saying. Try not to speak too fast, especially when speaking with someone who uses a different first language. Show interest when you are speaking to the other person or groups of people and respond appropriately to questions they may ask you.

Listening

Listening is very important, sometimes more important than speaking.

Good listeners:

- Avoid any distractions
- Concentrate on what is being said
- Think about what is being said
- Show interest in the person speaking and do not look bored
- Maintain eye contact with the person talking and acknowledge what is being said
- If necessary, ask questions to confirm what is being said
- Clarify what has been said, in their own words.

▲ Using good speaking and listening skills in the kitchen

Writing and reading

Written communication may be in use when:

- Dealing with food or drinks orders, including specific customer requests
- Following or adapting recipes
- Ordering food or equipment
- Following instructions on food products, equipment or cleaning chemicals
- Reading instructions or leaving instructions for others.

It is important that you write clearly so that others understand your meaning. When reading what someone else has written, ask for clarification if you do not understand it.

Non-verbal communication: body language

Communication can be unspoken. Body language plays an important part in communication and includes:

- How you dress and personal grooming
- Your posture – how you sit or stand
- How far you are from the person
- Your facial expressions
- Your movements and gestures
- Your eye movements.

Always think about how you approach people and what body language you use. Some gestures are open and positive – for example, leaning forwards hands extended shows interest, acceptance and a welcoming attitude. Leaning backwards, with your arms folded and head down might show that you are closed, uninterested, defensive and negative, or rejected.

Remember that in the hospitality industry you will work with people from a wide range of different countries and cultures. Body language can mean different things in different cultures and to different people:

- **Eye contact** – In Western cultures, people make eye contact every now and then while speaking to someone. This shows that they are interested. People in the Middle East look very closely into the eyes of people they are talking to but only if they are of the same gender – eye contact between the sexes is not acceptable. In some cultures direct eye contact is seen as invasion of privacy or rudeness, for example Japanese cultures.
- **Smiling** – People from many cultures smile automatically when greeting other people, while people from other cultures may interpret this as insincere. For example, Asian people generally smile less than those from the West.
- **Personal space** – The amount of personal space someone feels comfortable with can be influenced by their culture, social status, gender, age and other factors. If in doubt allow too much rather than too little.

What makes a good team?

A good team will be generally more effective and creative. There are a number of factors that contribute to a good team:

- Good communication
- Commitment from each member of the team – colleagues will expect you to play your part in the team as your performance will have an effect on the performance of the whole team. It is important that every member of the team performs to their best so as not to let the team down.
- Team members are all punctual
- Team members are all reliable
- Team members are all flexible
- Team members support one another
- All team members work together to achieve the aims and objectives of the organisation
- All team members understand the tasks that have to be achieved in the available time
- All team members are able to work with deadlines and are able to achieve the targets set
- The team has good leadership.

Asking for advice and assistance

If you are asked to do something you are unsure about, ask for help and advice so you will be able to perform the task well and to meet expectations. Asking for advice and assistance helps you to develop your skills and confirm that you have understood and performed a task correctly. It also means that you will not waste ingredients or cause damage to equipment by using it incorrectly. Listen carefully to instructions and write notes if this will help you to remember. Your supervisor is there to assist you and to show you the correct procedure.

KEY WORDS

Colleagues – The people you work with.

Courteous – Considerate and polite.

Workflow – Efficient and logical methods of work.

Pronunciation – the way you say words and speak.

Activity

1 List three things that will make a good team at work.
2 What is meant by good communication?
3 Suggest what may happen if members of a kitchen team did not communicate with each other.
4 Why is good time management crucial when working in the hospitality industry?
5 What makes a good listener?
6 What can someone's body language tell us?

Dealing effectively with customers

A hospitality business cannot exist without customers. Customers mean money, so customer care and customer service are very important to the success of the business. The main job of people working in the hospitality industry is to look after customers' needs, wants and expectations. For customers to be loyal to a business, the service must live up to or exceed their expectations. Happy customers are usually those who are pleased with the product or service and the price they paid for them. This means that they are likely to come back again, or tell other people about their positive experience, which helps the business to be profitable.

Even if a hotel has wonderful, luxurious facilities in comfortable surroundings, the business is doomed to failure if the customer service does not match the environment and the expectations of the customers. A bad experience can put someone off forever, and they may tell other people about their bad experience and put them off as well.

▲ Looking after customers

Communication with customers

Communicating well with customers is the key to good customer service. It is important to acknowledge the customer, understand them and anticipate their needs. It is also important to keep the customer informed so that they know what is happening to their order or their request, and to

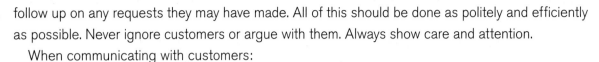

follow up on any requests they may have made. All of this should be done as politely and efficiently as possible. Never ignore customers or argue with them. Always show care and attention.

When communicating with customers:

- Listen to them carefully. Keep good eye contact and show that you are interested in what they are saying.
- Speak clearly with good pronunciation and voice projection.
- After taking an order or dealing with a request, respond in an appropriate way and confirm that you fully understand.
- When writing down a customer order or request do so clearly because someone else may be dealing with the order. Read it back to the customer to confirm that you have it right.
- If you are communicating directly with a customer in writing, once again make sure the message is clear. If you have received a written message from a customer make sure you understand the meaning (ask for help if necessary).

High standards of customer service will make the customer feel well cared for and important and will:

- Meet and hopefully exceed their expectations
- Show that you are there to meet with their requests and needs
- Encourage them to come back so there will be repeat sales
- Demonstrate that the business is customer focused.

Barriers to effective communication

There are some things that can make it difficult for people to communicate effectively:

- **Speaking unclearly, too quietly or too fast** may be a barrier to communication and understanding
- **Not listening properly** so the message is not or only partially understood
- **Inappropriate body language** – for example, someone shuffling, with hands in their pockets and looking down is not going to communicate well with customers
- **Poor personal appearance** – personal appearance communicates the standards of the establishment so needs to be good
- **Cultural barriers** – these can lead to a breakdown in communication. Something that is perfectly acceptable in one culture may cause insult or offence in another.
- **Misinterpretation**, such as not fully understanding what the other person said or getting the wrong meaning
- **Not speaking the same language** – there are many different cultures and nationalities which are employed in or are customers of the hospitality industry. It may be possible to find someone else in the building who speaks the same language to help.
- **Not understanding another person's accent** – speak clearly yourself and if you cannot understand the other person ask them to speak more slowly
- **Using too much unfamiliar terminology** and jargon – avoid using this
- **Having hearing difficulties** – if someone has hearing difficulties, speak clearly and slowly which may help

- **Intoxication** – being under the influence of alcohol or other substances may impair the ability to communicate properly
- **Personal problems or stress** – people may have these on their mind which means they are not fully concentrating on the conversation and then may not understand
- **Poor grammar and spelling, legibility, formatting and presentation** – this could be in written or electronic communication. Read through any letters or notes you write to check for possible errors. If you are unsure, get someone else to check it for you. Where possible use a computer and use the grammar and spellchecker but remember this is not foolproof, errors can still be there.

Professional tip

If a customer is clearly already intoxicated you are obliged by law not to sell them any more alcoholic drinks.

KEY WORDS

Cultural – ethnic or social beliefs and customs.

Jargon – terms, abbreviations or descriptions used by a particular group.

Intoxication – being under the influence of alcohol or other substance.

Electronic communication – includes a wide range of computer and mobile phone systems. Some electronic systems are designed specifically for hospitality businesses.

Revenue – money received (income).

Exceed – go further than expected.

Customer focused – everything is planned and carried out with the customer in mind.

Voice projection – making your voice carry a little further so you can be heard by more people.

Commitment – determined and keen to do something.

Activity •

1 Why is it important to communicate well with customers?

2 Suggest three ways that you could communicate with customers.

3 What are three things that would make customers want to return to an establishment and perhaps recommend it to friends?

4 Why is it important to look smart and well groomed when meeting customers?

5 When communicating with a customer who doesn't fully understand you, what should you do?

Test yourself

1 Use a diagram to show a full chef uniform and add a short description of each item.

2 Why is it so important that chefs wash their hands frequently and well? Suggest three occasions when chefs should wash their hands.

3 Why should oven cloths not be used if they are wet or damp?

4 Why should kitchen cloths not be placed on the shoulder?

5 Give three reasons why chefs should wear safety shoes with reinforced toecaps.

6 Why is it very important for chefs and other hospitality staff to arrive at work on time?

7 Suggest three characteristics that would make a good team member.

8 Listening is very important. Suggest three things that make a good listener.

9 There can be misunderstandings between people from different cultures. Give an example of this.

10 When writing down a customer order why is important to write clearly?

11 What would make a good service experience?

7 Boiling, poaching and steaming

This chapter covers Unit 107, Prepare and cook food by boiling, poaching and steaming.

By the end of the chapter you should be able to:

- Describe the process of cooking food items by boiling, poaching and steaming
- Identify the purpose of boiling, poaching and steaming
- Identify the food items which may be boiled, poached or steamed
- Identify the liquids which may be used when boiling, poaching or steaming foods
- State the importance of using the correct proportion of liquid to food to achieve the finished dish requirements
- State the importance of using associated techniques to achieve the finished dish requirements
- Describe the methods used to produce associated products
- List the methods used when boiling, poaching or steaming foods
- Identify suitable equipment for boiling, poaching and steaming
- Explain how time and the movement of liquids are determined by the item to be boiled, steamed or poached
- List the quality points to look for during selection of food items, preparation, cooking and finishing of dishes.

Boiling

Process

Boiling is when food is covered in liquid, which is then heated up until the liquid starts to bubble vigorously. At this point it is boiling. Usually the heat is then turned down so that the liquid is just bubbling gently.

> **Professional tip**
> Boiling is an economical way of cooking lots of food as it does not use too much fuel.

Purpose

Boiling is a healthy method of cookery as it does not use any fat, and when done properly will keep the flavour and nutritional value of the food. Boiling will:

- Make food easy to digest and pleasant to eat, providing food with an agreeable flavour
- Make food safe to eat
- Give food a good texture – tender, slightly firm and crisp (depending on the food).

Foods we often boil

The range of foods that can be cooked by boiling includes vegetables, eggs, pasta, pulses and grains. Meat and poultry can also be boiled.

▲ Boiling

Liquids used when boiling

There are four main liquids used when boiling foods:

- Water
- Milk
- Infused liquids
- Stock (fresh or convenience product).

The amount or type of liquid used is dependent on the type of food being boiled:

- When you put vegetables into boiling liquid, always make sure that there is enough liquid in the pot and that it is boiling before you add the food. The liquid should just cover the vegetables but not boil over during cooking.
- When boiling meat, **skim** the surface of the liquid regularly during the cooking; this will remove impurities and help enhance the finished dish.

You should simmer rather than boil vigorously whenever possible. This will mean that less water evaporates, so the amount of liquid will stay more or less the same and the food will not shrink too much.

Methods of boiling

There are two ways of boiling:

1 Place the food in boiling liquid. The liquid will stop boiling when you put the food in, so heat it up to bring it back to boiling. Then reduce the heat so that the liquid just bubbles gently (this is known as **simmering**) and boils the food.
2 Cover food with cold liquid. Heat it up and bring it to the boil, then reduce the heat to allow the food to simmer.

 Health and safety

When you place food into boiling water, you should lower it into the water gently to prevent splashing and scalding.

 Health and safety

Make sure that the handles on pots of boiling liquids are turned in when on stoves, so that sleeves and hands do not catch them. When removing the lid from the cooking pot, tilt it away from your face to allow the steam to escape safely. If you open it towards you the hot steam may burn your face.

Temperature and time control

For both methods of boiling, the temperature must be controlled so that the liquid is brought to the boil and then adjusted so that it goes to a gentle boil (simmer) until the food is cooked.

The time taken to cook food by boiling is dependent on the food being cooked.

- Stocks, soups and sauces must only simmer.
- Pasta should not be overcooked but left slightly firm (called *al dente*).
- Meat and poultry should be well cooked and tender.
- Vegetables should not be overcooked but left slightly crisp.

Equipment

Saucepans of various sizes can be used for boiling. Always choose pans that are the correct size for the item to be boiled – neither too small nor too large. Ensuring that the cooking pot is large enough for the water to cover the food without spilling over the edge once the water starts to boil will reduce the risk of being splashed by boiling water.

 Health and safety
Check the cleanliness and condition of the pan before use so as not to cause cross-contamination.

Associated techniques

There are a number of techniques associated with boiling which help the chef to prepare dishes correctly:

- **Soaking** – dried pulses and beans are pre-soaked prior to the cooking process to soften them.
- **Blanching** – food is cooked and then cooled rapidly to stop the cooking process. This is known as **refreshing** food.
- **Skimming** – scum or impurities often appear as foam or froth on the surface of the cooking liquid. To remove these, stir gently from the centre with a ladle to move the foam or froth to the edge of the pan; it can be collected by the edge of the ladle and placed into a bowl to be discarded.
- **Draining** – this is the process of removing food from the cooking liquid.
- **Chilling** – reducing temperature to holding or storage temperature.
- **Reheating** – bringing previously cooked food to the required temperature for serving.
- **Holding for service** – holding at a temperature above 63°C.

Products associated with boiling

Stock

Stock is important in several cooking methods. It is the basis of all meat sauces, gravies, soups and purées, as well as a cooking liquid in its own right.

There are three main types of stock:
- White stock is made from bones, vegetables and herbs
- Brown stock is the same as white stock, except the bones are browned in a pan or in the oven before adding the rest of the ingredients
- Vegetable stock is made from vegetables and herbs, without any bones.

Recipes for making stocks are included in the recipe section.

When making stocks:
- Only use fresh bones and vegetables
- Continually remove scum and fat from the surface of the stock as it cooks
- Always simmer gently
- Never add salt
- If the stock is going to be kept, strain and cool it quickly then store it in a refrigerator.

Convenience stocks are available in chilled, frozen, powder and condensed forms. It is important to taste these to check that you are satisfied with their quality before using them.

Soups

Stocks can be used to make a large variety of soups. A vast range of fresh vegetables and dried pulses (peas and beans) can be added to soups. Grains, pasta and many herbs and spices can also be used.

There are a variety of ready-prepared soups on the market, including soups in powdered and condensed form. If you have to make use of a convenience product, always taste and assess it first. In some situations, you can combine a freshly prepared soup with a suitable convenience product.

Sauces

A sauce is a liquid that has been thickened, either by a **roux**, cornflour or arrowroot (a roux is a combination of fat and flour gently cooked over a low heat for a short time). Sauces that will be used for coating foods (for example, jus lié – thickened gravy) should be as thin as possible and should only lightly coat the food.

Some types of accompaniment that are called sauces are not really sauces (for example, apple sauce, mint sauce, horseradish sauce). Recipes for several of this type of 'sauce' that is served with meat or poultry are included in the recipe section.

Poaching

Process

Poaching is when food is cooked in a liquid that is very hot but not boiling. It should be just below boiling point.

Purpose

The purpose of poaching is to cook food so that:
- It is very tender and easy to eat and digest
- The flavour of the dish is enhanced
- The nutritional content is retained.

Foods we often poach

The range of foods that can be cooked by poaching includes chicken, eggs, fish and fruit.

Liquids used when poaching

The same liquids used for boiling foods can be used for poaching, with a few additions:
- **Water** – eggs are usually poached in water, with a little vinegar added
- **Milk** – fish fillets, such as smoked haddock, may be poached in milk

- **Stock** – the stock should be suited to the food. For example, fish fillets can be poached in fish stock and chicken breast fillets in chicken stock. You can also poach poultry and fish in a rich vegetable stock.
- **Wine** – fruit, such as pears, may be poached in wine
- **Stock syrup** – this is sugar based and normally used for poaching fruits
- **Infused liquids** – flavouring a cooking liquor with seasoning, spice, herbs or wine.

> **Professional tip**
>
> Sometimes a tasty sauce can be made with the cooking liquid, for example, a parsley or other sauce can be made from the milk in which fish is poached.

 Health and safety

Although poaching liquids are not quite as dangerous as boiling liquids, they are still very hot and can cause serious burns or scalds. Be aware of pans of hot liquids – when you lower food into the poaching liquid, you should do so carefully to prevent splashes.

Methods of poaching

For most foods, the poaching liquid is heated first. When it reaches the right temperature, lower the prepared food into the barely simmering liquid and allow it to cook in the gentle heat.

There are two ways of poaching:

1 **Shallow poaching** – cook the food in only a small amount of liquid and cover it with greased greaseproof paper. Never allow the liquid to boil – keep it at a temperature as near to boiling as possible without actually boiling. To prevent the liquid from boiling, bring it to the boil on top of the stove, take it off the direct heat and then place the food in the water. Complete the cooking in a moderately hot oven (approximately 180°C). Foods poached using this method include cuts of fish and chicken.

2 **Deep poaching** – this can be used to cook eggs. Place eggs in approximately 8cm of gently simmering water. You can also deep poach whole fish (such as salmon), slices of fish on the bone (such as turbot), filleted cod and salmon, and whole chicken as well as whole fruits. All of these should be covered with the poaching liquid.

▲ Poaching

Temperature and time control

The temperature must be controlled so that the cooking liquid does not become too cool or too hot. Poaching is cooking at just below simmering point.

It is important to time the cooking correctly so that food is neither undercooked nor overcooked. If it is undercooked it will not be pleasant to eat and can sometimes be dangerous (for example, undercooked chicken). If it is overcooked it will break up and lose some of its nutrients.

The time and temperature needed to cook the food correctly will vary slightly for different types of food.

Equipment

A poaching pan should be used for this method of cooking. A spider, fish slice or slotted spoon can be used to remove poached items from the poaching liquid.

Associated techniques

There are a number of techniques associated with poaching which help the chef to prepare the dishes correctly.

Cutting – trimming and shaping food so it cooks efficiently and looks attractive.

Tying – food items are tied so that they stay in shape during the cooking process.

Folding – food such as fillets of flat fish which are shallow poached are folded to balance the thickness of the flesh, to make an even cooking time and to enhance presentation.

Reducing cooking liquid – with some dishes the liquid is strained and then reduced by boiling. This will then be used as the base for a sauce to accompany the dish.

Straining – removing food from cooking liquid and draining. This will enhance presentation as no poaching liquid weeps from the food item when served.

Holding for service – holding at a temperature above 63°C.

Steaming

Process

Steaming is another method of cooking using moist heat. Food is cooked under pressure in the steam produced by a boiling liquid (rather than placing the food itself in the boiling liquid).

Purpose

Steaming:

- Cooks food in a way that keeps it as nutritious as possible (most of the nutrients remain in the food)
- Changes the texture of food and makes it tender and edible – the texture will vary according to the type of food, type of steamer and level of heat
- Makes some foods lighter and easy to digest.

Liquids used when steaming

The following liquids can all be used to create a steam in which to cook food items:

- Water
- Stock (fresh or convenience)
- Infused liquids.

These liquids will add flavour and moisture to the dish.

> **Professional tip**
> The natural juices that result from steaming fish, for example, can be served with the fish or used to make the accompanying sauce.

Food items that can be steamed

The range of foods which can be cooked by steaming include chicken, fish, vegetables, and savoury and sweet puddings.

Methods and equipment

There are two main methods of steaming:

1 **Atmospheric steaming** – this is a low-pressure steaming method, in which steam is produced by placing water in the bottom of a saucepan and bringing it to a rapid boil. Food is placed in a container above the boiling water. The steam from the boiling water heats the container and cooks the food inside it. This could be done in a combi oven.

2 **High-pressure steaming** – this is done in high-pressure steamers such as pressure cookers or commercial steaming unit. The high pressure in the steamer produces higher temperatures and forces steam through the food, which makes the food cook faster.

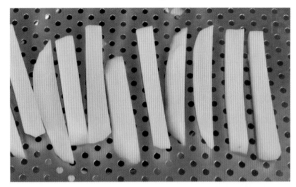
▲ Steaming

> **Professional tip**
>
> High-pressure steaming enables food to be cooked or reheated quickly. It is often used for 'batch' cooking, where small quantities of vegetables are cooked frequently throughout the service. This means the vegetables are always freshly cooked, so they keep their colour, flavour and nutritional content.

Temperature and time control

When using steamers it is important to make sure that the food is not undercooked or overcooked and therefore that the correct temperature and cooking time is used.

Food cooks much faster in high-pressure steamers and therefore there is a great danger of the food overcooking very quickly. When you are using a high-pressure steamer, wait until the pressure gauge shows that it has reached the correct pressure, then open the door very carefully to allow the steam to escape before you place the food in the steamer. This way you will be sure that the necessary cooking temperature has been reached.

Individual sponge puddings, for example, will cook in less time than when cooking in a large pudding basin to be portioned when cooked.

 Health and safety

Boiling water is used in the bottom of steamers, so the same safety points apply to steaming as to boiling. Steam is extremely hot and can cause serious burns and scalds. To avoid injuring yourself:

● Make sure you know how to use steamers properly and use them with great care

● Check the pressure in high-pressure steamers continually and allow the pressure to return to the correct level before opening doors or removing pressure-cooker lids

● Allow time for the pressure to return to normal before opening commercial steamers. Stand well away from the door as you open it, to avoid the full impact of the escaping steam.

Associated techniques

There are a number of techniques associated with steaming which help the chef to prepare the dishes correctly:

- **Preparation of containers** – ensure that the container being used to steam is fit for purpose (in good condition and the correct size)
- **Greasing** – lightly coat the inside of a mould to help provide a non-stick surface to allow puddings to be removed easily when cooked
- **Moulding** – placing food into a cooking mould. The food will take on the shape of the mould when cooked.
- **Traying up** – placing individual moulds onto a tray so multiple items can be steamed at the same time
- **Covering/waterproofing** – covering the food with greaseproof paper or foil to ensure that steam does not come into contact with the food during cooking
- **Loading** – placing moulds into the steamer.

Quality points for boiling, poaching and steaming foods

To ensure the quality of finished dishes there are a number of things that a chef should do to ensure the dish meets the customer's expectations:

- Selection of products – ensure that products are fresh, have a good appearance, smell as expected and are at the appropriate temperature
- Preparation – foods should be trimmed, shaped and sized according to dish requirements
- Cooking process – the temperature and cooking time should be checked, as should the amount of liquid to be used. These elements will impact on the flavour, colour, texture and taste of the dish
- Finishing of the final dish – consistency, appearance, portion size, seasoning and garnish if required should all be considered.

Test yourself

1 Briefly describe the process for the following methods of cooking:
   a Poaching
   b Steaming
   c Boiling
2 What is the purpose of poaching food?
3 List three vegetables that are cooked in boiling water.
4 What is the term for removing scum or foam from the top of a boiling liquid? How should you do this?
5 List three types of food that could be steamed.
6 List three cooking liquids that could be used as a sauce in the finished dish.
7 List five safety points for chefs to consider when cooking by boiling, poaching or steaming.
8 List four foods that can be cooked by poaching and indicate whether they are deep or shallow poached.
9 Describe one method of boiling.
10 What would you use to steam a pudding? Why are puddings for steaming covered?

Boiling recipes

Suffolk pork collar daube cooked in cyder

Ingredients	4 portions	10 portions
Pork collar, cleaned of excess fat, cut into portions and tied	1 kg	2½ kg
Olive oil	75 ml	200 ml
Carrots	4	10
Shallots	5	12
Leeks, small	2	5
Black peppercorns	8	20
Chicken stock or light pork stock	1 litre	2½ litres
Semi-sweet cyder	1 litre	2½ litres
Fresh parsley, sprigs	2	5

Get ready to cook

1 Prepare the vegetables into mirepoix.

2 Remove excess fat from the pork collar. Cut it into portions and tie it. Season the meat.

Cooking

1 Heat the oil in a large pan and seal the meat all over.

2 Add the vegetables, herbs, peppercorns, cyder and stock to the pan with the sealed pork. Bring up to the simmer.

3 Cover and cook in the oven until the pork is cooked through, about 2 hours.

4 Remove the pork from the cooking liquor, set aside, cool and refrigerate. Strain and chill the stock overnight. (This recipe could also be prepared and served straight away.)

To serve

1 Take the stock from the fridge, remove the fat from the surface and decant the stock from the container, leaving the sediment behind.

2 Untie the pork, place in a tray and cover with 300 ml of stock.

3 Cover with foil and place in the oven at 180°C for about 15 minutes until the pork is heated through.

4 Reduce the remaining stock to 450 ml and set aside.

5 Heat some vegetables ready for serving.

6 Divide the pork between four plates, garnish with the vegetables and spoon over the reduced stock. Finish with picked herbs.

 Note: This regional recipe was contributed by Carmel Asbury, Head of School of Hospitality at West Suffolk College.

Recipe 2

White stock

Ingredients	To make 4½ litres	To make 10 litres
Raw, meaty bones	1 kg	2½ kg
Water	5 litres	10½ litres
Onion, carrot, celery, leek	400 g	1½ kg
Bouquet garni		

Get ready to cook

1 Chop the bones into small pieces and remove any fat or marrow.
2 Wash and peel the vegetables.
3 Prepare a bouquet garni.

Cooking

1 Place the bones in a large pot, cover with cold water and bring to the boil.
2 As soon as the water comes to the boil, take pot to the sink and drain away the water.
3 Wash the bones and clean the pot.
4 Return the bones to the pot, cover them with water and bring them back to the boil again.
5 Reduce the heat so that the water is simmering gently.
6 Skim the surface to remove any scum as and when required. Also wipe round the top and inside of the pot.
7 After 2–3 hours add the vegetables and the bouquet garni.
8 Simmer for 3–4 hours, skimming regularly.
9 When the cooking is finished, skim the stock again and strain it.

Storage suggestion

If you are going to keep the stock, cool it quickly, pour it into a suitable container and put it in the fridge.

Try something different – chicken stock

Chicken stock can be made in the same way, using either chicken carcasses and/or winglets, or an old boiling fowl.

● Simmer the carcasses and/or winglets for one hour, then add the vegetables and simmer for a further hour.
● Allow the boiling fowl to three-quarters cook before adding the vegetables. The time will vary according to the age of the bird.

Recipe
3

Brown stock

Ingredients	To make 1 litre	To make 3 litres
Raw, meaty bones	250 g	750 g
Water	1¼ litres	3¾ litres
Onion, carrot, celery, leek	100 g	300 g
Bouquet garni	1	1

Get ready to cook

Chop the bones into small pieces.

Cooking

1 Brown the chopped bones well on all sides. You can do this by frying them in a little fat or oil in a frying pan, or by roasting them in a hot oven.

2 Strain off any fat and place the bones in a large pot.

3 If there is any sediment in the bottom of the frying pan or roasting tray, brown this and then deglaze (swill out) the pan with ½ litre of boiling water.

4 Simmer for a few minutes and then add this liquid to the bones.

5 Cover the bones with cold water and bring it to the boil.

6 Reduce the heat so that the water is simmering gently.

7 Simmer for 2–3 hours, skimming the surface to remove any scum as and when required.

8 Fry the vegetables in a little fat or oil until brown. Drain off any fat and add them to the bones with the bouquet garni.

9 Simmer for 3–4 hrs, skimming regularly.

10 When the cooking is finished, skim the stock again and strain it.

Storage suggestion

If you are going to keep the stock, cool it quickly, pour it into a suitable container and put it in the fridge.

Try something different

You could add some squashed tomatoes or washed mushroom trimmings to this stock.

Recipe 4 — Fish stock

Ingredients	To make 1 litre	To make 3 litres
Oil, butter, margarine	10 g	30 g
Onions	50 g	150 g
Fresh white fish bones	500 g	1½ kg
Lemon juice	¼	1
Parsley stalks	2	6
Bay leaf	1	1
Water	1 litre	3 litres

Get ready to cook

1 Slice the onions.
2 Wash the fish bones thoroughly.

Cooking

 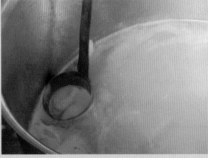 

1 Place the oil, butter or margarine in a thick-bottomed pan.
2 Add the onions, fish bones, lemon juice, bay leaf and parsley stalks.
3 Cover the ingredients with oiled greaseproof paper and a tight-fitting lid and sweat them gently without colouring for five minutes.
4 Add the water and bring it to the boil.

5 Reduce the heat so that the water is simmering gently.
6 Simmer for 20 minutes, skimming regularly.

7 Strain the stock.

Storage suggestion

If you are going to keep the stock, cool it quickly, pour it into a suitable container and put it in the fridge.

 Note: Cooking the stock for longer than 20 minutes will spoil the flavour.

Split pea soup

Ingredients	4 portions	10 portions
Split peas	200 g	500 g
White stock or water	1½ litres	3¾ litres
Onions, chopped	50 g	125 g
Carrots, chopped	50 g	125 g
Bouquet garni		
Knuckle of ham or bacon (optional)		
Salt		
Stale bread sliced (to make croutons)	1 slice	2½ slices
Butter, margarine or oil	50 g	125 g

Get ready to cook

1 Check and wash the peas. If pre-soaked, change the water.
2 Wash, peel and chop the onions and carrots.
3 Prepare a bouquet garni.
4 Prepare the croutons.

Cooking

1 Place the peas in a thick-bottomed pan.
2 Add the stock or water. Bring to the boil and skim.
3 Add the remainder of the ingredients and a little salt.
4 Simmer until tender, skimming when necessary.
5 Remove the bouquet garni and ham.
6 Liquidise the soup and pass it through a chinoise.
7 Return the soup to a clean pan and bring it back to the boil.
8 Taste and correct the seasoning and consistency. If too thick, dilute with stock.

Note: Any type of pulse can be made into soup, for example, split pea (yellow or green), haricot beans, lentils.

Some pulses may need to be soaked overnight in cold water.

Serving suggestion

Serve with fried or toasted croutons.

Try something different

Add either of the following:

● A chopped fresh herb from parsley, chervil, tarragon, coriander, chives
● A spice or a combination, such as garam masala.

Activity •

Name as many types of pulse as you can (there are at least 21).

Recipe 6 Mutton broth

Ingredients	4 portions	10 portions
Scrag end of mutton, off the bone	400 g	1 kg
Mutton or lamb stock or water	800 ml	2 litres
Barley	30 g	80 g
Carrot, turnip, leek, celery, onion	300 g	750 g
Bouquet garni		
Parsley, chopped		

Get ready to cook

1 Trim off any fat from the meat.
2 Wash the barley.
3 Wash and peel the vegetables and cut into small neat squares (brunoise).
4 Prepare a bouquet garni.

 Note: Instead of chopped parsley, you could use basil and oregano if you prefer.

Cooking

1 Place the meat in a saucepan and add cold water.
2 Heat this to a fast boil.

3 As soon as the water starts to boil, remove the pan from the heat. Lift out the meat and wash it under cold running water.
4 Pour away the cooking water and clean the pan.
5 Replace the meat and cover with cold water or stock. Bring to the boil and skim.
6 Add the barley to the pan and then reduce the heat and simmer for one hour.

7 Add the vegetables, the bouquet garni and seasoning.

8 Continue simmering for 30 minutes or until meat is tender. Skim off any fat or scum as necessary.

9 Once cooked, remove the meat from the pan and allow it to cool.

10 Cut the meat into neat cubes the same size as the vegetables. Return the meat to the broth.

11 Skim off any fat, taste and correct the seasoning.

Serving suggestion

This is a traditional, rustic recipe, which may be served as a substantial dish.
Add fresh chopped parsley and serve.

Try something different

For a more delicate dish, the vegetables and meat may be diced smaller.
- **Scotch broth** – use lean beef and beef stock in place of mutton.
- **Chicken broth** – use chicken and well-flavoured chicken stock. Add washed rice 12–15 minutes before the broth is cooked. Leave out the barley.

Activity •

Suggest a different broth of your own choice.

Recipe

7

Leek and potato soup

Ingredients	4 portions	10 portions
Butter, margarine or oil	25 g	60 g
Leeks	400 g	1½ kg
White stock	750 ml	2 litres
Bouquet garni		
Potatoes	200 g	½ kg
Salt		

Get ready to cook

1 Wash and trim the leeks and cut the white and light green part into ½ cm squares (paysanne).

2 Wash and peel the potatoes and cut into ½ cm squares 2 mm thick.

3 Prepare a bouquet garni.

Cooking

1 Melt the fat in a saucepan. Add the leeks, cover with a lid and cook slowly without colouring until soft.

2 Add the stock, potatoes, bouquet garni and a little salt.

3 Simmer for approximately 15 minutes.

4 Remove the bouquet garni. Liquidise the soup and pass through a chinoise, then taste and correct the seasoning before serving.

Recipe 8 Sweet potato soup

Ingredients	4 portions	10 portions
Red peppers, deseeded and diced	2	5
Sweet potatoes, peeled and diced	1 kg	2½ kg
Onions, peeled and diced	1	3
Garlic cloves, chopped	2	5
Vegetable or chicken stock	1 litre	2½ litres
Salt and pepper to season		

Get ready to cook

1 Remove the seeds from the peppers and dice into even-sized pieces.
2 Peel and dice the sweet potato.
3 Peel and dice the onions and chop the garlic.

Cooking

1 Sweat the onions until soft and translucent.

2 Add the sweet potato, peppers and garlic and cook gently for 10–15 minutes on a low heat.

3 Add the stock and simmer for approximately 40 minutes.
4 Purée the vegetables either in the pan with stick blender or in a liquidiser.

5 Pass through a conical strainer.
6 Return to pan and season to taste.

Recipe
9

Tomato soup

Ingredients	4 portions	10 portions
Butter, margarine or oil	50 g	125 g
Bacon trimmings (optional)	25 g	60 g
Onion and carrot, washed peeled and roughly chopped	100 g of each	250 g of each
Flour	50 g	125 g
Tomato purée	100 g	250 g
Large tomatoes, chopped	2	5
Stock	1½ litres	3½ litres
Bouquet garni		
Salt		
Stale bread sliced (to make croutons)	1 slice	3 slices

Get ready to cook

1 Peel, wash and roughly chop the vegetables.
2 Prepare a bouquet garni.
3 Prepare the croutons.

Note: A slightly sweet/sharp flavour can be added to the soup by preparing what is known as a gastric (gastrique). In a thick-bottomed pan, reduce 100 ml of malt vinegar and 35 g caster sugar until it is a light caramel colour. Mix this into the completed soup.

Some tomato purée can be stronger than others, so you may have to add a little more or less when making this soup.

Cooking

1 Melt the fat in a thick-bottomed pan.

2 Add the bacon, carrots and onions and lightly brown these.

3 Mix in the flour and cook to a sandy texture.

4 Mix in the tomato purée, then remove the pan from the heat and allow the mixture to cool.

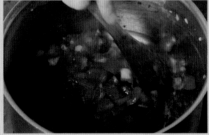

5 Return the pan to the heat and add the chopped tomatoes.

6 Mix well.

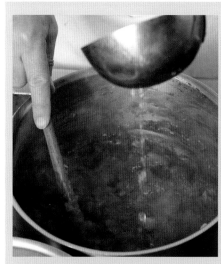  

7 Gradually mix in the hot stock. Stir it until it is boiling.

8 Add the bouquet garni and a little salt and simmer for one hour.

9 Skim the soup and remove the bouquet garni.

10 Liquidise the soup, then pass through a medium-mesh conical strainer.

11 Return the soup to a clean pan and reheat it.

12 Taste the soup and check seasoning and consistency.

Serving suggestion

Serve with fried or toasted croutons.

Try something different

Try adding:

- The juice and lightly grated peel of 1–2 oranges
- Cooked rice
- A chopped fresh herb, such as chives.

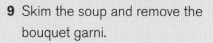

Activity

1 Prepare, cook and taste the recipe for tomato soup with and without a gastric. Discuss and assess the two versions.

2 Name and prepare a variation of your own.

3 Review the basic recipe for tomato soup and adjust to meet dietary requirements for a low fat vegetarian customer.

Recipe 10 — Garden marrow soup

Ingredients	4 portions	10 portions
Onions, peeled and roughly diced	1	2
Olive oil	90 ml	225 ml
Marrow (large), cut into cubes	1	2½
Mild curry powder	½ tbsp	2½ tbsp
Chicken or vegetable stock	1 litre	2½ litres

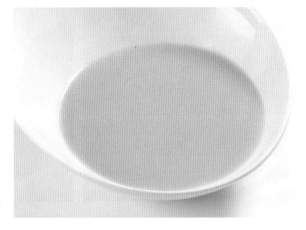

Get ready to cook

1 Peel and roughly dice the onion.
2 Peel and cube the marrow.

Cooking

1 Sweat the onion in the olive oil until translucent.
2 Add the cubed marrow and fry gently.
3 Stir in the curry powder.
4 Add the stock and simmer for approximately 40 minutes.
5 Purée the soup either in the pan with a stick blender or in a liquidiser.
6 Pass through a chinoise or conical strainer. Season with salt and pepper.
7 Adjust the consistency if necessary by adding a little water.

 Note: Courgette may be used instead of marrow. Courgettes are available all year round.

Velouté

Ingredients	4 portions	10 portions
Margarine, butter or oil	100 g	400 g
Flour	10 g	40 g
Stock, chicken, fish	1 litre	4½ litres

Note: This is a basic white sauce made from white stock and a blond roux.

Cooking

1 Melt the fat in a thick-bottomed pan.
2 Mix in the flour.
3 Cook out to a sandy texture over a gentle heat, allowing the lightest shade of colour (blond roux).
4 Remove the pan from the heat to allow the roux to cool.
5 Return the pan to stove and, over a low heat, gradually add the hot stock.
6 Mix until smooth and simmering.
7 Cook gently for one hour and pass through a fine conical strainer.

Storage suggestions

To prevent a skin from forming, brush the surface with melted butter. When ready to use, stir this into the sauce. Alternatively, cover the sauce with a circle of oiled greaseproof paper, or baking parchment. You are advised not to use cling film for this purpose.

Try something different

A velouté-based sauce can be used for egg, fish, chicken and mutton.

Sauce	Served with	Additions per ½ litre
Caper	Boiled leg of mutton or lamb	2 tbsp capers
Aurora	Poached eggs, chicken	1 tsp tomato purée 60 ml cream or natural yoghurt 2–3 drops of lemon juice
Mushroom	Poached chicken	100 g sliced button mushrooms lightly cooked in a little fat or oil

Activity

Suggest an alternative of your choice. Prepare, taste, discuss and assess it.

Recipe 12 Béchamel (basic white sauce)

Ingredients	1 litre	2½ litres
Margarine, butter or oil	80 g	200 g
Flour	100 g	400 g
Milk, warmed	1 litre	4½ litres
Onion	½	1
Clove	1	1
Bay leaf	1	2

Get ready to cook

Push a clove into an onion, with the sharp end going into the onion, leaving the round end studding the outside of the onion.

Cooking

1 Add the studded onion and a bay leaf to the milk. Simmer, allowing it to infuse, for five minutes.
2 Melt the fat in a thick-bottomed pan.
3 Mix in the flour with a wooden spoon.
4 Cook for a few minutes, stirring frequently. When making white roux you should not allow the mixture to colour.
5 Remove the pan from the heat to allow the roux to cool.

6 Return the pan to stove over a low heat. Gradually ladle the milk into the roux – stir the mixture back to a smooth paste each time you add a ladleful of milk.

7 Continue adding the milk, one ladleful at a time.

8 Allow the mixture to simmer gently for 30 minutes, stirring frequently.

9 Remove from the heat and pass the sauce through a conical strainer.

Storage suggestions

To prevent a skin from forming, brush the surface with melted butter. When ready to use, stir this into the sauce. Alternatively, cover the sauce with a circle of oiled greaseproof paper, or baking parchment. You are advised not to use cling film for this purpose.

Try something different

Béchamel is a basic white sauce that can be used as the basis for many other sauces. The suggestions below are for half a litre of béchamel, which is enough for 8 to 12 portions of sauce:

Sauce	Served with	Additions per ½ litre
Egg	Poached or steamed fish	2 diced hard-boiled eggs
Cheese	Poached fish or vegetables	50 g grated cheddar cheese
Onion	Roast lamb or mutton	100 g chopped onions cooked without colouring, either by boiling or sweating in fat
Parsley	Poached fish or boiled ham	1 teaspoon chopped parsley
Cream	Poached fish or vegetables	Add cream or natural yoghurt to give the consistency of double cream
Mustard	Grilled herrings	Add diluted English or continental mustard to give a spicy sauce

Activity

1 As a group, make all six of these sauces. Taste, discuss and assess them.

2 Suggest a variation of your own, using béchamel and a dish with which it might be served.

Recipe
13 Roast gravy

Ingredients	4 portions	10 portions
Raw meat bones	200 g	500 g
Brown stock or water	500 ml	1½ litres
Onions	50 g	125 g
Carrots	50 g	125 g
Celery	25 g	60 g

 Note: Roast gravy is traditionally made from the residue that roast joints leave in their roasting pans, but it can also be made with raw bones if you need a larger quantity, as in this recipe.

Get ready to cook

1 Chop the bones into small pieces.
2 Wash, peel and roughly chop the vegetables.

Cooking

1 Brown the bones in a little fat in a roasting tray in the oven or in a heavy frying pan on the stove.
2 Drain off the fat and place bones in a saucepan.
3 Deglaze the tray or pan with stock or water to ensure that all of the tasty brown residue is not wasted.
4 Pour the deglaze liquid into the saucepan with the bones and cover the bones with stock or water.
5 Bring to the boil, skim and allow to simmer.
6 Lightly fry the vegetables in a little fat in a frying pan or add them to the bones when these are partly browned.
7 Simmer for 1½–2 hours and strain.
8 Skim off any fat that settles on the surface.

Try something different

If your roast gravy does not have enough flavour when tasted, add a little of a suitable convenience product to help. Many convenience gravy products are available, but you should taste and assess these before using them.

Recipe 14

Thickened roast gravy

Ingredients	Amount per ½ litre of gravy
Gravy	
Tomato purée	1 tsp
Mushroom trimmings	1 heaped tsp
Thyme	a small pinch
Arrowroot or cornflour	1 heaped tsp

 Note: You can make a light brown sauce by lightly thickening a well-flavoured roast gravy with arrowroot or cornflour dissolved in water.

Cooking

1 Simmer the required amount of gravy in a thick-bottomed pan.
2 Add the tomato purée, mushroom trimmings and thyme.
3 Dilute the arrowroot or cornflour in a basin with a little cold water and gradually add this to the simmering gravy, stirring continuously until it re-boils.
4 Simmer for 5–10 minutes and pass through a fine-mesh chinoise.

Try something different

- This basic sauce can be used for a number of variations; it is more commonly known as *jus-lié* and is used in many other sauces as a base.
- Rosemary or lavender can be used in place of thyme.

Recipe 15

Boiled eggs

Ingredients

Allow one or two eggs per portion

Cooking soft-boiled eggs

1 Place the eggs in a saucepan. Cover with cold water and bring to the boil.
2 Simmer for 2–2½ minutes.
3 Remove from the water and serve in egg cups.

Cooking medium soft eggs

1 Place the eggs carefully into a pan of boiling water.
2 Re-boil, simmer for 4–5 minutes and remove.

Cooking hard-boiled eggs

1 Place the eggs carefully into a pan of boiling water.
2 Re-boil and simmer for 8–10 minutes.
3 Refresh until cold under running water.

Recipe 16

Farfalle with chives and bacon

Ingredients	4 portions	10 portions
Farfalle	400 g	1 kg
Streaky bacon rashers	10	25
Fresh chives	2 tbsp	5 tbsp
Butter or oil	50 g	125 g
Parmesan	50 g	125 g

Get ready to cook

1 Grill the bacon until crisp then cut into small pieces.
2 Chop the chives.
3 Grate the Parmesan.

Cooking

1 Cook the pasta in lightly salted boiling water until al dente (firm to the bite).
2 Drain the pasta and place in a warm bowl.
3 Mix in the butter, chives and Parmesan.
4 Taste, correct the seasoning and serve.

Recipe 17 **Plain boiled rice**

Ingredients	4 portions	10 portions
Basmati rice or similar long-grain rice, dry weight	100 g	250 g

Get ready to cook

Pick and wash the rice. (Picking the rice means checking that there is nothing in it that should not be there!).

Cooking

1 Place the washed rice in a saucepan.
2 Add to plenty of lightly salted boiling water.
3 Stir to the boil then simmer gently until tender (approximately 12–15 minutes).
4 Pour into a sieve and rinse well, first under cold running water then very hot water.
5 Drain off all water and leave the rice in a sieve placed over a bowl and covered with a clean tea cloth.

 Health and safety

Once rice is cooked, it should be kept at a temperature above 65°C, but for no longer than two hours. If it is kept at a lower temperature than this, or for longer than two hours, the spores of a bacterium found in the soil may change back to bacteria and could result in food poisoning.

Avoid storing and reheating cooked rice unless it has it has been done in strict hygiene and temperature-controlled conditions.

Recipe 18 — Boiled chicken with rice and suprême sauce

Ingredients	4 portions	10 portions
Chicken:		
Boiling fowl, 2–2½ kg	1	2–3
Onion	50 g	125 g
Cloves		
Carrot	50 g	125 g
Celery	50 g	125 g
Bouquet garni	50 g	125 g
Salt, pinch		
Sauce:		
Butter, margarine or oil	75 g	180 g
Flour	75 g	180 g
Chicken stock	1 litre	1½ litres
Cream or non-dairy cream	4 tbsps	10 tbsps
Lemon juice – a few drops		
Braised rice:		
Onion	50 g	125 g
Butter, margarine or oil	50 g	125 g
Rice, long grain	200 g	500 g
Chicken stock	500 ml	1¼ litres

Get ready to cook

1 Wash and peel the carrot and celery. Leave them whole.
2 Peel the onions for the chicken and stud with one clove per onion.
3 Prepare a bouquet garni.
4 Peel and chop the onion for the rice.
5 Wash the chicken and truss it. Trussing is a way of tying the chicken to hold and improve its shape so that it is easier to carve.

Cooking

1 Place the prepared chicken into a saucepan. Cover it with cold water. Bring to the boil and skim.
2 Add the peeled whole vegetables, bouquet garni and a little salt.
3 Simmer gently until cooked (approximately 1–1½ hours).
4 While the chicken is cooking, prepare the supreme sauce as per the velouté recipe (Recipe 11), and the braised rice as per the recipe on page 161.
5 Cook the velouté for 30–45 minutes.
6 Once the sauce is cooked, taste it and correct the seasoning.
7 Pass it through a fine chinoise and mix in the cream.
8 To check that the chicken is cooked, insert a two-pronged fork between a drumstick and a thigh and remove the chicken from the stock. Hold it over a plate and allow the juices to come out. There should be no trace of blood in the juices. Also pierce the drumstick with a trussing needle or a skewer, which should easily slide in as far as the bone.

Serving suggestion

1 Remove the legs and cut each leg into two (drumstick and thigh).
2 Remove the breasts and cut each one in two.
3 A portion for one person is one piece of leg and one piece of breast.
4 Place the rice and chicken portions carefully on plates. The chicken can be placed on top of the rice or beside it. Coat the chicken with the sauce.

The skin may be removed before the chicken is served.

 Note: This dish can be prepared using suprêmes (breasts) of chicken, instead of whole birds. In that case, poach the chicken in stock instead of water.

Recipe
19 # Pease pudding

Ingredients	4 people	10 people
Yellow split peas (dried), soaked	200 g	500 g
Water	½ litre	1¼ litre
Onion, studded with a clove	50 g	125 g
Carrot	50 g	125 g
Bacon trimmings	50 g	125 g
Butter or margarine	50 g	125 g
Salt		

Get ready to cook

1 Soak the split peas overnight and then drain.
2 Peel the onion and then push a clove into it, sharp end first, so the round end is on the outside of the onion.

Cooking

1 Place all ingredients except the butter in a thick-bottomed saucepan. Cover with a tight-fitting lid.
2 Bring to the boil and skim the water.
3 Allow the peas to cook, preferably in an oven at 180–200°C, for 2 hours.
4 Remove the onion, carrot and bacon and either pass the peas through a sieve or use a food processor.
5 Return the peas to a clean pan and mix in the butter. Taste and correct the consistency, which should be firm.

Recipe 20 — Boiled bacon

Ingredients

You can use a hock, collar or gammon joint for this recipe

Get ready to cook

Prepare the joint as follows:

- Hock: cook it whole, or bone it and tie it with string.
- Collar: remove a bone and tie the joint with string.
- Gammon: cook it whole or cut it into two or three pieces and tie it with string if necessary.

Depending on how salty the bacon joint is, you may need to soak it in cold water for 2–3 hours (or longer) before cooking.

Cooking

1 Place the joint in a suitably sized pan and cover with water.
2 Bring to the boil, skim and simmer gently. The cooking time will depend on the size of the joint: simmer for approximately 25 minutes per ½ kg plus another 25 minutes.
3 Remove the pan from the heat and allow the joint to cool in the liquid.
4 Remove the rind and brown skin and any excess fat.

Serving suggestion

Carve into thick slices and serve with a little of the cooking liquor.

It can be accompanied by a traditional dish of puréed peas, known as pease pudding (see Recipe 19), and a suitable sauce, such as parsley or mustard.

Recipe 21 — Pastry cream

Ingredients	Approx. 1 litre
Milk	1 litre
Vanilla pod (can be replaced with a few drops of vanilla arome)	1
Eggs	4
Caster sugar	200 g
Flour (strong)	100 g
Custard powder	30 g

Cooking

1 Split open the vanilla pod and scrape out the seeds. Place the pod and seeds in a heavy stainless steel pan, add the milk and place on the heat.
2 Whisk the eggs and sugar together.
3 Sieve the flour and custard powder onto paper and then add to the eggs. Whisk them all together to form a liaison.
4 When the milk has boiled, pour about one-third of it into the egg mixture and whisk in.
5 Bring the rest of the milk back to the boil, then pour in the liaison. Whisk hard until the mixture comes back to the boil again.
6 Simmer gently for 5 minutes.
7 Pour into a sterilised tray and stand on a wire rack. Stir occasionally to help the mixture cool quickly.
8 When cold, store in a plastic container in the fridge. Use within 3 days.

Poaching recipes

Recipe 22

Mulled cider poached pear with shortbread

Ingredients	4 portions	10 portions
Mulled cider poached pears:		
Northamptonshire cider	500 ml	1¼ litres
Granulated sugar	200 g	500 g
Root ginger	50 g	125 g
Zest from oranges	½	1½
Zest from lemons	½	1½
Pears	4	10
Shortbread:		
Unsalted butter	250 g	625 g
Caster sugar	75 g	190 g
Soft flour	250 g	625 g
Ground rice	50 g	125 g
Hazelnuts	50 g	125 g

 Note: Regional recipe contributed by Mike Coppock, Curriculum Manager Hospitality and Catering at Northampton College.

Get ready to cook

1 Peel and slice the ginger.
2 Grate the orange and lemon zest.
3 Finely chop the hazelnuts.

Note: Northamptonshire cider is made by David and Elizabeth Bates at Welland Valley Vineyard in Marston Trussell.

Northampton College source local pears from Sima Johnston at Windmill Orchards, Sulgrave.

Cooking

Cooking the pears

1 Bring to the boil the cider, ginger, zests and sugar, remove from heat.
2 Peel the pears whole and core out the centre without damaging the outside, remove the stalks if damaged.
3 Place all the pears into the hot syrup at the same time, making sure there is sufficient to just cover them.
4 Place a disc of silicone paper over the top and use a small plate to hold the pears under the surface.
5 Return to the heat, bring up to a gentle simmer. Cooking time depends on the ripeness of the pears. They are ready when the blade of a knife sinks easily into them (possibly 25 to 30 minutes).
6 Remove the pears from the syrup and allow to cool. The syrup can be reduced to make a sauce for accompanying the dessert.

Making the shortbread

1 Cream together the butter and sugar until just mixed but not lightened.

2 Gently add the flour, ground rice and hazelnut then bring the ingredients together to form a smooth paste. Allow to chill for 15 to 20 minutes.

3 Roll out on a lightly floured surface to 5mm thickness.

4 Cut into desired shape and place onto a tray with baking parchment, leaving a gap between each one.

5 Bake at 180°C for 20 minutes until golden brown (the edges should be golden leaving the centre of the shortbread paler in colour).

6 While still warm, cut through the shortbread to portion, remove from the tins and allow to cool.

Serving suggestion

Serve the pears and shortbread plated together with a vanilla-flavoured whipped cream.

Recipe 23 Poached eggs

Ingredients

Allow one or two eggs per portion

Malt vinegar – one tablespoon per litre of water

Note: Only use top-quality fresh eggs for poaching because they have thick whites, which help them to stick together in the simmering water.

Using vinegar (an acid) helps to set the egg white and also makes it more tender and white.

Cooking

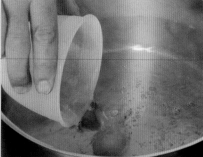

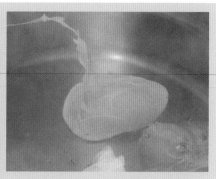

1 Heat a shallow pan of water at least 8 cm deep.

2 Add one tablespoon of malt vinegar per litre of water.

3 Break the eggs into small pots.

4 Carefully tip the eggs into the gently simmering water.

5 You will see each egg form a ball shape.

7 Remove carefully using a perforated spoon. Place into ice water to stop the cooking process, then place on a clean dry cloth to drain off any water. Poached eggs may be cooled, stored and then re-heated – see Chapter 11.

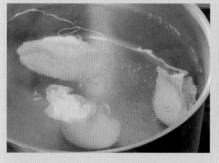

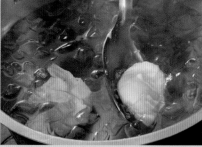

6 Cook for approximately 3–3½ minutes, until lightly set.

Serving suggestion

Serve on hot, buttered toast.

Activity

Poach two eggs: one as fresh as possible, the other stale and out of its 'best before' date. Assess the results.

Poached salmon

Ingredients	4 portions	10 portions
Salmon fillets (100–150 g)	4	10
Butter or margarine	25 g	60 g
Salt		
Fish stock	Sufficient to come halfway up the fish – this will depend on the size and type of cooking vessel.	

Get ready to cook

1 Wash and dry the fish fillets.
2 Grease an ovenproof dish with butter.

Cooking

1 Arrange the washed and dried fish fillets in the ovenproof dish and season lightly.
2 Cover with buttered greaseproof paper.
3 Add sufficient fish stock to come halfway up the fish.
4 Cook in a moderate oven at 170°C for approximately 10 minutes. The cooking time will vary according to the thickness of the fillets. Fish should *not* be overcooked.
5 When cooked, remove the fillets, drain well and keep warm and covered with greaseproof paper.
6 Strain off the cooking liquor into a small pan. Place on a hot stove and allow to reduce by half. Strain.

Serving suggestion

Serve with a little of the cooking liquid spooned over the fish.

Try something different

- Enrich the cooking liquid to give a light sauce. When the cooking liquid has been reduced, gradually add 25 g of softened butter, mixing well until combined. Taste and correct seasoning.
- Add chopped fresh herbs to the sauce, such as chives, parsley, dill or fennel.
- When the salmon is prepared for cooking, sprinkle a few finely cut slices of white button mushrooms on the top before covering with the buttered greaseproof paper. When the fish is finally presented for serving, add a light sprinkle of freshly chopped parsley.

Activity

In groups, prepare, cook and serve five variations of poached salmon. Then taste, assess and discuss the findings.

Recipe 25 Poached pears in red wine

Ingredients	4 portions	10 portions
Water	100 ml	250 ml
Red wine	300 ml	50 ml
Granulated sugar	125 g	300 g
Lemon zest	1	2
Cinnamon stick	1	3
Pears (firm e.g. Williams/ Comice)	4	10

 Note: Poaching of fruits is completed in flavoured liquids, that is, stock syrup or wines with the addition of spices to enhance the flavour of the fruits. The fruit can be cooked whole or in pieces, depending on how it is going to be used.

Get ready to cook

Grate the lemon zest.

Cooking

1 Place the water, wine and sugar in a saucepan and heat gently to dissolve the sugar.
2 Add zest of lemon and cinnamon.
3 Peel the pears neatly without removing the stalks.
4 Place upright in the pan, ensure fully covered with liquor, cover with greaseproof paper and lid.
5 Bring to the boil and simmer until pears are cooked – they should be tinged red and tender when pricked with a skewer.
6 Pears can be removed from syrup to cool, or cooled quickly in liquid to store.
7 Reduce some of the cooking liquor to make a sauce or glaze to serve with the pears.

Chef's tip

When peeling white fruit, like pears, you can place them into acidulated water to stop them oxidising and going brown.

Steaming recipes

Recipe 26 'Tiny Tip' raspberry steamed sponge pudding

Ingredients	4 portions	10 portions
Butter	75 g	185 g
Caster sugar	75 g	185 g
Lemon zest	pinch	pinch
Beaten egg	75 g	185 g
Vanilla essence		
Self-raising flour	125 g	310 g
Milk	30 ml	75 ml
'Tiny Tip' raspberry jam	100 g	250 g
Lemon juice	1 dessertspoon	2½ dessertspoons

Get ready to cook

Prepare an individual pudding mould for each portion.

Cooking

1 Mix together the lemon juice and jam. Divide the mixture evenly between the pudding moulds.
2 Cream together the butter, sugar, lemon zest and vanilla until light and white.
3 Gradually add the eggs.
4 Fold in the flour.
5 Add milk to form a dropping consistency.
6 Divide the mixture evenly into the moulds, seal them and steam until cooked.
7 Serve with crème Anglaise or custard.

 Note: This regional recipe was supplied by Chris Barker at the Colchester Institute. 'Tiny Tip' raspberry jam is made by the well-known local firm Wilkin & Sons of Tiptree Jam.

Recipe 27 — Steamed fish with garlic and spring onion

Ingredients	4 portions	10 portions
White fish fillets, e.g. plaice, lemon sole	400 g	1.5 kg
Salt		
Ginger, peeled and freshly chopped	1 tbsp	2½ tbsp
Spring onions, finely chopped	2 tbsp	5 tbsp
Light soy sauce	1 tbsp	2½ tbsp
Garlic, peeled and thinly sliced (optional)	1 clove	2 cloves
Light oil	1 tbsp	2½ tbsp

Get ready to cook

1 Peel and chop the ginger.
2 Peel and thinly slice the garlic.
3 Chop the spring onions.
4 Wash and dry the fish well.

Cooking

1 Rub the fish lightly with salt on both sides.
2 Put the fish onto plates or dishes. Sprinkle the ginger evenly on top.
3 Put the plates into a steamer, cover tightly and steam gently until just cooked (5–15 minutes, according to the thickness of the fish). Do not overcook.

4 Remove the plates and sprinkle on the spring onions.

5 Brown the garlic slices in hot oil in a small frying pan, if required.

6 Sprinkle the garlic slices and soy sauce over the fish.

Activity

Suggest two or three variations, then prepare, cook, serve, taste, assess and discuss them.

Recipe 28 Steamed steak pudding

Ingredients	4 portions	10 portions
Suet paste:		
Flour, soft or self-raising	200 g	500 g
Baking powder	10 g	25 g
Salt, pinch		
Prepared beef suet	100 g	250 g
Filling:		
Prepared stewing beef – chuck steak	400 g	1½ kg
Worcester sauce	3–4 drops	8–10 drops
Parsley, chopped	1 tsp	2½ tsp
Onion, chopped (optional)	50–100 g	200 g
Salt		
Water	125 ml approx	300 ml

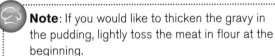

Note: If you would like to thicken the gravy in the pudding, lightly toss the meat in flour at the beginning.

Get ready to cook

1 Cut the meat into 2 cm strips and then into squares.
2 Peel and chop the onion.
3 Grease a half-litre basin.

Cooking

1 Sieve the flour, baking powder and salt together.
2 Add the suet, then make a well in the mixture and add the water.
3 Mix lightly to a fairly stiff paste.
4 Lightly flour the rolling surface and rolling pin.
5 Roll out three-quarters of the suet paste and use this to line a greased half-litre basin.
6 Mix all of the filling ingredients except the water. Season lightly with salt.
7 Place in the lined basin and add the water so that the basin is filled to within 1 cm of the top.
8 Moisten the edge of the paste at the top of the basin. Roll out the remaining paste, cover the filling with this and seal firmly.
9 Cover with greased greaseproof paper or foil or a pudding cloth tied securely with string.
10 Cook in a steamer for at least 3½ hours.

Serving suggestion

When serving, offer extra thickened gravy separately.

Recipe 29 — Steamed sponge pudding

Ingredients	6 portions	12 portions
Butter or margarine	100 g	200 g
Caster or soft brown sugar	100 g	200 g
Eggs, medium, well beaten	2	4
Flour	150 g	300 g
Baking powder	10 g	20 g
Milk	A few drops	Several drops
Flavouring		

Flavourings for the pudding

- For vanilla sponge pudding, add a few drops of vanilla essence.
- For jam sponge pudding, add a good measure of jam to the moulds before putting in the mixture. When cooked and turned out there should be an appetising cap of jam on top.
- For fruit sponge pudding, add dried fruit to the mixture – raisins, sultanas, currants or a mixture.

Cooking

1 Cream the fat and sugar in a bowl until almost white.

2 Gradually add the eggs, mixing vigorously.

3 Sieve the flour and baking powder. Lightly fold this into the mixture and a little milk if necessary. It should be dropping consistency (this means that if you lift a spoonful of the mixture and turn the spoon on its side, the mixture will drop off).

4 Place the mixture in a greased pudding basin or individual moulds.

Recipe continues overleaf.

5 Make a foil cover for the basin. The fold will allow the foil to expand during cooking.

6 Cover the basin securely with greaseproof paper, then tie the foil cover over the top. Steam for 1–1½ hrs.

Serving suggestion

Turn the puddings out of the moulds to serve accompanied with a suitable sauce, such as jam, lemon, chocolate or custard.

▲ Atmospheric steaming video, http://bit.ly/YDBMdF

Recipe 30 — Boiled/steamed cauliflower

Ingredients	4 portions	10 portions
Cauliflower, prepared	1 medium sized	2 large

 Note: All vegetables that can be boiled can also be steamed. The vegetables are prepared in the same way for boiling and steaming. To steam vegetables, place them in steamer trays and salt lightly. Steam them under pressure for as short a time as possible. The less time they are cooked for, the more nutritional value and colour they will keep.

Cooking

1 Place the cauliflower in lightly salted water. Bring the water to the boil.
2 Boil or steam for approximately 10–15 minutes if you have left the cauliflower whole, or 3–5 minutes if you are using florets. Do not overcook.
3 Drain well. If you have cooked it whole, cut it into four even portions before serving.

Get ready to cook

1 Remove the outer leaves.
2 Trim the stem.
3 Hollow out the stem using a potato peeler or cut into florets and wash.

Serving suggestion

- Serve plain or lightly coated with melted butter.
- Serve with a cream sauce (page 111).
- Place the portioned cauliflower on a tray or dish. Coat it with cream sauce and sprinkle with grated cheddar or Parmesan cheese. Lightly brown the topping under the salamander or in a hot oven.

Recipe 31 — Boiled/steamed broccoli

Ingredients	4 portions	10 portions
Broccoli, prepared	½ kg	1¼ kg

Cooking

1 Place the broccoli in lightly salted water. Bring the water to the boil.
2 Boil or steam for approximately ½–1 minute. This should leave the broccoli slightly crisp and not mushy. Do not overcook. As they are in florets they require very little cooking.
3 Drain well.

Get ready to cook

Break the broccoli into florets, removing the main stem.

Recipe 32 — Boiled/steamed spinach

Ingredients	4 portions	10 portions
Spinach	2 kg	5 kg

Get ready to cook

1 Remove the stems from fully grown spinach. You do not need to remove them from young or baby spinach.
2 Wash the leaves carefully in deep water, several times if the spinach feels gritty. When washing, lift the spinach out of the deep water into a colander with your hands.

Cooking

1 Place the spinach into a saucepan and season lightly with salt. If you are cooking the spinach immediately after washing it there should be no need for extra water. If it is dry add a little water.
2 Cover it with a lid and cook for 1–3 minutes (according to its age), over a fierce heat.
3 Tip it into a colander over the sink and press it several times to remove all the water.
4 Squeeze the spinach into portion-sized balls ready for service.

 Note: Boil green, leafy vegetables like spinach in the smallest possible amount of lightly salted boiling water until slightly crisp. Do not let them go mushy.

Serving suggestion

- Reheat the spinach in a steamer. Use a two-pronged fork to separate the leaves loosely.
- Or you could heat the spinach in a thick-bottomed pan containing 25g butter per portion.

Try something different

- Make spinach purée by passing the cooked spinach through a sieve or mouli (vegetable puréeing mill), or using a food processor. Reheat in 25g butter per portion.
- You can halve the amount of butter you use and add a tablespoonful of cream instead.

Recipe 33 — Boiled/steamed potatoes

Ingredients

1 kg of old potatoes will yield 4–6 portions

Cooking

1 Place the potatoes in a pan of lightly salted cold water and bring it to the boil.
2 Cook carefully for approximately 15–20 minutes.
3 Drain well and serve.

 Note: To boil potatoes or other root vegetables, just cover them with lightly salted cold water. Bring the water to the boil and cook until the vegetables are slightly firm. Do not let them go mushy. The one exception to this is potatoes that you are boiling to mash, which should be allowed to cook until they are a bit softer.

Get ready to cook

1 Wash, peel and re-wash the potatoes.
2 Cut into evenly sized pieces, 2–3 pieces per portion.

Try something different

- You can steam the potatoes rather than boiling them.
- Brush 10g melted butter per portion onto the potatoes.
- Sprinkle lightly with freshly chopped parsley.

Recipe 34 — Plain steamed rice

Ingredients	4 portions	10 portions
Basmati rice or similar long-grain rice, dry weight	100 g	250 g

Get ready to cook

Wash the rice.

Cooking

1 Place the rice in a saucepan. Add cold water until the water level is 2½ cm above the rice.
2 Bring to the boil over a fierce heat until most of the water has evaporated.

! Health and safety

Make sure you follow the health and safety points on reheating and storing rice (see Recipe 20).

3 Turn down the heat as low as possible. Cover the pan with a lid and allow the rice to complete cooking in the steam.
4 Once cooked, the rice should be allowed to stand in the covered pan for 10 minutes.

8 Stewing and braising

This chapter covers Unit 108, Prepare and cook food by stewing and braising.

By the end of the chapter you should be able to:

- Describe the process of cooking food items by stewing or braising
- Identify the purpose of stewing or braising
- Identify the food items which may be stewed or braised
- Identify the liquids which may be used when stewing and braising foods
- State the importance of using the correct proportion of liquid to food to achieve the finished dish requirements

- Explain how time and temperature are determined by the item to be stewed or braised
- List the methods used when stewing or braising foods
- State the importance of using associated techniques to achieve the finished dish requirements
- Identify suitable equipment for stewing or braising
- List the quality points to look for during selection of food items, preparation, cooking and finishing of dishes.

Stewing

Process

Stewing is a slow, gentle, moist-heat method of cooking in which the food is completely covered by a liquid. Both the food and the sauce are served together. Stews are cooked on top of the stove. When stews are cooked in the oven they are called casseroles.

Purpose

The purpose of stewing is to:

- Make food tender and palatable. Stewing is an ideal method for cheaper cuts of meat and poultry as they often have more flavour than more tender cuts of meat, which tend to dry out in stews due to the long cooking times.
- Keep the nutritional value of food. During stewing, meat and vegetable juices that escape from the food during cooking stay in the liquid. This means that any vitamins and minerals are not lost, but are served up in the tasty and nutritious sauce.
- Give a rich, deep flavour to the food. Because it is a gentle cooking method the food does not shrink much and keeps its flavour.

Food items that can be stewed

- Meat (beef, lamb and pork)
- Poultry (chicken and turkey)
- Vegetables
- Fruit.

Liquids used for stewing

Liquid, other than stock, could include:

- **Stock syrup** – a water and sugar base, which could be infused with herbs and spices for cooking fruits in
- **Wine** – the alcohol cooks off to leave a rich flavoured sauce to cook the meat in
- **Beer and cider** – used in the same way as wine, but often associated with regional dishes; these add flavour to the dish.
- **Sauce** – this includes ready-made sauces, for example velouté, or even convenience sauces such as a curry sauce. Sauces are used to stew vegetables in for a vegetable curry.

Liquids are added to stews at various points through the cooking process dependent upon the recipe. Some are thickened during the cooking process; others are thickened once the main ingredient is cooked, as in a blanquette.

If stews and casseroles are cooked correctly, very little liquid will evaporate, leaving plenty of sauce to serve up as part of the stew. The amount of liquid used should be enough to cover the food items to keep them moist throughout the process. Consistency should be monitored to ensure that there is sufficient liquid/sauce for each portion of the finished dish.

Temperature and time control

Time required will vary according to the type and quality of foods to be stewed. As a guide, red meat will need longer than poultry and some vegetables will take longer than fruits.

▲ Stewing

Good stews are cooked slowly, so it is important to control the temperature properly. The liquid must barely simmer. Use a tight-fitting lid to keep in the steam. This helps to keep the temperature correct and reduces evaporation.

Methods

Stews can be cooked on a hob or in an oven dependent upon the recipe and foods being cooked.

When cooked on a hob, meat and vegetables are placed in a saucepan and covered with liquid (water or stock). The liquid is brought to the boil then turned down to a low simmer. A lid is placed on the pan and the food is left to cook slowly.

A stew may also be cooked in the oven, when it is referred to as a casserole.

 Health and safety

Place large stews on stovetops carefully to avoid splashes and spills. When you lift the lid from a pan, lift it away from you to avoid burning yourself on the steam.

Searing, browning and refreshing

Meat dishes may require the meat to be sealed first. This can be done to various degrees:

- **Browning or searing with colour** – meat is placed in hot fat or oil to seal and colour the meat.
- **Searing without colour** – meat or chicken is placed in moderately hot fat or oil to start to cook the surface of the meat.
- **Blanching and refreshing** – where the meat is placed in cold water and brought to the boil; it is then refreshed in running cold water.

Thickening

All stews should have a thickened consistency. This comes from thickening agents:

- Unpassed ingredients can cause thickening. For example, in an Irish stew all of the vegetables are left in the stew and help to make it the right consistency.
- Flour can be added to the sauce. For example, for brown lamb stew (navarin) you will cook the meat, then mix flour with the meat, browning the flour before adding the cooking liquid.
- In fricassées (white stews), the cooking liquid is thickened using a roux (flour and butter mixture).
- Egg yolks and cream can also be used to thicken white stews, such as blanquette.

However, stews should not be over-thickened and the sauce should stay light. Make sure you use the correct amount of thickening agents and adjust the consistency during cooking if necessary by adding more liquid or more thickening agent.

> **Professional tip**
> Do not overcook stews as this causes too much liquid to evaporate. The food also breaks up, loses its colour and spoils the flavour.

Associated techniques

There are a number of techniques associated with stewing which help the chef to prepare the dishes correctly:

- **Skimming** – removing scum or impurities which appear as foam or froth on the surface of the cooking liquid. Stir gently from the centre with a ladle to move impurities to the edge of the pan. Collect them with the edge of the ladle and place them into a bowl to be discarded.
- **Reduction** – with some dishes the liquid is strained and then reduced by boiling. The liquid will then be used as the base for a sauce to accompany the dish.
- **Straining** – removing food from the cooking liquid and draining.

KEY WORDS

Velouté – a basic white sauce made using stock and a blond roux

Mirepoix – a mixture of roughly cut onion, carrot, leek and celery

Navarin – a brown lamb stew; the sauce is thickened as part of the cooking process

Fricassée – a white stew; the sauce is thickened as part of the cooking process

Blanquette – a white stew; the sauce is made by thickening the cooking liquor at the end of the cooking process

Braising

Process

Braising is a moist-heat method used for cooking larger pieces of food. The food is only half covered with liquid and can be cooked on the stovetop or in the oven. The food is cooked very slowly in a pan with a tightly fitted lid, using very low temperatures. A combination of steaming and stewing cooks the food. Food is usually cooked in very large pieces and carved before serving.

Purpose

The purpose of braising food is:

- To enhance the flavour – cooking foods in the braising liquid helps to retain the maximum flavour.
- To change the texture to make the food more tender and edible – braising breaks down the tissue fibres in certain foods, which softens them and makes them tender. This means that tougher, less expensive cuts of meat and poultry can be used.

Foods that are often braised

- Meat (beef, lamb and pork)
- Vegetables
- Rice.

Liquids used when braising foods

- Stock, including fresh and convenience stocks
- Wine
- Beer and cider
- Water
- Sauce.

Always use the correct portion of these liquids to achieve the requirements of the finished dish.

Temperature and time control

When braising food, the temperature should be controlled so that the liquid is barely simmering.

The length of time required to cook individual dishes will depend on the item being braised, its size, shape and the type of food. For example, if lamb shanks are cooked too quickly the meat can detach from the bone before it is tender enough for the customer to enjoy.

The following is a guide to braising correctly:

- Cook the food slowly. The liquid must barely simmer.
- Use a tight-fitting lid to reduce evaporation and maintain the temperature.
- The time needed for braising will vary according to the quality of the food.
- The ideal oven temperature for braising is approximately 160°C.

Methods

There are two methods of braising:

- **Brown braising** is used, for example, for joints and portion-sized cuts of meat. Meat must be sealed and browned first (use the same method as given for stewing). The sealed and browned meat is then placed over browned vegetables (mirepoix). During the cooking process, the vegetables prevent the meat from touching the base of the pan. If it does come into contact with the pan, the meat may become tough and dry.
- **White braising** is used, for example, for vegetables. First blanch the vegetables, and then place them in a braising pan with mirepox and white stock. Add the liquid to the braising pan so that it half covers the food being braised. Once you have added the liquid, place a heavy, tight-fitting lid on the cooking pan. The lid keeps the moisture in the pan and around the food, and creates steam. This prevents the food from becoming dry and tough.

> **! Health and safety**
>
> Use heavy, dry oven cloths whenever you remove the pot from the oven or lift the lid. When you lift the lid from the pan, lift it away from you to avoid burning yourself on the steam. The contents can become extremely hot, so take great care to prevent splashing when you stir them.

Once food has been braised the liquid is normally strained from the food. For foods other than vegetables this is then normally made into a sauce by reducing or thickening.

When braising a joint of meat to be served whole, remove the lid three-quarters of the way through cooking and baste the joint frequently to glaze it – this makes it look attractive when it is served.

▲ Braising

Associated techniques

There are a number of techniques associated with braising which help the chef to prepare the dishes correctly:

- **Skimming** – removing scum or impurities that appear as foam or froth on the surface of the cooking liquid. Stir gently from the centre with a ladle to move the impurities to the edge of the pan; they can then be collected by the edge of the ladle, placed in a bowl and discarded.
- **Basting** – spooning the cooking liquid over food items during the cooking process, to help keep them moist and glaze them to enhance the presentation of the finished dish.
- **Reducing cooking liquid** – with some dishes the liquid is strained and then reduced by boiling. This liquor will then be used as the base for a sauce to accompany the dish.
- **Straining** – removing food from cooking liquid and draining.

Equipment for stewing and braising

- Saucepans, sauté pans and, where large numbers of portions are being cooked, bratt pans are all considered to be traditional types of equipment for stewing and braising. These should be clean and in good repair, with no loose handles and with correct fitting lids.
- A number of kitchens are now using non-traditional equipment to stew and braise foods; this includes slow cookers and steamers.
- Casserole dishes are usually deep, round, ovenproof dishes with handles and a tight-fitting lid. They can be made of glass, metal (cast iron), ceramic or any other heatproof material. They are available in various sizes, some of which are then used to serve the food at the table. Always make sure you use the appropriate size and type of dish for the food that you are cooking.

Quality points

To ensure the quality of finished dishes:

- Select products that are fresh, have a good appearance and smell and are at the correct temperature
- Trim, shape and size ingredients according to dish requirements
- Ensure that the correct temperature, time and amount of liquid are used as this will impact on the flavour, colour, texture and taste of the dish
- Ensure when finishing the dish that it has the correct consistency, appearance and portion size, and that seasoning and garnish are added if required.

Test yourself

1 Briefly describe the process for the following methods of cooking:
   a Stewing
   b Braising
2 What is the purpose of stewing?
3 List three cooking liquids that could be used as a sauce in the finished dish.
4 List three types of stew.
5 List five safety points that chefs should consider when cooking by stewing or braising.
6 What is the term for removing scum or foam from the top of a boiling liquid? Why do we do this?
7 List four foods that can be cooked by braising.
8 List three types of food that could be stewed.
9 What is a mirepoix?
10 List two pieces of equipment that are traditionally used for stewing and braising.

Stewing recipes

Traditional scouse

Ingredients	4 portions	10 portions
Lamb shoulder	500 g	1¼ kg
Salted butter	10 g	25 g
Onions	1	3
Garlic cloves	1	2–3
Carrots	1	3
Tomato purée	1 tbsp	2½ tbsp
Black treacle	1 tbsp	2½ tbsp
Chicken stock	1 litre	2½ litres
Bouquet garni (black peppercorns, bay leaf, parsley, thyme)		
Potatoes	1	3
Celeriac	¼	¾
Worcester sauce	1 tbsp	2½ tbsp
Ground white pepper and sea salt		

Note: Contributed by Paul Robinson, Curriculum Leader, Hospitality at Grimsby Institute of Further and Higher Education.

This recipe is based on the traditional lamb dish called scouse, which was brought to England by Scandinavian sailors, and then changed by the people of Liverpool.

Get ready to cook

1 Remove the bone and fat from the lamb.
2 Cut the lamb into cubes of equal size (2 cm square) with minimal waste.
3 Wash, peel, then re-wash the vegetables. Cut the carrots and potatoes into macédoine, the celeriac into jardinière and the onions and garlic into brunoise.

Cooking

1 Melt the butter in a thick-bottomed deep pan and seal the meat until it starts to brown.
2 In the same pan soften the onions for a few minutes with the garlic, then add the carrots.
3 Add the tomato purée, black treacle and stir, then pour in the stock and bring to the boil.
4 Once the liquid starts to boil turn back the heat and allow it to simmer with the bouquet garni.
5 Simmer for 40 minutes until the meat is almost tender then add the celeriac and potato.
6 Add the Worcester sauce and continue to simmer gently until the meat is tender.
7 Once the potato starts to break down reduce the sauce, then remove the bouquet garni.
8 Finish the stew by skimming any excess fat that has risen to the surface.
9 Check the consistency of sauce then adjust the flavour (season), present and garnish.

Stewed fruits

Ingredients	4 portions	10 portions
Seasonal fruits: rhubarb, apricots, apples, plums, strawberries, pears	500 g	1.25 kg
Caster sugar	50 g (75 g for rhubarb)	125 g (190 g for rhubarb)
Water	30 ml	75 ml
With rhubarb add some fresh grated ginger to bring out the flavour (optional)	2 cm piece	5 cm piece

Get ready to cook

1 Peel the fruit if necessary. Hull the strawberries (remove the tops).

2 Chop up all the fruit to even sizes, discarding any stones.

▲ Peeling rhubarb

▲ Hulling a strawberry

Cooking

1 Place the fruit in a pan and add the sugar.

2 Add water and cook on a medium heat with the lid on.

3 Once the fruit has softened, remove the lid and let the liquid reduce - you want to end up with a fairly thick consistency.

Serving suggestion

Serve over cereal, yoghurt, pancakes, granola or muesli. Also great to use as a crumble filling or with apple to serve with roast pork.

 Chef's tip: When you are stewing fruit it is best to decide how much sugar to add by tasting the fruit. If your fruit is really ripe and sweet, you'll need less than suggested in the recipe above.

Recipe
3

Brown lamb or mutton stew (navarin)

Ingredients	4 portions	10 portions
Stewing lamb: shoulder, neck end, breast	500 g	1½ kg
Oil	2 tbsp	5 tbsp
Salt		
Carrot, roughly chopped	100 g	250 g
Onion, roughly chopped	100 g	250 g
Flour, white or wholemeal	25 g	60 g
Tomato purée	1 level tbsp	2¼ level tbsp
Brown stock, mutton stock or water	500 ml	1.25 litres
Bouquet garni	1	1
Garlic clove (optional)	1	2–3
Parsley, chopped		

Get ready to cook

1 Trim the meat of any excess fat and bone and cut into even pieces.
2 Peel and roughly chop the onion and carrot.
3 Prepare a bouquet garni.

Cooking

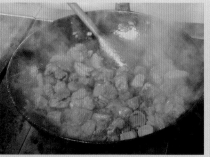

1 Season the meat lightly with salt. Heat some oil in a frying pan and fry the meat quickly until just coloured.

2 Add the onion and carrot and continue frying until well browned.
3 Drain off any surplus fat and discard.

4 Mix in the flour with a wooden spoon and cook on a low heat, stirring continuously, for 3–4 minutes.

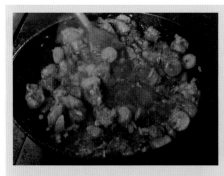  

5 Mix in the tomato purée, then allow the meat mixture to cool slightly.

6 Put it back on the heat and gradually add the stock and stir to the boil.

7 Add the bouquet garni and garlic. Skim and cover with a lid.

8 Simmer gently, in a moderate oven at 180°C or on the side of the stove, for approximately 1½–2 hours.

9 When cooked, pick out the meat and put it into a clean pan.

10 Taste and correct the sauce and pass it through a strainer on to the meat.

Serving suggestion

Serve lightly sprinkled with chopped parsley.

Try something different

- Either separately or in with the stew, cook a garnish of small neat vegetables, such as carrots, turnips, button onions, potatoes, peas. If cooking them with the stew, add them approximately 30 minutes before the meat is cooked.
- Brown beef stew can be made by using this recipe and substituting prepared stewing beef cut into 2 cm pieces in place of the lamb.

Activity

As a group, prepare, cook, serve, taste and assess the recipe using:

1 An ordinary brown stock (page 99)
2 A well-flavoured lamb or mutton brown stock
3 Water.

Recipe 4 Irish stew

Ingredients	4 portions	10 portions
Stewing lamb, shoulder, neck-end, breast	500 g	1½ kg
Water or white stock	400 g	1 kg
Bouquet garni	1	1
Salt		
Potatoes	100 g	250 g
Onions	100 g	250 g
Celery	100 g	250 g
Savoy cabbage	100 g	250 g
Leeks	100 g	250 g
Button onions (optional)	100 g	250 g

Get ready to cook

1 Trim the meat of any excess fat and bone and cut into even pieces.

2 Peel and wash the vegetables.

Cooking

1 Place the meat in a shallow saucepan, cover with water and bring to the boil.

2 Place the meat under running water until meat is clean then return it to the cleaned pan.

3 Cover with water or white stock, season lightly with salt and add the bouquet garni.

4 Skim, cover with a lid and allow to simmer for three-quarters of an hour.

5 Peel and wash the vegetables and cut into neat, small pieces and add to the meat.

6 Simmer for 30 minutes, skimming frequently.

7 Add the button onions and simmer for a further 20–30 minutes.

8 Skim, taste and correct the seasoning.

Serving suggestion

Serve lightly sprinkled with chopped parsley. You could also accompany it with Worcester sauce and/or pickled red cabbage.

Beef goulash

Ingredients	4 portions	10 portions
Prepared stewing beef	500 g	1½ kg
Lard or oil	35 g	100 g
Onions, chopped	100 g	250 g
Flour	25 g	60 g
Paprika	10–25 g	25–60 g
Tomato purée	25 g	60 g
Stock or water	750 ml	2 litres

Get ready to cook

1 Trim the meat and cut it into 2 cm square pieces.

2 Peel and chop the onion.

Cooking

1 Heat the fat in a thick-bottomed pan, season the meat lightly with salt and quickly fry it until lightly coloured.

2 Add the onions, cover with a lid and cook gently for 3–4 minutes until the onions are soft.

3 Mix in the paprika and flour using a wooden spoon.

4 Allow to cook out on top of the stove or in an oven for 2–3 minutes.

5 Mix in the tomato purée and then gradually add the stock, mixing well.

6 Bring to the boil, skim, taste, correct seasoning and cover.

7 Simmer, preferably in the oven, for approximately 1½–2 hours, until the meat is tender.

8 Skim, taste and correct the seasoning again.

Try something different

Add a little cream or yoghurt at the last moment.

Recipe 6 Beef olives

Ingredients	4 portions	10 portions
Stuffing:		
White or wholemeal breadcrumbs	50 g	125 g
Parsley, chopped	1 tbsp	3 tbsp
Thyme, a small pinch		
Suet, prepared and chopped	5 g	25 g
Onion, finely chopped and lightly sweated in oil	25 g	60 g
Salt		
Egg	½	1
Olives:		
Lean beef, topside	400 g	1¼ kg
Salt		
Dripping or oil	35 g	100 g
Carrot, chopped	100 g	250 g
Onion, chopped	100 g	250 g
Flour	25 g	60 g
Tomato purée	25 g	60 g
Brown stock	500–700 ml	1¼–1½ litres
Bouquet garni		

Get ready to cook

1 Cut the meat into four thin slices across the grain and, using a meat bat, carefully thin out the slices.
2 Trim the slices to approximately 10 cm x 8 cm and chop the trimmings.
3 Peel and chop the onions and carrots.
4 Prepare a bouquet garni.
5 Prepare and chop the suet.

 Note: Beef olives are thin slices of beef filled with stuffing and rolled up before being cooked. They resemble a stuffed olive!

Cooking

1 Combine all the stuffing ingredients.
2 Add the meat trimmings and make sure the stuffing is thoroughly mixed.
3 Season the meat lightly with salt.
4 Spread a quarter of the stuffing down the centre of each slice. Neatly roll up each slice and tie with string.

5 In a thick-bottomed pan, heat a little dripping or oil and fry the rolls a light golden brown on all sides.

6 Add the chopped onions and carrots halfway through.

7 Place the olives and vegetables into a suitable ovenproof pan or casserole.

8 Drain off any remaining fat into a clean pan and if necessary add more to make it up to 25 ml. Mix in the flour and, stirring continuously, brown lightly.

9 Mix in the tomato purée, then cool and mix in the boiling stock.

10 Bring to the boil, skim and pour onto the olives.

11 Add the bouquet garni, cover and simmer gently, preferably in a moderate oven at 160°C, for approximately 1½–2 hours.

12 Once cooked, remove the meat and cut off the strings.

13 Skim, taste and correct the sauce and pass through a fine strainer onto the meat and serve.

Activity

As a group, use four variations to the stuffing of your choice. Prepare one without salting the meat then taste, assess and discuss.

Recipe 7
Vegetable casserole with herb dumplings

Ingredients	4 portions	10 portions
Casserole:		
Vegetable oil	2 tbsp	5 tbsp
Onion, chopped	50 g	125 g
Garlic cloves, crushed	2	5
Carrots, diced	100 g	250 g
Parsnip, diced	100 g	250 g
Swede, diced	100 g	250 g
Turnip, diced	100 g	250 g
Jerusalem artichokes, diced	60 g	150 g
Fresh thyme, chopped	1 tsp	2½ tsp
Fresh parsley, chopped	1 tsp	2½ tsp
Button mushrooms, quartered	100 g	250 g
Vegetable stock	1 litre	2½ litre
Yeast extract (e.g. Marmite)	1 tsp	2½ tsp
Ground pepper		
Dumplings:		
Plain flour	200 g	500 g
Baking powder	10 g	25 g
Vegetable suet	100 g	250 g
Herbs, freshly chopped:		
Parsley	1 tsp	2½ tsp
Chervil	1 tsp	2½ tsp
Tarragon	1 tsp	2½ tsp
Oregano	1 tsp	2½ tsp
Rosemary	1 tsp	2½ tsp
Basil	1 tsp	2½ tsp
English mustard powder	2 tsp	4 tsp
Water	60 ml	180 ml

Get ready to cook

1 Peel and chop the onion.

2 Peel the carrots, parsnip, swede, turnip and Jerusalem artichokes and cut into ½ cm pieces.

3 Clean the mushrooms and cut into quarters.

4 Chop all of the fresh herbs.

Cooking

1 Shallow fry the onion, garlic, carrots, parsnips, swede, turnip and artichoke for 5–10 minutes. Stir continuously.

2 Sprinkle with the fresh herbs. Add the mushrooms and cook for a further 5 minutes.

3 Add the vegetable stock, yeast extract and season with ground pepper. Simmer until the vegetables are tender.

4 Prepare the dumplings by sifting the flour with the baking powder.

5 Mix in the shredded suet.

6 Dilute the mustard powder in half of the water and add this and the herbs. Mix well.

7 Add the mustard and the remaining water to the flour and suet and mix to a soft dough.

8 Knead and form into small dumplings.

9 Cook the dumplings in the casserole, or separately in vegetable stock, for 10–15 minutes.

Serving suggestion

Serve the casserole with the dumplings in a suitable dish.

Braising recipes

Recipe 8 | Braised belly pork

Ingredients	4 portions	10 portions
Belly pork, boned and skinned	500 g	1¼ kg
Marinade:		
Ginger, finely chopped	10 g	25 g
Red chilli, chopped	½	1
Garlic cloves	1	2
Soy sauce	15 ml	40 ml
Five spice powder	½ tsp	1 tsp
Honey	1 tbsp	2 tbsp
Tomato ketchup	1 tbsp	2 tbsp
Zest and juice of oranges	½	1
Worcester sauce	1–2 tsp	5 tsp
Arrowroot	5 g	12 g

Note: Regional recipe contributed by Iain Middleton, Team Leader for Hospitality and Catering at New College Stamford, Lincolnshire.

Get ready to cook

1 Bone and skin the pork belly, unless this has been done by the butcher.
2 Mix together the ingredients for the marinade. Marinade the pork overnight.

Cooking

1 Remove the pork from the marinade and drain well.
2 Sear the meat on all sides in small amount of oil in a shallow pan.
3 Place in braising pan.
4 Add marinade to pan and enough water or white stock to come halfway up meat and bring to simmer.
5 Cover with tight fitting lid or foil and braise in oven at 160°C for approx 2½ hours (or until tender).
6 Drain off meat and allow to rest.
7 Reduce cooking liquor or thicken with a little arrowroot dispersed in cold water.
8 Slice the pork and serve on a plate with the sauce and garnish.

Serving suggestion

Serve with fondant potatoes and braised red cabbage.

To make crackling, cut rind into thin strips, place on tray, salt, cover with silicone paper and another tray and bake in oven at 190°C until crispy.

Recipe 9 — Braised rice (pilaff)

Ingredients	4 portions	10 portions
Oil, butter or margarine	50 g	125 g
Onion, finely chopped	25 g	60 g
Rice, long grain	100 g	250 g
White stock, vegetable or chicken	200 ml	500 ml
Salt		

Cooking

1 Place half the fat into a thick-bottomed pan.

2 Add the onion and cook gently without colouring until the onion is soft (2–3 minutes).

3 Add the rice and stir to mix. Cook over a gentle heat without colouring for 2–3 minutes.

4 Add *exactly* twice the amount of stock to rice.

5 Season lightly, cover with greased paper and bring to the boil.

6 Place in a hot oven (230–250°C) until cooked (approximately 15 minutes).

7 When cooked, remove immediately to a cool container or pan. (If the rice is left in the hot pan, it will continue cooking, which will result in it overcooking and being spoilt.)

8 Carefully mix in the remaining half of the fat using a two-pronged fork.

9 Taste, correct the seasoning and serve.

Try something different

- Add sliced mushrooms, at the same time as the onions
- Add freshly grated cheese (10–100 g) with the fat at the end.

Activity

Cook two dishes of pilaff, one with a good, richly flavoured chicken stock and the other with water. Taste and compare them.

Recipe 10 Braised lamb shanks

Ingredients	4 portions	10 portions
Lamb shanks	4	10
Oil	3 tbsp	7 tbsp
Red onions	50 g	125 g
Garlic cloves	2	5
Plum tomatoes (canned)	400 g	1 kg
Lamb stock	250 ml	625 ml
Flageolet beans (canned)	400 g	1 kg
Rosemary, fresh	1 tbsp	2½ tbsp
Honey, clear	1 tbsp	2½ tbsp
Salt		

Cooking

1 Lightly season the shanks.
2 Heat the oil in a suitable braising pan.
3 Quickly fry the shanks on all sides until golden brown. Remove from the pan and set aside.
4 Add the chopped onion and garlic to the pan (if there is insufficient oil, add a little more). Allow to sweat gently over a moderate heat until soft.
5 Stir in the tomatoes and stock.
6 Place the shanks back in the pan.
7 Bring to the boil, then reduce the heat so that the cooking is at a gentle simmer. Cover and put in the oven at 160°C for one hour.
8 Check the shanks to see that they are cooked by using a two-pronged fork, which should slide in as far as the bone in the thickest part of the shank.
9 Remove the shanks and stir in the beans, honey and rosemary.
10 Replace the shanks and reheat to a gentle simmer. Skim, taste the liquid and correct the seasoning.

Get ready to cook

1 Peel and finely chop the onions.
2 Peel and crush the garlic.
3 Drain and chop the tomatoes.
4 Rinse and drain the beans.
5 Chop the rosemary.

Serving suggestion

Serve in an earthenware dish sprinkled with freshly chopped parsley.

Activity

1 You can make many variations to this recipe, using different beans, additional vegetables, different herbs and so on. Create your own recipe. Then prepare, cook, taste, assess and discuss it.
2 Suggest what accompaniments you would like to serve with the shanks.

Recipe 11 — Braised mushrooms 'East–West'

Ingredients	4 portions	10 portions
Olive oil	2 tbsp	5 tbsp
Shallots	4	10
Fresh young ginger	3 cm	7 cm
Dried ceps	50 g	125 g
Black Chinese mushrooms	50 g	125 g
White button mushrooms	400 g	1 kg
Light soy sauce	2 tbsp	5 tbsp
Chives	2 tbsp	5 tbsp
Chicken stock	120 ml	300 ml
Salt and freshly ground black peppercorn to taste		

 Note: Ceps are a type of wild mushroom.

Get ready to cook

1 Place the ceps in a bowl, cover them with hot water and leave to soak for 30 minutes.
2 Squeeze the water out and cut them into wide strips. Set aside.
3 Peel and finely chop the ginger and shallots.
4 Clean and slice the button mushrooms.
5 Chop the chives.

Cooking

1 Heat the olive oil in a medium-sized frying pan. Add the shallots, ginger and then all the mushrooms and sauté for 3 minutes.
2 Add in the soy sauce, chives and chicken stock. Cook over a medium heat for a further 10 minutes to completely reduce the liquid.
3 Season with salt and pepper to taste.

Recipe 12 Traditional braised beef

Ingredients	4 portions	10 portions
Lean beef (topside or thick flank)	500 g	1½ kg
Dripping or oil	25 g	60 g
Onions, sliced and lightly fried	100 g	250 g
Carrots, sliced and lightly fried	100 g	250 g
Brown stock	500 ml	1¼ litres
Salt, pepper		
Bouquet garni		
Tomato purée	25 g	60 g
Demi-glace or jus-lié	250 ml	625 ml

Get ready to cook

1 Pre-heat the oven to 150–180°C.

2 Wash, peel and slice the onions and carrots. Lightly fry them.

3 Trim and tie the joint.

  Note: About one-third of the meat weight gives you the weight of vegetables needed.

▲ Braised beef video,
http://bit.ly/10lIYyU

Cooking

1 Season the meat and colour quickly on all sides in hot fat to seal the joint.

2 Place the lightly fried vegetables into a small braising pan (any pan with a tight-fitting lid that may be placed in the oven) or in a casserole.

3 Place the joint in with the vegetables.

4 Add the stock, which should come two-thirds of the way up the meat, and season lightly.

5 Add the bouquet garni and tomato purée and, if available, add a few mushroom trimmings.

6 Bring to the boil, skim and cover with a lid; cook in a moderate oven at 150–180°C.

7 After approximately 1½ hours' cooking, remove the meat.

8 Add the demi-glace or jus-lié, reboil, skim and strain.

9 Replace the meat; do not cover, but baste frequently and continue cooking for approx. 2–2½ hours in all. Braised beef should be well cooked (approx. 35 minutes per ½ kg plus 35 minutes). To test if cooked, pierce with a trussing needle, which should penetrate the meat easily and there should be no sign of blood.

10 Remove the joint and correct the colour, seasoning and consistency of the sauce.

Serving suggestion

- Remove the string and carve slices across the grain. Pour some of the sauce over the slices and serve the remainder of the sauce in a sauceboat.
- Serve with plenty of potatoes and vegetables, or with pasta.

9 Baking, roasting and grilling

This chapter covers Unit 109, Prepare and cook food by baking, roasting and grilling.

By the end of the chapter you should be able to:

- Describe the process of cooking food items by baking, roasting and grilling
- Identify the purpose of baking, roasting and grilling food
- Identify the food items which may be baked, roasted and grilled
- State the importance of using associated techniques to achieve the finished dish requirements
- Describe associated products

- State the points requiring consideration when baking, roasting and grilling foods
- Describe the methods used when baking, roasting and grilling
- Identify suitable equipment for baking, roasting and grilling
- List the quality points to look for during selection of food items, preparation, cooking and finishing of dishes.

Baking

Process

Baking is cooking food with dry heat in an oven. Although the food is cooked in a dry oven, steam plays a big part in this method of cookery.

Purpose

The purpose of baking is:

- To produce tender, tasty food with deep flavours that is digestible and enjoyable to eat
- To make food visually appealing, with a good colour and texture
- To maintain the nutritional value of the dish
- To make food safe to eat.

Food items which may be baked

The range of foods that can be baked includes:

- Flour-based products (both sweet and savoury), which may contain meat, fish or fruits
- Milk and egg-based products
- Fruit
- Vegetables
- Pre-prepared products (such as lasagne).

> **Professional tip**
> Baked goods can be produced in bulk, all cooked for the same amount of time and all coming out the same colour.

▲ Lining a flan, pressing the edges

Points to consider when baking

- Temperature control is essential. Always preheat ovens to the required temperature before putting the food in, otherwise the product will be spoiled. Make sure the oven reaches the required temperature before each additional batch of goods is placed in the oven.
- Most products contain water and once heated this will create moisture or humidity in the oven. Bakers' ovens often inject steam into the oven at the start of baking some dough products.
- The time required will vary according to the type and quality of foods to be baked. As a guide, loaves of bread will need longer than bread rolls.
- You will need to think about shelf position. In general-purpose ovens, the top part of the oven is the hottest. In convection ovens, the temperature is the same in all parts of the oven, so you can place the shelves anywhere.
- Be accurate in your weighing and measuring.
- Prepare trays and moulds correctly. Keep baking trays level in the oven so that the product bakes evenly. Do not overload trays.

 Health and safety

Use thick, dry oven cloths when removing trays from the oven.

- Avoid opening oven doors whenever possible. Draughts may affect the quality of the product, and the oven temperature will drop. Opening the oven door too quickly may also adversely affect the presentation of products such as Yorkshire puddings and soufflés.

 Health and safety

Do not open oven doors too quickly as there is likely to be a lot of steam, which may burn your face.

- Use oven space effectively.
- Avoid jarring products (particularly fruit cakes, sponges and soufflés) before and during baking as the quality may be affected.

Methods

There are three methods of baking:

- **Dry baking** – this is done in a dry oven. The water that is naturally found in food turns to steam when it is heated. This steam combines with the dry heat of the oven to cook the food. This method is used for cakes, pastry and baked jacket potatoes.
- **Baking with increased humidity** – certain foods, such as bread, need to be baked with increased humidity. To do this, place a bowl of water in the oven or inject steam into the oven (there will be a switch on the oven to do this). The humidity of the air (the moisture in it) is increased, which in turn increases the water content of the food, keeping it moist and good to eat.
- **Baking with modified heat** – food such as baked egg custard requires the heat in the oven to be modified (reduced). To do this, place the food in a bain-marie (a tray of water). This makes

the food cook more slowly and means that it does not overheat. In the case of egg custard, it also means that the egg mixture is less likely to overcook.

Associated techniques

There are a number of techniques associated with baking which help the chef to prepare the dishes correctly:

- **Aeration** – to create light textures, products are aerated through whisking (for example, when using eggs and sugar); chemical aeration is provided with the addition of baking powder (for example when baking scones); fermentation produces gas for aeration (this is used for dough).
- **Mixing** – ensures the correct finished texture of the dish, providing an even balance of ingredients before cooking.
- **Rolling and shaping** – bread rolls, for example, are shaped into even sizes prior to cooking; pastry is often rolled out to line or cover a dish.
- **Cutting** – products are cut to shape prior to baking. This process is used when baking biscuits or Chelsea buns.
- **Resting** – some products cook better after relaxing (for example, scones and biscuits); resting helps maintain their shape.
- **Greasing** – using oil or butter on the tray or dish to prevent food from sticking.
- **Marking or scoring** – this is done to pastry to enhance the appearance of the finished dish (for example, on shortbread).
- **Loading** – how items are placed in the oven. Space should be used efficiently.
- **Brushing and glazing** – products are coated with milk, water, egg-wash or syrup either before or after baking.
- **Cooling** – to prevent baked items going soggy they are placed on cooling racks to stabilise.
- **Finishing** – finishes include glacé, dusting with sugar or even splitting and filling with cream.

Roasting

Process

Roasting is cooking in dry heat, in an oven or on a spit, with the aid of fat or oil. The initial heat of the oven seals the food. This prevents too many of the natural juices from escaping. Once the food is lightly browned, the oven temperature (or the temperature of the heat source when spit roasting) should be reduced to cook the inside of the food without hardening the surface.

Purpose

Roasting:

- Creates a distinctive taste
- Creates food that is tender, easy to digest and palatable to the customer
- Enhances the flavour and colour of the food, adding to the presentation
- Makes the food safe to eat.

Food items which may be roasted

The range of foods that can be roasted includes:

- Meats such as beef, pork and lamb
- Poultry, including chicken and turkey
- Vegetables.

Points requiring consideration when roasting foods

- Always preheat ovens to the required cooking temperature. Follow the oven temperature given in the recipe.
- Adjust the shelf position according to the instructions given in the recipe. In general-purpose ovens, the top part of the oven is the hottest; in convection ovens, the temperature is the same in all parts of the oven.
- The cooking time will be affected by the shape, size, type, bone proportion and quality of the food you are cooking.
- Meat thermometers or probes can be inserted to determine the exact temperature in the centre of the joint (the core temperature).

Methods

There are two main methods of roasting food.

1 **Roasting on a spit** – place prepared meat or poultry on a rotating spit, over or in front of fierce radiated heat.
2 **Roasting in an oven** – place whole joints and large pieces of meat and fish on a trivet (see page 160). This will prevent the base of the product burning or overcooking. A trivet can consist of chopped vegetables (a bit like braising, but larger than mirepoix), or can be made up from the bones or skeleton of the product you are roasting.

> **Professional tip**
>
> With spit roasting, you can see exactly how the cooking is progressing and you have easy access to the food.

Health and safety

Take care when removing a joint of meat from the oven. It may have released a lot of fat that could cause burns or scalds. Always use thick, dry oven cloths.

Health and safety

When roasting in an oven there is minimal fire risk because a thermostat is used to control the temperature, so there is no risk of overheating.

Associated techniques

There are a number of techniques associated with roasting which help the chef to prepare the dishes correctly:

- **Stuffing** – a meat, vegetable, cereal or grain-based mix is placed into the cavity or rolled into the meat to add flavour and texture to the finished dish.

- **Trussing and tying** – using string or skewers to hold poultry or joints in shape and ensure an even cooking; this helps to keep joints moist.
- **Trivet** – using a rack or base of vegetables to keep the meat from having direct contact with the tray when roasting.
- **Basting** – spooning the fat and cooking juices over the food during cooking to help keep the food moist and enhance the colour and appearance of the finished dish.
- **Relaxing before carving** – joints of meat carve and eat better if they have been given time to relax once they are taken out of the oven.

> **Health and safety**
> When basting the product, try to avoid splashing hot fat on yourself, as this could cause burns.

Meat carving tips

Joints should be allowed to rest for at least 15 minutes beforehand, as this will allow the joint to 'set', making it easier to carve.

To carve meat properly, a good, well-balanced and properly sharpened carving knife is essential. It should not be serrated, as this encourages a sawing action and gives an unattractive appearance to the meat slices.

Bone-in-joints: Hold the joint at the end of the bone, using a towel or kitchen paper for a firmer grip if necessary. Carve the meat away from the bone, into approximately 1 cm thick slices.

Boneless joints (for example, short saddle of lamb): Hold the joint in place with a carving fork or tongs. Carve the meat across the grain into slices approximately ½ cm thick.

Racks and rib roasts: Hold the meat with the bones facing upward, using a towel or kitchen paper for a firmer grip if necessary. Carve down between the bones into even-sized cutlets. Or remove the bones completely by cutting along the bones through the meat. This will enable you to carve the roast into thin slices.

 DONALD RUSSELL

Images and text courtesy of Donald Russell: www.donaldrussell.com.

Accompaniments and associated products

- Roast gravy is made by de-glazing the roasting pan (see Recipe 23)
- Sauces that enhance the dish and are considered to aid digestion, including: apple with pork, mint with lamb, horseradish with beef and bread with poultry.

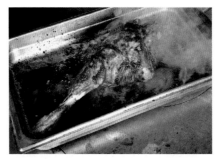

▲ Roasting

Grilling

Process

This is a fast method of cooking using radiant heat. The heat source transfers heat directly towards the food being grilled.

Purpose

Grilling creates a distinctive taste and provides interesting variety to the menu; the smell of grilling foods can whet the appetite and some restaurants have grill areas that are open to view so the aroma travels through to diners as they wait. Other purposes of grilling are:

- To create food that is tender, easier to digest and palatable for the customer
- To char foods, adding colour and giving food a distinctive appearance, which adds to the presentation
- To improve the flavour of the food
- To make food safe to eat
- To maintain the nutritional value of the food. Grilling is often considered to be the best cooking method for reducing fat and retaining nutrients because the food is cooked so quickly.

Food items which can be grilled

The range of foods that can be grilled include:

- Meat (beef, pork and lamb). When grilling meat, the fierce heat seals the surface of the meat, helping to keep the juices in the meat as long as it is not pierced by a fork while cooking. Grilling is only suitable for certain cuts of best-quality meat – inferior meat cooked this way will be tough and inedible.
- Poultry (chicken and turkey)
- Vegetables
- Fish
- Pre-prepared products.

> **Professional tip**
>
> When grilling you have good control of the cooking process because the food is visible and accessible while it is being grilled.

Points to consider when grilling foods

- Do not grill foods for too long. Cooking the food slowly will dry it out.
- Smaller, thinner items should be cooked very quickly.
- The amount of time the food is grilled for should be determined by the degree of cooking required – rare and medium cooking takes less time than well-cooked foods.
- Seal and colour food on the hot part of the grill, then move to a cooler part to complete cooking.
- Basting of food and oiling of bars will help to prevent the food from drying out and sticking to the grill.
- The positioning of the shelf or grill above or below the heat will influence the amount of time the item takes to cook.

Method

Grilled foods can be cooked over heat (charcoal, barbecues, gas or electric heated grills/griddles), under heat (gas or electric salamanders, over-heated grills) or between heat (electrically heated grill bars or plates).

▲ Grilling

1. **Grilling over heat** – preheat grill bars and brush with oil prior to use, otherwise food will stick to them. The bars should char the food on both sides to give the distinctive appearance and flavour of grilling. When using solid fuel, allow the flames and smoke to die down before placing food on the bars, otherwise the food will be tainted and spoiled. You can marinate certain foods (such as skewered kebabs and chicken) before cooking. You should brush other foods (such as pork spare ribs) liberally with a barbecue sauce on both sides before and during cooking.

2. **Grilling under heat/salamander** – preheat salamanders and grease the bars. Steaks, chops and items that are likely to slip between the grill bars of an under-heated grill may be cooked under a salamander.

3. **Grilling between heat** – this is grilling between electrically heated grill bars or plates, and is used for small cuts of meat.

 Health and safety

When reaching over to turn a steak at the back of the grill, be careful of the heat coming up from underneath, which may burn your forearm.

Associated techniques

There are a number of techniques associated with grilling which help the chef to prepare the dishes correctly:

- **Batting out** – cuts of meat are hit with a meat hammer to give an even thickness and start breaking down the connective tissue to help cooking.

- **Oiling, greasing and basting** – these techniques prevent items from sticking to the bars of the grill; food items are often oiled or greased lightly prior to cooking, with additional basting during cooking to ensure that items do not dry out.
- **Traying up** – items are placed on to trays prior to placing under a salamander; trays are normally lightly greased, allowing space for items to be turned to ensure even cooking.
- **Marinating** – items are pre-soaked or coated in a marinade to help flavour, tenderise and in some cases colour food before the cooking process starts.

Health and safety

If meat or fish has been marinated in an oil marinade, ensure that it is well drained before you place it on the grill. Food with too much oil on it may be a fire hazard if it is moved directly from the marinating container to the grill.

Equipment used for baking, roasting and grilling

There are a number of pieces of equipment that are used for baking, roasting and grilling:

- **Ovens** – general purpose, convection and combination
- **Grills** – under-fired or traditional grills, salamander, infra-red and contact grills
- **Small equipment** – tongs, probes, slices, palette knives and skewers.

More information on these types of equipment is provided in Chapter 5.

Health and safety

Always use the correct equipment to turn and lift food on the grill. Use tongs to turn and lift cutlets and steaks; use fish slices to turn and lift tomatoes, mushrooms and whole or cut fish.

Quality points

To ensure the quality of finished dishes there are a number of things that the chef can do during the process:

- Select products that are fresh, have a good appearance and smell and are at the appropriate temperature
- Prepare foods according to dish requirements: trim, shape and size as required
- Ensure the correct temperature, time and amount of liquid are used. These will have an impact on flavour, colour, texture and taste of the dish
- When finishing the final dish ensure consistency of appearance and portion size; add any seasoning and garnish if required.

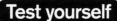

Test yourself ••

1 Briefly describe the process for the following methods of cooking:
   • Baking
   • Roasting
   • Grilling

2 List three ways in which heat is applied to food by grilling.

3 List three types of oven that could be used in a kitchen for baking or roasting foods.

4 List five safety points a chef should consider when baking or roasting foods.

5 What are the traditional accompaniments to the following roast meats:
   • Chicken
   • Leg of lamb
   • Sirloin of beef?

6 List four foods that can be cooked by grilling.

7 List three types of food that could be baked.

8 What are the four main degrees of grilling for a steak?

9 What is trussing?

10 What is the purpose of marinating food before grilling?

•••

Baking recipes

Millionaire's shortbread

Ingredients	20 pieces	40 pieces
Shortbread:		
Butter	175 g	345 g
Plain flour	265 g	525 g
Caster sugar	85 g	165 g
Filling:		
Butter	265 g	525 g
Caster sugar	175 g	345 g
Golden syrup	4 tbsp	9 tbsp
Condensed milk	600 g	1200 g (3 tins)
Topping:		
Milk chocolate	300 g	600 g
White chocolate	75 g	150 g

Cooking

1 Place butter, flour and sugar together, and bind together.

2 Press shortbread mixture into lined rectangular frame 40 cm × 20 cm (for 40 pieces) and prick the top with a fork.

3 Bake in the oven (preheated at 180°C/gas 4) for 20–25 minutes until thoroughly baked and golden brown.

4 To make the filling, place the butter, sugar, golden syrup and condensed milk into a thick-bottomed saucepan and heat gently until the sugar has dissolved.

5 Bring to the boil and simmer for 6–8 minutes, *stirring constantly* until the mixture becomes a light sand colour.

6 Pour over the baked shortbread base and leave to set.

7 Melt the milk chocolate over a pan of warm water. Spread the milk chocolate over the caramel with a palette knife so it is all evenly distributed. Melt the white chocolate in the same way and pour into a piping bag. Pipe the white chocolate over the milk chocolate.

8 Allow to set.

9 Portion into 2 cm × 10 cm slices using a large cook's knife.

 Note: Regional recipe contributed by Moira Hinde, Pastry Lecturer and Course Leader for the Professional Cookery programme at level 1, City College Norwich. This recipe is used in City College Norwich's Café Debut and is a very popular product.

Recipe 2

Red onion and sweetcorn frittata

Ingredients	4 portions	10 portions
Oil for frying	5 ml	15 ml
Red onions	½ (or 1 if small)	1
Carrots	50 g	125 g
Ground paprika	⅛ tsp	¼ tsp
Potatoes	100 g	250 g
Sweetcorn	20 g	50 g
Fresh, ripe tomatoes	2	5
Parsley	1 tsp	1½ tsp
Eggs	3	5
Milk	250 ml	625 ml
Cheddar cheese	100 g	250 g

Get ready to cook

1 Finely chop the onion and carrot.
2 Peel the tomatoes, then deseed and finely dice them.
3 Peel the potatoes and dice them (cut into 1 cm cubes).
4 Cook the diced potatoes in boiling water. Drain well.
5 Grate the cheese and chop the parsley.

Cooking

1 Shallow fry the onions and carrots in the oil without colouring.
2 Sprinkle with paprika and drain off any excess oil.
3 Add the diced tomatoes, sweetcorn, potatoes and chopped parsley to the pan and combine all the ingredients.
4 Place the mixture into a suitable ovenproof dish.
5 Whisk the eggs and milk together and season with black pepper.
6 Pour the eggs and milk over the vegetables in the ovenproof dish.
7 Sprinkle with cheddar cheese.
8 Bake in the oven at 180°C for approximately 15 minutes or until the mixture has set.
9 Allow to rest slightly before cutting into portions and serving.

Serving suggestion

Serve hot, or cold with salad.

Recipe 3   Arlie potatoes

Ingredients	4 portions	10 portions
Potatoes	4	10
Butter, soft	50 g	125 g
Salt and pepper		
Parsley	1 tsp	2½ tsp
Cheese (e.g. Parmesan)	60 g	150 g

Get ready to cook

1 Bake the potatoes in their jackets:

   a Preheat the oven to 230–250°C.

   b Select good, evenly sized potatoes and scrub well.

   c With the point of a small sharp knife, cut an incision skin deep around the potatoes.

   d Place the potatoes on a tray in the hot oven for about an hour. Turn the potatoes after 30 minutes.

   e Test by holding the potato in a clean teacloth and squeezing gently. If it is cooked, it should feel soft. (The cloth will protect your hand, in case the potato bursts.)

2 Chop the parsley and grate the cheese.

Cooking

1 Cut off the top of each potato, about one-third of the way down.

2 Scoop out the flesh from the potatoes and place it in a bowl. Keep the jackets. Mash or purée the flesh.

3 Add the butter and a little parsley. Season with salt and pepper. Mix.

4 Use a piping bag and star tube to pipe the mixture into the empty jackets.

5 Sprinkle with grated cheese and cook in the oven at 200°C until golden brown.

 Note: If you use a microwave to cook the potatoes, be sure to prick the skins first, otherwise they could burst open in the oven.

Recipe 4

Savoury (Boulangère) potatoes

Ingredients	4 portions	10 portions
Potatoes, peeled and washed	400 g	1¼ kg
Onions, peeled and sliced	100 g	250 g
Salt		
White stock	½ litre	1¼ litre
Butter, margarine or oil	25–50 g	60–100 g
Parsley, chopped		

Get ready to cook

1 Using a mandolin, and taking great care, cut the potatoes into 2 mm slices.
2 Using a large knife, peel, halve and finely slice the onions.
3 Preheat the oven to 230–250°C.

Cooking

1 Put the neatest slices of potato to one side. Mix the remainder with the onions.
2 Season lightly and place in a well-greased shallow earthenware dish or a roasting tin. Make sure the top layer consists of neatly overlapping slices of potato.
3 Brush lightly with oil or dab with butter. Just cover with stock.
4 Cook in a hot oven (230–250°C) for approximately 20 minutes, until lightly coloured.

5 Reduce the heat to 180°C and continue to cook for approximately another ¾–1¼ hours. Press down the potatoes from time to time with a clean, flat-bottomed pan.
6 When cooked, all the stock should have been absorbed.
7 If cooked in an earthenware dish, clean the edges with a damp cloth dipped in salt.

Serving suggestion

Sprinkle with freshly chopped parsley and serve.

Recipe 5 — Macaroni pasta bake

Ingredients	4 portions	10 portions
Macaroni	100 g	250 g
Oil or butter (optional)	25 g	60 g
Grated cheese	100 g	250 g
Thin béchamel sauce	500 ml	1¼ litres
Diluted English or Continental mustard	¼ tsp	1 tsp
Salt, milled pepper		

Get ready to cook

1 Prepare the béchamel sauce, as described on page 110.

2 Dilute the mustard powder.

Cooking

1 Plunge the macaroni into a saucepan of lightly salted boiling water.

2 Boil gently, stirring occasionally, for approximately 10–15 minutes (until al dente).

3 Drain well in a colander.

4 Return to a clean dry pan and add the oil or butter.

5 Mix with half the cheese, the mustard and the béchamel. Season lightly and taste to check.

6 Place in an earthenware dish and sprinkle with the remainder of the cheese.

7 Brown lightly under a grill or in a hot oven.

Try something different

Add a layer of sliced tomatoes or lightly cooked sliced mushrooms to the top of the finished macaroni before adding the final grated cheese and browning.

Recipe 6

Shepherd's pie

Ingredients	4 portions	10 portions
Oil	35 g	100 g
Onions	100 g	250 g
Cooked lamb or mutton (minced)	400 g	1¼ kg
Worcester sauce	2–3 drops	5 drops
Thickened gravy	125–250 ml	300–600 ml
Salt		
Potato	400 g	1¼ kg
Milk or eggwash		

 Note: The ideal lamb joint for this is shoulder cooked by roasting, but any leftover lamb can be used provided all fat and gristle is removed.

Get ready to cook

1 Remove all the fat and gristle from the cooked meat and then mince it.
2 Peel, cook and mash the potatoes.
3 Peel and finely chop the onions.
4 Make the thickened gravy (see page 113) and eggwash.

Cooking

1 Gently cook the onion in the oil in a thick-bottomed pan, without colouring, until soft.
2 Add the cooked meat and season lightly.

3 Add Worcester sauce and sufficient thickened gravy to bind the mixture. This should not be too dry or too sloppy.
4 Bring to the boil, stirring frequently, and simmer for 10–15 minutes.

5 Place into an ovenproof dish.
6 Pipe or neatly arrange the mashed potato on top and brush with eggwash or milk.
7 Colour to a golden brown in a hot oven and under the salamander.

Serving suggestion

- Serve accompanied with a sauceboat of thickened gravy and a suitable vegetable.
- It can also be served with a light sprinkling of garam masala and grilled pitta bread.

Try something different

Many variations can be made to this basic dish.

- Cover the meat with canned baked beans before adding the potato.
- Sprinkle with grated cheese before browning.
- Vary the flavour of the meat by adding herbs or spices.
- Vary the potato topping by mixing in grated cheese or chopped spring onion.
- This dish can also be prepared from leftover cooked beef or raw minced beef, which would require extra cooking time until the meat was quite soft. This is known as cottage pie.

Activity

Prepare, cook, serve and taste your own variation. Assess and discuss.

Recipe 7

Baked cod with a cheese and herb crust

Ingredients	4 portions	10 portions
Cod fillet portions, 100 g each	4	10
Fresh white breadcrumbs	100 g	250 g
Butter, margarine or oil	100 g	250 g
Cheddar cheese	100 g	250 g
Parsley	1 tbsp	1 tbsp
Salt		
Herb mustard	1 heaped tsp	2 heaped tsp

Get ready to cook

1 Prepare, skin, clean, wash and thoroughly dry the fish.

2 Grate the cheese and chop the parsley.

Cooking

1 Place the fillets on a greased tray or ovenproof dish.

2 Combine all the other ingredients thoroughly. Season lightly with salt.

3 Press an even layer of the mixture onto the fish.

4 Bake in an oven at 180°C for approximately 15–20 minutes until cooked and the crust is a light golden brown.

Serving suggestion

Serve with quarters of de-pipped lemon, or a suitable sauce such as tomato or egg.

Try something different

- Add a good squeeze of lemon juice before cooking.
- Add 2 tbsp/5 tbsp milk before cooking.
- Brush with beaten egg before adding the topping.
- Cover with slices of peeled tomato before cooking.
- Add chopped fresh herbs, such as chives, dill, fennel, or a touch of spice, such as garam masala.

Activity

In groups, prepare, cook, taste and assess four variations of your choice.

Recipe 8 — Steak pie

Ingredients	4 portions	10 portions
Stewing beef, preferably chuck steak	400 g	1½ kg
Oil or fat	50 ml	125 ml
Onion (optional)	100 g	250 g
Worcester sauce	3–4 drops	8–10 drops
Parsley	1 tsp	3 tsp
Stock or water	125 ml	300 ml
Cornflour or arrowroot	10 g	25 g
Salt		
Short pastry using flour weight of	200 g	500 g

Get ready to cook

1 Make your pastry (see Recipe 9).
2 Cut the meat into 2 cm strips and then into squares.
3 Chop the onion and parsley.

Cooking

1 Heat the oil in a frying pan, add the meat and quickly brown on all sides.
2 Drain the meat in a colander.
3 Lightly sweat the onion.
4 Place the meat, onion, Worcester sauce, parsley and the liquid in a saucepan. Season lightly with salt.
5 Bring to the boil, skim and allow to simmer gently until the meat is tender.
6 Dilute the cornflour with a little water and stir in to the simmering meat.
7 Re-boil, taste, correct seasoning.
8 Place the mixture in a pie dish.
9 Carefully roll the pastry onto the rolling pin and then unroll it over the top of the pie, being careful not to stretch it.
10 Seal the pastry onto the dish rim firmly and cut off any extra pastry.
11 Place the pie on a baking sheet and bake at 200°C for approximately 30–45 minutes. If the pastry colours too quickly, cover it with greaseproof paper or foil.

Recipe 9

Short pastry

Ingredients	5–8 portions	10–16 portions
Flour, soft	200 g	500 g
Salt	Pinch	Large pinch
Lard or vegetable fat	50 g	125 g
Butter or margarine	50 g	125 g
Water	2–3 tbsp	5–8 tbsp

Get ready to cook

1 Ensure that your hands are well scrubbed, rinsed under cold water and dried.

2 Cut the fat into small pieces.

Note: Short pastry is made from soft flour and fat, which gives the pastry a crumbly 'short' texture

The amount of water required can vary according to the type of flour: a very fine soft flour can absorb more water.

Heat (such as warm weather conditions, contact with hot hands) will affect the quality.

Preparation

1 Sieve the flour and salt into a bowl or onto a cool surface.

2 Using your fingertips, lightly rub in the fat to the flour until it is a sandy texture.

3 Make a well in the centre of the mixture.

4 Add enough water to make a fairly firm paste. Mix it together, handling it as little and as lightly as possible.

5 Keep working it gently with your hands until it has formed a dough.

6 Allow the pastry to rest, covered with a damp teacloth, in a cool place (refrigerator) before using. This allows the pastry to relax, which means there is less chance of it shrinking when it is rolled out.

Recipe
10

Sweet pastry

Ingredients	4 portions	10 portions
Egg, medium sized	1	2–3
Sugar, caster	50 g	125 g
Butter or margarine	125 g	300 g
Flour, soft	200 g	500 g
Salt	Pinch	Large pinch

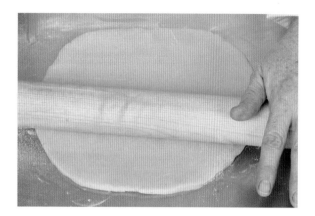

 Note: Sweet pastry can be used for flans, tartlets and tarts.

Preparation

1 Cream the fat and sugar together until the fat is completely combined.
2 Beat in the egg. Mix well.
3 Add the flour gradually, then bring the mixture together lightly to form a smooth dough.
4 Allow to rest in the refrigerator covered with cling film or a damp cloth.

Troubleshooting when making short or sweet pastry

If your pastry is too hard, you may have:
• Added too much water
• Added too little fat
• Not rubbed in the fat sufficiently
• Handled and rolled it too much
• Over-baked it.

If your pastry is too soft and crumbly, you may have:
• Added too little water
• Added too much fat.

If your pastry is blistered, you may have:
• Added too little water
• Added the water unevenly
• Rubbed in the fat unevenly.

If your pastry is soggy, you may have:
• Added too much water
• Had the oven too cool
• Not baked it for long enough.

If your pastry is shrunken, you may have:
• Handled and rolled it too much
• Stretched it while handling it.

Recipe 11 Fruit tartlets

Ingredients	4 portions	10 portions
Sweet pastry	100 g	250 g
Pastry cream	4 tbsp	10 tbsp
Fruit, fresh or tinned	100 g	250 g
Arrowroot for glaze (optional)		

 Note: Soft fruits (such as strawberries, raspberries) and tinned fruits (such as pineapple, peaches, pears) are popular for tartlets.

The pastry cases are cooked 'blind', which means that they are cooked before the filling is added.

Get ready to cook

1 Prepare the sweet pastry as per Recipe 10.

2 Prepare the pastry cream (see page 119), or prepare custard.

3 Prepare the fruit if it is fresh. Strawberries should be well washed, completely dried and, depending on size, either kept whole or cut into slices.

4 Preheat the oven to 200°C–220°C.

Cooking

1 Roll out sweet pastry 3 mm thick.

2 Using a fluted (wavy) cutter, cut out rounds.

3 Place the pastry rounds in lightly greased tartlet moulds.

4 Neaten them carefully to shape, using a light coating of flour on the fingers only if necessary.

5 Prick the bottoms gently with a fork in 2–3 places.

6 Cut rounds of greaseproof paper to fit comfortably in each lined tartlet case. Place the paper on top of the pastry and fill the centres with dried peas, beans or pieces of stale bread.

7 Place the tartlets on a baking sheet. Bake at 200°C–220°C for approximately 20 minutes until cooked and nicely browned.

8 Remove from the oven onto a cooling rack.

9 When cooled, remove the papers and beans.

10 Place a thin layer of pastry cream or thick custard in the bottom of each tartlet case.

11 Neatly arrange the fruit on top. Work methodically. In this picture, the chef has spaced out the first blueberries evenly.

12 Now he fills in the gaps. The pattern of fruit is neat and regular.

13 Dilute some arrowroot in a basin with a little fruit juice (10 g arrowroot to ¼ litre of the juice). If you used tinned fruit, use the juice from the tin.

14 Boil the remainder of the juice in a small pan and gradually stir in the diluted arrowroot, stirring continuously until it re-boils. Allow the glaze to cool before use.

15 Use this glaze to thinly mask (coat or cover) the fruit in the tartlets.

Try something different

For soft fruits, a red glaze can be made by diluting a matching jam with a little water or syrup, heating it gently until mixed, then passing it through a fine strainer.

Recipe 12 Fruit pies

Ingredients	4 portions	10 portions
Fruit	400 g	1 kg
Sugar, granulated	100 g	250 g
Water	2 tbsp	5 tbsp
Short pastry using flour weight of	100 g	250 g

Get ready to cook

1 Prepare and wash the fruit. Remove any stalks, leaves or stones. If using apples, peel, cut into quarters, remove the core and slice.
2 Make the short pastry and keep refrigerated until you need it.
3 Preheat the oven to 220°C.

Cooking

1 Place the fruit in a half-litre pie dish.
2 Add the sugar and water (for an apple pie, add a clove).
3 Roll out the pastry ½ cm thick to the shape of the pie dish. Use as little dusting flour as possible on the table surface, the pastry and rolling pin. Allow the pastry to relax for a few minutes.
4 Dampen the rim of the pie dish with water or milk and press a thin strip of pastry onto it.
5 Carefully roll the pastry onto the rolling pin and then unroll it over the top of the fruit, being careful not to stretch it.
6 Seal the pastry onto the dish rim firmly and cut off any extra pastry.
7 Brush the pastry with milk and sprinkle with sugar.
8 Place the pie on a baking sheet and bake in a hot oven at 220°C for about 10 minutes.
9 Reduce the heat to 180°C and cook for a further 20–30 minutes (if the pastry colours too quickly, cover it with greaseproof paper or foil).

Serving suggestion

Serve with custard, cream or ice cream.

Fruit fillings for pies

Bramley apples are ideal. They could be combined with either blackberries, damsons or gooseberries.
Rhubarb pie or cherry pie will also work well.

Recipe 13 — Bread rolls

Ingredients	8 rolls	20 rolls
Flour, strong	200 g	500 g
Yeast	5 g	12 g
Liquid – ½ water, ½ milk	125 ml	300 ml
Butter or margarine	10 g	25 g
Caster sugar	¼ tsp	½ tsp
Salt	Small pinch	Large pinch
Egg, beaten for eggwash	1	2

Cooking

1 Sieve the flour into a bowl and warm in the oven or on the stove.
2 Cream the yeast in a basin with a quarter of the liquid.
3 Make a well in the flour and add the dissolved yeast.
4 Sprinkle over a little of the flour, cover with a cloth and leave in a warm place until the yeast ferments (bubbles).
5 Add the remainder of the warmed liquid, the fat, sugar and salt.
6 Knead firmly until smooth and free from wrinkles.
7 Return to the basin, cover with a cloth and leave in a warm place to prove (double in size).
8 Knock back (lightly knead) the dough to remove the air and bring it back to its original size.
9 Mould the dough in a roll and cut into even pieces.
10 Mould the pieces into the shapes you want. Place them on a lightly floured baking sheet and cover with a cloth.
11 Leave in a warm place to double in size.
12 Brush gently with eggwash.
13 Bake in a hot oven at 220°C for approximately 10 minutes.
14 Remove from the oven and place the rolls on a cooling rack.

Try something different

Gently add 50 g of sultanas and 50 g of chopped walnuts at stage 8.

Recipe 14 Simple white loaf

Ingredients	10 portions
Strong flour, plain	375 g
Yeast, dried or fresh	10 g
Water, warm	125 ml
Milk, warm	125 ml
Caster sugar	2 tsp
Salt	1 tsp
Melted butter, margarine or vegetable oil	30 g

 Note: Most bread today is leavened (made to rise) by yeast or baking powder (bread made with baking powder is called soda bread). Yeast produces carbon dioxide, which collects in small bubbles throughout the dough and causes the dough to rise.

It is important that yeast is fresh and is in the correct proportion to the amount of flour used. Mixing and kneading must be thorough to incorporate the yeast. The second kneading should not be too heavy or too much gas will be lost.

Always use strong flour when making bread. Soft flour is unsuitable because it contains less gluten.

Bread made without yeast or baking powder is known as 'unleavened' bread. Unleavened bread is flat, such as pitta bread.

Cooking

1 Combine the yeast, water and sugar in a bowl and whisk until the yeast is dissolved. Cover and stand in a warm place to ferment (bubble) for about 10 minutes or until the mixture is frothy.

2 Sift the flour and salt into a mixing bowl. Add the melted butter, milk and yeast mixture.

3 Mix to form a dough, using the hook attachment on the mixer. Start on low speed for 6 minutes, then turn up to medium for 4 minutes.

4 Add the salt and mix for 2 minutes.

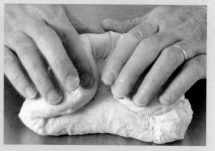

5 Place the dough into a lightly floured bowl. Stand in a warm place covered with a damp cloth and allow to prove (to rise and increase in size) until it has doubled in size.

6 It may take up to one hour for the dough to double in size.

7 Turn the dough out onto a floured surface and knock it back (re-knead) to its original size and until it is smooth.

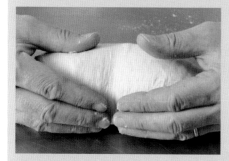

8 Roll the dough into a rectangle 18 cm × 35 cm. Roll this up like a Swiss roll. Place it in a greased bread tin 14 cm × 21 cm. Cover and stand in a warm place for about 20 minutes until it has doubled in size.

9 Brush the top of the loaf with milk to give a rich brown colour. Place it in a preheated hot oven (180°C–200°C) for approximately 30 minutes.

10 Turn out the bread onto a wire rack.

Troubleshooting in bread making

If your bread is heavy, you may have:
- Used stale yeast
- Destroyed the yeast with hot liquid or hot conditions during the making process
- Made or proved the dough in a place that was too cool
- Not have used enough liquid
- Not have proved the dough for long enough.

If your bread has an uneven texture, you may have:
- Not kneaded the dough enough
- Over-proved the dough

- Placed the bread in an oven that was too cool for the initial cooking, allowing fermentation to proceed for too long.

If your bread is sour, you may have:
- Used stale yeast
- Used too much yeast
- Over-risen or over-proved the dough.

Storage

Uncooked bread and dough products should be kept in the refrigerator until ready for baking. Always keep frozen bread and dough products in the deep freeze until ready for baking.

Recipe 15 — Gluten-free bread

Ingredients	10 portions
Gluten-free plain flour	450 g
Baking powder	2 tsp
Salt	1½ tsp
Oat bran	180 g
Sunflower seeds	160 g
Butter, margarine or vegetable oil	70 g
Milk	375 ml
Egg	2
Poppy seeds	2 tsp

 Note: Some people are allergic to gluten, a protein found in wheat. Coeliac disease is caused by a reaction to gluten. Gluten-free is a safe alternative to ordinary bread for coeliacs and those allergic to gluten.

Cooking

1 Sift the flour, baking powder and salt into a large bowl. Add the oat bran and stir well. Mix in the sunflower seeds.

2 Rub in the butter or mix in the vegetable oil.

3 Beat the eggs and milk. Add this to the mixture.

4 Mix to a dough.

5 Press the dough into a greased loaf tin measuring 14 cm x 21 cm. Brush with milk. Sprinkle with poppy seeds.

6 Bake in a pre-heated oven at 160°C–180°C for approximately one hour.

7 When baked, allow the bread to stand in the loaf tin for 10 minutes. Turn it out onto a wire rack to cool.

Recipe 16 Banana loaf

Ingredients	10 portions
Soft brown sugar	125 g
Margarine or butter or vegetable oil	140 g
Eggs	2
Wholemeal flour	200 g
Baking powder	12 g
Cinnamon	⅛ tsp
Ripe bananas, mashed	2
Sultanas	50 g

Get ready to cook

1 Beat the egg.
2 Peel and mash the banana.

Cooking

1 Cream together the sugar and margarine, butter or vegetable oil.

2 Slowly add the beaten egg and beat well after each addition.

3 Sift the baking powder with the wholemeal flour.

4 Gradually add the flour with the baking powder to the sugar, margarine and egg mixture.

5 Carefully incorporate the mashed bananas and the sultanas. Gently mix well.

6 Place the mixture into a bread tin approximately 20 cm × 12 cm lined with silicone paper.

7 Bake in an oven at 180°C for approximately 30 minutes.

8 Remove and allow to cool. Cut into portions.

Recipe 17 — Fruit buns

Ingredients	8 buns	20 buns
Bun dough:		
Flour, strong	200 g	500 g
Yeast	5 g	12 g
Milk and water (approximately)	60 ml	150 ml
Egg, medium sized	1	2–3
Butter or margarine	50 g	125 g
Caster sugar	25 g	60 g
Dried fruit (e.g. currants, sultanas)	50 g	125 g
Mixed spice		
Bun wash:		
Sugar	100 g	
Water or milk	125 ml	

Get ready to cook

1 Wash the dried fruit.

2 Beat the egg.

Cooking

1 Sieve the flour into a bowl and warm.

2 Rub the yeast into the flour.

3 Rub in the fat.

4 Make a well in the centre of the flour and pour in the beaten egg.

5 Pour in the mixture of milk and water.

6 Fold together. As you work, add the sugar, dried fruit and mixed spice.

7 Knead well to form a soft, slack dough.

8 Continue kneading until smooth and not sticky.

9 Keep covered in the bowl and allow to prove. The dough will double in size.
(This photo shows the same amount of dough, before and after proving. There was no fruit in that dough.)

10 Mould the dough into balls. Place these on a lightly greased baking tray. Cover with a cloth and allow to prove again.

11 Bake in a hot oven (220°C) for 15–20 minutes

12 Boil together the ingredients for the bun wash until it is a thick syrup.

13 Remove the buns from the oven and brush liberally with bun wash.

14 Remove onto a cooling rack.

Try something different

To make hot cross buns:

- Make fruit buns as above, but use a little more spice.
- When moulded, make a cross on top of each bun with the back of a knife.
- Alternatively, make a slack mixture of flour and water in a greaseproof paper cornet and pipe on neat crosses.

Scones

Ingredients	8 scones	20 scones
Self-raising flour	200 g	500 g
Baking powder	5 g	12 g
Salt	Small pinch	Large pinch
Butter or margarine	50 g	125 g
Caster sugar	50 g	125 g
Milk or water	65 ml	175 ml
Sultanas	50 g	125 g

Note: Because of the small amount of fat in the dough, it is essential that you mix gently and handle the dough lightly to produce a light scone.

Get ready to cook

Wash the sultanas. Dry them well.

Cooking

1. Sieve the flour, baking powder and salt into a basin.
2. Gently rub in the fat until the mixture has a sandy texture.
3. Dissolve the sugar in the liquid.
4. Gently and lightly mix in the flour.
5. Divide the dough into two.

6. Using as little flour as possible, gently roll out the dough to 1 cm thick.
7. Cut out the rounds using a cutter.
8. Place the rounds on a lightly greased baking sheet.
9. Cut a cross with a sharp knife halfway through the rounds. Brush with milk and bake at 200°C for 15–20 minutes.

Try something different

Sprinkle with icing sugar to enhance the presentation. For wholemeal scones, use half self-raising flour and half wholemeal flour.

Recipe 19
Apple crumble

Ingredients	4 portions	10 portions
Crumble filling:		
Bramley apples	600 g	2 kg
Sugar, granulated or brown	100 g	250 g
Cloves	1	2
Topping:		
Butter or margarine	50 g	125 g
Soft brown sugar	100 g	250 g
Plain flour	150 g	400 g

Cooking

1 Peel, core and slice the apples.

2 Cook them gently with a few drops of water, sugar and clove in a covered saucepan.

3 Place the cooked apple in a pie dish or in individual moulds. Remove the cloves.

4 Make the topping by lightly rubbing the fat into the flour. Combine this with the sugar.

5 When the fruit is cool, sprinkle on the topping and bake at 190°C for about 30 minutes, until lightly browned.

Serving suggestion

Serve with custard, cream or vanilla ice cream.

Try something different

Try some fruit combinations, such as:

- Apple and blackberry
- Apple and gooseberry
- Apple and rhubarb.

Try some topping variations:

- Add a little spice, such as cinnamon, nutmeg, mixed spice, ground ginger
- Use half flour and half porridge oats.

Baked rice pudding

Ingredients	4 portions	10 portions
Rice, short grain	50 g	125 g
Caster suger	50 g	125 g
Milk, whole or skimmed	½ litre	1½ litres
Butter	12g	30 g
Vanilla essence	2–3 drops	6–8 drops
Nutmeg, grated		

Cooking

1 Wash the rice and place it in a pie dish.

2 Add the sugar and milk and mix well.

3 Add the butter, vanilla essence and the nutmeg.

4 Place the dish on a baking sheet. Clean any milk from the rim of the pie dish.

5 Bake at 180°C–200°C until the milk starts to simmer.

6 Reduce the heat to 150°C and allow the pudding to cook slowly for 1½–2 hours.

Roasting recipes

Roast rump of Glamorgan lamb on lava bread potato cake – Welsh stout and berry sauce

Ingredients	4 portions	10 portions
Pembroke new potatoes	400 g	1 kg
Rump of Glamorgan Lamb	4	10
Rapeseed oil	2 tbsp	5 tbsp
Vegetables for mirepoix (carrot, leek, onion, celery)	100 g	250 g
Welsh black beer (Bullmastif brewery)	1 bottle	2 bottles
Redcurrant jelly	1 tsp	2 tsp
Lamb stock	400 ml	1 litre
Tarragon	1 tbsp	2 tbsp
Leeks	100 g	250 g
Lardons of bacon	100 g	205 g
Orange	1	2
Lava bread (pre-prepared product)	200 g	500 g
Fresh blackcurrant or blackberries	1 punnet	2 punnets

Note: Recipe contributed by Kevin Fairlie, Senior Chef/Lecturer at Cardiff and Vale College.

Welsh Mountain Sheep are local to Glamorgan and are lean with good flavour. Pembroke new potatoes are a popular variety in Wales. Local beer from a micro-brewery in Cardiff adds a very local dimension to this dish and using locally reared bacon gives this dish a very South Wales appeal. Lava bread is now being found in a variety of dishes across Wales, not just as a breakfast ingredient.

Method

1. Cook the potatoes in boiling salted water for about 15 mins until cooked through. Crush lightly with a fork. Cover and put aside in a warm place.
2. Season the lamb rumps with salt and freshly ground black pepper.
3. Heat the rapeseed oil in an ovenproof frying pan and fry the lamb rumps until lightly browned all over.
4. Transfer the rumps to the oven and roast for 8–10 minutes (for medium rare).
5. Remove from the oven and set aside to rest in a warm place, keep pan for next stage.
6. Place the reserved lamb trimmings and mirepoix of vegetables into the roasting pan and cook over a high heat until all ingredients begin to brown and caramelise.

Get ready to cook

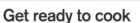

1. Prepare and trim the lamb (keep the trimmings to one side). Score the fat if you are going to present the rumps whole for service.
2. Wash the potatoes and vegetables.
3. Cut the vegetables into mirepoix.
4. Chop the tarragon and finely grate the orange zest.
5. Pre-heat oven to 185–195°C.

7 Pour in enough beer to cover the ingredients in the pan and add the redcurrant jelly. Deglaze by scraping up any browned bits from the bottom of the pan with a wooden spoon.

8 Cook until the beer has reduced in volume by half, then add the lamb stock and tarragon. Reduce by half again, checking for flavour. Cook until the consistency of a jus is achieved. Adjust seasoning as necessary.

9 Strain the sauce and keep warm for service.

10 Pre-heat a heavy bottomed pan and fry the lardons of bacon, leek and orange zest in the pan quickly, using the fat from the lardons as the cooking medium (dry-frying). Fry until the lardons are lightly browned and a little crisp.

11 Add the potatoes and lava bread to the pan and mix carefully, crushing down the potatoes a little further. Taste for seasoning and adjust if needed.

12 Place a portion of the potato mixture into a small ring mould in the centre of a plate and de-mould. Put the roast rump of lamb carefully on top (sliced or whole) then pour the jus around the plate. Finish by scattering a garnish of blackberries or blackcurrants around the plate.

Try something different

● This recipe uses potatoes with the skin on – try making it with peeled potatoes for a smoother texture.

● Add the berries to the sauce after passing it. When the sauce is re-heated, this will soften the fruit, changing the texture of the garnish.

Recipe **22**

Roast potatoes

Ingredients

Potatoes, washed, peeled and cut (1 kg of old potatoes will yield 4–6 portions)

Oil or dripping for roasting

Salt, pinch

Cooking

1 Heat a good measure of oil or dripping in a roasting tray.

2 Add the well-dried potatoes and lightly brown on all sides.

3 Season *lightly* with salt and cook for ¾–1 hour in a hot oven (230–250°C).

4 Turn the potatoes halfway through cooking.

5 Cook to a crisp, golden brown, then drain off the fat and serve.

Get ready to cook

1 Wash, peel and re-wash the potatoes.

2 Cut into evenly sized pieces, 3–4 pieces per portion.

3 Dry the potatoes well.

4 Preheat the oven to 230–250°C.

Traditional roast beef and gravy

Ingredients

Joint of beef of your own choice and size

Salt

Dripping or oil

Roughly chopped onion, carrot and celery

Brown stock

Get ready to cook

1 Trim the joint to remove sinew, excess fat and any bones that may make carving difficult. Depending on the joint and the way you prepare it, you may want to tie it with string to keep its shape.
2 Wash, peel and roughly chop the vegetables.
3 Prepare a brown stock (page 99).
4 Preheat the oven to 250°C.

Note: Suitable roasting joints are:
- First class – sirloin, wing ribs, fore ribs, fillet
- Second class – middle ribs, topside.

Cooking

1 Season the joint lightly with salt and place on a trivet (metal or bones) in a roasting tray.
2 Place a little dripping or oil over the meat and cook it in a hot oven at 230–250°C for around 15 minutes, then reduce the heat to 200–220°C, depending on the size of the joint. Roasting time is approximately 15 minutes per ½ kg plus 15 minutes.
3 Baste frequently and, for large joints, gradually reduce the heat by 5–10°C (depending on the size of the joint.
4 Roughly chopped onion, carrot and celery can be added to the roasting tray approximately 30 minutes before the joint is cooked, to give extra flavour to the gravy.
5 Remove the tray from the oven and place the joint onto a dish or plate to check whether it is cooked (see below).
6 Once you are happy that the meat is cooked, cover it with foil and leave to rest in a warm place for at least 15 minutes. This allows the meat to set and become tender for carving.

Testing whether a joint is cooked

If you do not have a temperature probe:

- Remove the joint from the oven and place on a dish or plate.
- Firmly press the meat surface to force out some meat juice.
- Check the colour of the juice:
  - Red – indicates that the meat is underdone
  - Pink – indicates that the meat is medium done
  - Clear – indicates that the meat is cooked through

If you are using a temperature probe:

- Set the required internal temperature and insert the probe horizontally into the centre of the meat.
- Leave the probe inside the joint during cooking.
- It will set off a beeper alerting you when your meat is cooked to perfection.

When using a meat temperature thermometer:

- Insert it into the part of the joint that was the thickest before it was placed in the oven.
- The internal temperature reached should be as follows:
  - Rare or underdone meat 52–55°C
  - Medium done (pinkish) 66–71°C
  - Just done (slightly pink) 78–80°C.

Making the gravy

1 While the meat is resting you can make the gravy by carefully pouring off as much fat as possible, leaving any meat juice or sediment and vegetables in the tray.

2 Place this over a low heat and add sufficient brown stock for the amount of gravy required and allow it to simmer for 5 minutes, scraping off all the sediment and meat juice from the joint with a non-metal spoon.

3 Taste the gravy, correct the seasoning and pass it through a fine strainer. If the gravy is lacking in flavour, a little commercial product can be added.

Serving suggestion

- Carve the meat against the grain, as per the carving guidance given on page 160.
- Lay your table with sharp, un-serrated steak knives that will cut cleanly through the meat. A blunt knife makes the meat seem less tender, and a serrated knife encourages your guests to 'saw', both of which can ruin even the most beautifully cooked meat.
- Serve with Yorkshire pudding, gravy and a selection of roast and steamed vegetables.

Recipe 24 — Yorkshire pudding

Ingredients	4 portions	10 portions
Plain flour	85 g	215 g
Eggs	2	5
Milk	85 ml	215 ml
Water	40 ml	100 ml
Salt, pinch		
Beef dripping from the joint or a light oil	20 g	50 g

Cooking

1 Place the flour and eggs into a mixing bowl and mix to a smooth paste.

 Note: Yorkshire pudding is the traditional accompaniment to roast beef.

2 Gradually add the milk and water, beating strongly to incorporate air, which should start to appear in small bubbles on the surface. Add the salt and allow the mixture to rest for one hour.

3 Heat the pudding trays in a hot oven at 190°C. Add a little dripping in each tray, preferably from the meat as this will give flavour. Otherwise, use oil.

4 Ladle in the mixture so each tray is two-thirds full.

5 Place in the oven for 20–30 minutes. When checking, only open the oven door sufficiently to glance at the puddings, and then close it slowly without banging.

6 For the last 10 minutes of cooking, take the trays out, turn the puddings over and return them to the oven to dry out and complete cooking. Serve immediately.

Recipe 25 — Horseradish sauce

Ingredients	4 portions	10 portions
Horseradish, grated	25 g	65 g
Cream, lightly whipped	120 ml	300 ml
Malt vinegar or lemon juice	1 tbsp	2½ tbsp
Salt		

Making the sauce

 Note: Horseradish sauce is the traditional sauce offered with roast beef.

1 Thoroughly wash the horseradish, peel and grate finely.

2 Mix all the ingredients, season lightly with salt and taste.

Recipe 26 — Roasted beetroot

Ingredients	4 portions	10 portions
Small young beetroot	4	10
Olive oil	2 tbsp	5 tbsp
Crème fraîche	150 ml	375 ml
Grated horseradish	2 tbsp	5 tbsp
Chives, finely chopped	1 tbsp	2½ tbsp

Get ready to cook

1 Trim and thoroughly wash the beetroot. Dry well.
2 Preheat the oven to 200°C.

 Note: It is not necessary to peel the beetroots. If peeled they will lose colour (bleed).

Cooking

1 Place the beetroot in a roasting tray and sprinkle with olive oil.
2 Roast at 200°C for approximately 1½ hours until cooked.
3 Mix the horseradish in the crème fraîche.

Serving suggestion

- When the beetroot is cooked, place on a serving dish. Cut a criss-cross in the top, half way through.
- Spoon some crème fraîche onto each beetroot and sprinkle with chopped chives.

Try something different

You can use natural yoghurt or half-whipped cream as alternatives to crème fraîche.

Recipe 27 — Roast loin of pork with apple and onion sauce

Ingredients	4 portions	10 portions
Loin of pork on the bone	1 kg	2.5 kg
Salt		
Cooking apples, peeled, de-cored and quartered	2	5
Onion, peeled and quartered	1	2–3
Cider	60 ml	150 ml

Get ready to cook

1 Use a loin that is on the bone. Saw down the chine bone to make it easier to carve. The chine bone is the bone along the back of the loin that attaches the two loins together.

2 Trim off all sinew and excess fat.

3 If it has not been done by the butcher, score the skin (cut deep with the point of a small sharp knife) in the direction that the loin will be carved. Season lightly with salt.

4 Secure it by tying a string through the chine bone.

5 Peel, core and quarter the apples, and peel and quarter the onion.

6 Preheat the oven to 250°C.

▲ Scoring the skin

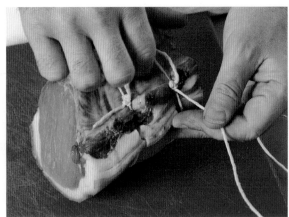

▲ Tying the joint

Cooking

1 Heat some oil in a frying pan. Place the pork into the oil and seal it on all sides.

2 Remove the pork from the pan. Cook the apples and onions in the same pan.

3 Deglaze the pan with some of the cider.

 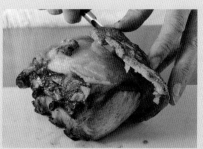

4 Place the meat, apples and onions in a roasting tin. Add the rest of the cider and roast at 200°C for 25 minutes, then reduce the temperature to 170°C and continue to cook until done, approximately 45 minutes.

5 Remove the joint from the tray and put on a plate or dish.

6 Check that it is cooked by pressing the lean meat – no signs of blood should be in the juice.

7 Cover the joint loosely with foil and allow it to rest for 10–15 minutes before carving. Remove the crisp skin (crackling) and break it up.

8 Purée the apples and onions in a processor, then reheat. This should be a thickish consistency – if too thick, adjust with cider.

Serving suggestion

Slice the pork and serve with sauce and roast gravy. A piece of the crisp skin (crackling) should be served with each portion of pork.

Recipe 28 Roast rack of lamb

Ingredients

Rack of lamb

Salt

Vegetable oil

Brown stock for gravy (see page 99)

Preparing the joint

1 Remove the skin from head to tail (top to bottom) and breast (front) to back, leaving as much fat as possible on the joint.

2 Remove the sinew and the tip of the blade bone.

3 Clean the sinew from between the rib bones and on the bones.

4 Score (lightly cut with the tip of a sharp knife) a line through the fat, 2 cm from the end of the bone.

5 If necessary, trim the overall length of the rib bones to two and a half times the length of the nut of lean meat. (The nut is the main part of the meat.)

6 Score down the middle of the back of each bone.

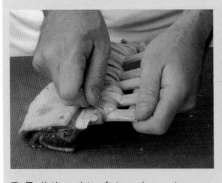

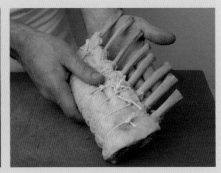

7 Pull the skin, fat and meat away from the end of each bone, so that the bones will be visible after cooking. Clean away any sinew.

8 Cut off the sinew along the other edge.

9 Tie the joint.

Cooking

1 Season the rack lightly with salt and place fat side up on a bed of bones or a metal trivet in a roasting tray.
2 Add a little vegetable oil on top and cook in a hot oven at 175–185°C.
3 Roast for approximately 20–25 minutes. Baste (spoon fat over the joint) two or three times during cooking.
4 To test if cooked, remove the rack, place on a warm plate and press the lean meat to force out a little juice. If the juice does not show any pinkness (sign of blood) it is cooked right through. If the lamb is to be cooked pink, then reduce the cooking time by approximately 5 minutes.

Serving suggestion

- If you are going to make roast gravy with this dish (see Recipe 23 for roast beef, which includes instructions for making gravy), add a peeled sliced onion, celery and carrot to the roasting tin with the lamb rack. This will give the gravy more flavour. There are a number of commercial gravy products that can also be used to boost the gravy if it is not tasty enough.
- In addition to roast gravy, offer mint sauce and/or redcurrant jelly.

Recipe 29	**Mint sauce**	

Ingredients	Quantity
Mint leaves, chopped	2–3 tablespoons
Caster or demarara sugar	1 tsp
Water	125 ml
Malt vinegar	to taste

Making the sauce

1 Boil the water and dissolve the sugar in it. Allow to cool.
2 Add the chopped mint leaves and enough malt vinegar to give a slightly sharp but pleasant taste.

Grilling recipes

Recipe 30 Grilled pollock with allspice and lime

	4 portions	10 portions
Scotch bonnet chillies	12 g	30 g
Onions	12 g	30 g
Ginger	8 g	20 g
Fresh thyme	1½ g	3 g
Oregano leaves	1½ g	3 g
Paprika powder	1½ g	3 g
Salt	1½ g	3 g
Turmeric (haldi powder)	1½ g	3 g
Allspice	1 g	10 g
Black pepper powder	2 g	5 g
Lime juice	12 ml	30 ml
Orange juice	12 ml	30 ml
Pollock fillets, skinless	4	10
Vegetable oil	12 ml	30 ml

Get ready to cook

1 Chop the chillies and thyme.

2 Dice the onions.

3 Peel and thinly slice the ginger.

Cooking

1 Mix together the chillies, onions, ginger, herbs, spices and juices.

2 Marinade the fish in this mixture for 30 minutes.

3 Brush the fish with oil and grill it. Turn it once. Cook until a core temperature of 75°C is reached.

4 Serve on a suitable plate.

 Note: This recipe has been supplied by Gerard O'Sullivan. It was developed specially for the athletes' village at the London 2012 Olympic Games. The culinary operations team produced a range of nutritious meals inspired by dishes from around the world. The standard recipe was for 24 portions; it has been scaled down for this book.

9

Grilled sardines

Ingredients

Sardines, three or four per portion depending on their size

Flour

Light oil

 Note: Grilling is cooking under radiant heat. It is a fast method suitable for small whole fish or fillets, whole or cut in portions.

Get ready to cook

Prepare, clean, wash and thoroughly dry the fish. Fillet them if required.

Cooking

1 Pass the fish through flour, shake off surplus and place on an oiled baking sheet.
2 Brush the tops with oil and cook carefully under a hot grill, ensuring they do not burn.
3 After 2–3 minutes, remove the tray and turn the sardines with a palette knife. Return to the grill and cook for 2 minutes, until lightly browned.

Serving suggestion

Serve with quarters of lemon (pips removed).

Activity

Name six other fish that could be grilled whole or in fillets.

Recipe 32 — Lamb kebabs

Ingredients	4 portions	10 portions
Lamb, lean meat	600 g	1½ kg
Red pepper	2	5
Onion	1	3
Bay leaves	4	10
Thyme, dried	½ tsp	1 tsp
Vegetable oil	2 tbsp	5 tbsp

Get ready to cook

1 Cut the meat into cubes.

2 Deseed the red pepper and cut into cubes.

3 Peel the onion and cut into cubes.

Note: The ideal cuts of lamb are the nut of the lean meat of the loin or rack.

Kebabs, a dish of Turkish origin, are pieces of food impaled on skewers and cooked on or under a grill or barbecue. They are made using tender cuts of various meats with pieces of vegetables or fruits in between.

Cooking

1 Push the squares of meat on skewers, alternating these with squares of red pepper, onion and a bay leaf.

2 Brush with oil and lightly sprinkle with dried thyme.

3 Cook over or under a grill.

Serving suggestion

Serve with pilaff rice (page 151) and finely sliced raw onion.

Try something different

Different flavours can be added by marinating the kebabs. This involves soaking the meat, before cooking, in a combination of oil, vinegar, lemon juice, spices and herbs, for two hours at room temperature or four hours in the refrigerator.

Activity

Each member of the group should devise their own kebab from a range of ingredients: meat, vegetables, herbs and spices.

The group then cooks, serves, tastes and assesses each version.

Recipe 33 Grilled pork chops

Ingredients

Pork chops

Salt

Oil

Parsley

Get ready to cook

Preparing a chop from a loin:

- Remove the skin, excess fat and sinew.
- Cut, saw or chop through the loin in approximately 1 cm slices.
- Remove any excess bone and neatly trim.

 Note: You can buy chops ready prepared, or you can prepare them from a loin as described above.

Cooking

1 Season the chops lightly with salt.
2 Brush with oil or fat and cook on both sides on or under a moderately hot grill or salamander for approximately 10 minutes, until cooked through.

Serving suggestion

Garnish with a sprig of parsley. Serve with hot apple sauce.

Recipe 34 — Grilled beef steak

Ingredients

Steaks
Salt
Oil

Get ready to cook

Preheat the grill.

Cooking

1 Season steaks lightly with salt and brush both sides with oil.
2 Place on hot, preheated greased grill bars.
3 Turn the steaks over halfway through cooking and brush occasionally with oil.
4 Cook to the degree ordered by the customer (see guidance in Chapter 10, page 231).

Serving suggestion

Serve garnished with a small bunch of well-washed and dried watercress, a deep-fried potato and a suitable sauce, such as a compound butter sauce.

Using a barbecue

Instead of grilling the steaks you could barbecue them. Marinate them using a good oil, seasoning and/or herbs before cooking.

To prepare the barbecue:

● If possible, use gas rather than charcoal as it is easier to control the temperature with gas.
● Secure a layer of tin foil over the barbecue.
● Wait until the grill bars are hot or the charcoal embers glow. (If using charcoal, always wait for the glow before starting to cook. A gas barbecue will take about 30 minutes to pre-heat.)
● Remove the tinfoil and brush the grill bars with a firm, long-handled wire brush to remove any unwanted debris.

▲ Grilled steak video,
http://bit.ly/XVkyZX

Recipe

35

Grilled gammon rashers

Ingredients

Thick-cut gammon rashers

Oil

Get ready to cook

Preheat the grill.

Cooking

1 Brush the rashers on both sides with a little fat or oil.

2 Place the rashers on the preheated grill bars and cook for approximately 5 minutes on each side.

Serving suggestion

Serve accompanied by fried egg(s), grilled open mushrooms and grilled tomatoes. Garnish with a sprig of parsley.

Try something different

- Instead of cooking gammon on grill bars, you can cook them on a tray under a salamander. Lightly grease the tray first.
- Gammon rashers can be cooked by gently frying them in a little oil or fat. Use a thick-bottomed frying pan or a sauté pan.
- Rashers of back or streaky bacon can be cooked on lightly greased trays under a preheated grill. Turn them over when they are half cooked. When they are ready they will be lightly browned and slightly crispy. Do not add any fat: they will make their own while they are cooking.
- Bacon rashers can also be fried in a frying pan with just a little fat or oil to prevent them from sticking.

Recipe 36 Grilled vegetable bake

Ingredients	4 portions	10 portions
Aubergines	250 g	725 g
Courgettes	400 g	1 kg
Red peppers	3	8
Vegetable oil	90 mls	225 mls
Pesto	1 tbsp	2½ tbsp
Garlic cloves	2	5
Breadcrumbs	60 g	150 g
Parsley	1 tbsp	5 tbsp
Basil	1 tbsp	5 tbsp
Cheshire cheese	80 g	200 g

Get ready to cook

1 Peel and crush the garlic.
2 Cut the aubergine and courgettes into 5 mm slices.
3 Deseed the peppers and cut into 1 cm dice.
4 Chop the parsley and basil.
5 Grate the cheese.
6 Preheat the oven to 150–180°C.

 Note: Pesto is a green sauce made from fresh basil leaves, garlic, toasted pine nuts, Parmesan cheese and olive oil. It can be bought ready-made.

Cooking

1 Sprinkle the vegetables with oil, pesto and the crushed and chopped garlic.
2 Lightly grill the vegetables on a griddle pan.
3 Line a suitable shallow dish with half the breadcrumbs and chopped parsley and basil.
4 Arrange in the dish the courgettes and the aubergines overlapping in rows with the peppers.
5 Add the rest of the breadcrumbs to the grated cheese. Sprinkle this mixture over the vegetables.
6 Bake in a moderate oven (150–180°C) for approximately 20 minutes.

Serving suggestion

Serve with a suitable salad, such as mixed leaves with rice noodles seasoned with soy sauce garnished with tomato, chopped onion and avocado.

Recipe 37 — Rice pudding with dried fruit and nuts

Ingredients	4 portions	10 portions
Rice, short grain	50 g	125 g
Caster sugar	50 g	125 g
Milk, whole or skimmed	½ litre	1½ litres
Butter	12 g	30 g
Vanilla essence	2–3 drops	6–8 drops
Nutmeg, grated		
Dried fruit	50 g	125 g
Nuts	50 g	125 g

Cooking

1 Boil the milk in a thick-bottomed pan, stirring occasionally to stop the milk from burning.

2 Add the washed rice and stir to the boil.

3 Simmer gently, stirring frequently until the rice is cooked.

4 Remove from the heat and mix in the sugar, vanilla, butter and dried fruit and nuts.

5 Pour the mixture into a pie dish, lightly grate with nutmeg and brown under a grill (salamander).

 Note: Any mixture of dried or candied fruits, cut into small dice, can be used.
The best nuts for this recipe are lightly toasted sliced almonds.

10 Deep frying and shallow frying

This chapter covers Unit 110, Prepare and cook food by deep frying and shallow frying.

By the end of the chapter you should be able to:

- Describe the process of cooking food items by deep or shallow frying
- Identify the purpose of deep and shallow frying
- Identify the food items which may be deep or shallow fried
- Identify the frying mediums which may be used when deep and shallow frying foods
- State the importance of using associated techniques to achieve the finished dish requirements

- Describe associated products for deep and shallow frying
- State the points requiring consideration when deep and shallow frying
- List the methods used when deep and shallow frying
- Identify suitable equipment to deep and shallow fry food
- List the quality points to look for during selection of food items, preparation, cooking and finishing of dishes.

Deep frying

Process

Deep frying is the process by which small, tender pieces of food are totally immersed in hot fat or oil, and cooked quickly. The heat of the oil penetrates the food and cooks it. Although oils and lards are 'wet', deep frying is classified as a dry method of cookery. This is because it has a drying effect on the food.

Deep fried foods can be cooked quickly and handled easily for service.

▲ Deep frying

Purpose

The purpose of deep frying is to produce food with an appetising golden-brown colour, that is crisp and enjoyable to eat. Deep frying:

- Tenderises and makes food items more digestible
- Ensures food is safe to eat
- Enhances the colour, flavour and texture of the finished dish
- Enhances the presentation of the dish
- Protects items from absorbing the fat it is cooked in by applying a coating (usually milk, egg, crumbs or batter). Applying a coating means a variety of foods can be cooked in this way and prevents the enclosed food from becoming greasy.

Foods which may be deep fried

Fish and chips are probably the most popular kind of deep fried food in the UK. However, many things can be deep fried, including:

- Meat (beef, lamb, pork)
- Poultry (chicken and turkey)
- Vegetables
- Fish
- Fruit
- Flour-based products (sweet and savoury)
- Ready-made products.

Frying mediums: types of oil used

A variety of oils and fats can be used for deep fat frying. Often a mix of vegetable oils is used. There are several varieties of vegetable oil:

- Sunflower
- Corn
- Maize
- Rapeseed
- Olive.

Some establishments deep fry in goose fat, duck fat or beef dripping. This has become popular because of the flavour it adds to the fried food, in particular chips.

Points to consider when deep frying

Health and safety

Hot fat can cause serious burns, either through spills or accidents. Deep frying can be a very dangerous method of cooking, especially if people are not correctly trained. Only trained people should use deep fryers.

Commercial deep fryers have built-in safety features, such as thermostatic controls and fat-level indicators. These safety features make commercial fryers preferable to pots on stoves.

- Never overfill fryers with fat or oil, or with the food to be cooked.
- When deep fat frying it is essential to maintain the fat at the right temperature. The normal frying temperature is between 175°C and 195°C. A slight heat haze will rise from the fat when it reaches this temperature. When using free-standing fryers without a thermometer, never allow the fat to get so hot that smoke rises from it. This will give the food a bad taste and smell.

Health and safety

Monitor the temperature – if it is too high, the fat may easily ignite and cause a fire. Never allow fat to heat up so much that it starts to smoke. Smoke means that the hot oil could burst into flames and is very dangerous.

- Timing is important too. If you are cooking thicker pieces of food, you should lower the temperature. This allows the food to cook thoroughly on the inside without burning on the outside. The reverse is also true – the smaller the pieces of food, the hotter the frying temperature needs to be and the shorter the cooking time.

- Ensure that food to be fried is dry.
- After removing a batch of food, allow the fat/oil to heat up again before adding the next batch. The temperature of the fat/oil must be allowed to recover before the next batch is cooked. If not, the food will look pale and unappetising and will be soggy to eat.
- Ensure that you are using the right amount of fat/oil for the amount of food you are cooking. Too much food in too little fat/oil will reduce the temperature drastically and spoil the food.
- Do not fry the food too far in advance of serving it – fried foods soon lose their crispness.
- Strain oil and fat after use to remove any food particles. If these are left in the fat they will burn when the fat is next heated, spoiling the appearance and flavour of the food.
- Always cover oil or fat when not in use to prevent the air from making it rancid.

Health and safety

Do not move a deep fryer that is either on or still hot. Avoid sudden movements around deep fryers, as they may be bumped or items may be dropped into the hot fat.

Methods

To deep fry:

- Pre-heat the oil or fat
- Coat the food as required (see associated techniques below)
- Once it has reached the required temperature, place the food carefully into the oil or fat.

Health and safety

Always keep a close eye on a deep fryer and never leave it unattended.

Health and safety

Stand back when placing food into the fryer to avoid steam and splash burns. Avoid putting your face, arms or hands over the deep fryer.

- Fry it until it is cooked and golden brown.
- Drain the food well before serving.

Health and safety

Before using a deep fryer, know how to put out a fat fire. Do not try to put out a fat fire with water. Cover the pot or fryer with a lid or fire blanket, and then use the correct fire extinguisher. Fire extinguishing equipment should be kept nearby and staff should be trained how to use it.

Partially cooking food before deep frying is known as **blanching**. The food is partly cooked (by boiling, steaming or frying) in advance of service and then finished by deep frying to order. This works particularly well with certain types of potato, giving chips a floury texture inside and crisp exterior. Preparing in advance and cooking later helps during a busy service and saves time.

Associated techniques

There are a number of techniques associated with deep frying, which help the chef to prepare the dishes correctly:

- **Coating** – covering food items prior to frying to help seal items, protecting the food surface from intense heat of the fat or oil, slowing down the penetration of heat and preventing moisture and nutrients from escaping. Coatings include breadcrumbs, batter and flour.

- **Draining and drying** – items to be fried should be free from excess water; once cooked, fried foods should be drained to ensure any oil/fat drains off the food before service.
- **Immersion** – placing the food item in the fat, with or without a basket. This is dependent upon the dish – normally larger items can be cooked without a basket, whereas small items would be in a basket.
- **Holding for service** – when fried foods are to be held for service they shouldn't be covered as moisture caused would turn the food soggy.

Associated products

- Accompaniments and associated products include the traditional items that would be offered with specific dishes.
- Sauces and garnishes are normally indicated in recipes, and include tartare sauce with fish or deep fried parsley and lemon with other fried dishes.

Shallow frying

Process

Shallow frying is cooking food in a small quantity of pre-heated fat or oil in a shallow pan (a frying pan or a sauté pan) or on a flat surface (a griddle plate). As the food is in direct contact with the fat, it cooks rapidly. The high temperature used in shallow frying seals the surface of the food almost instantly and prevents the natural juices from escaping.

▲ Shallow frying

Purpose

The purpose of shallow frying is to brown food, giving it a different colour and an interesting and attractive flavour. Shallow frying:

- Tenderises and makes food items more digestible
- Ensures food is safe to eat and maintains its nutritional value
- Enhances the colour, flavour and texture of the finished dish
- Enhances the presentation of the finished dish.

▲ Shallow frying video, http://bit.ly/Xt1t1R

Food items which may be shallow fried

- Meat, (beef, lamb, pork)
- Poultry (chicken and turkey)
- Vegetables
- Fish

- Eggs
- Fruit
- Flour-based products (sweet and savoury)
- Ready-made products.

Frying mediums

The same fats and oils are used as in deep frying.

If shallow-fried food needs to be cooked in butter, you should use clarified butter, which has a higher burning point than unclarified butter, so it will not burn as easily. To clarify butter, melt it and then carefully strain off the fat, leaving behind the clear liquid.

Points to consider when shallow frying

- When shallow frying continuously over a busy period, prepare and cook the food in a systematic way.
- Cleaning the pans after every use, even in batch cooking, will ensure the best presentation.
- Food should be dry to ensure that it fries correctly and that oil/fat is not spat out of the pan towards the chef.
- Food items should be placed in the pan presentation side down first so that turning once will help enhance presentation of the finished dish.

Health and safety

Add food to the pan carefully, away from you, to avoid being splashed by hot fat. Always keep your sleeves rolled down to prevent splashing fat from burning your forearm.

Temperature and time control are particularly important as all shallow-fried foods should have an appetising golden-brown colour on both sides. The temperature should initially be hot; the heat should then be reduced and the food turned when necessary.

Methods

There are four methods of shallow frying:

- **To shallow fry** (meunière), cook the food in a small amount of fat or oil in a frying pan or sauté pan. Fry the presentation side of the food first (the side that will be seen when it is on the plate). The side that is fried first will have the better appearance because the fat is clean. Then turn the food to cook and colour the other side.
- **To sauté** (toss or jump) tender cuts of meat and poultry, cook them in a sauté pan or frying pan in the same way as for shallow frying. Once the food is cooked on both sides, remove it from the pan, discard the fat and deglaze the pan with stock or wine. This liquid is then used to make the sauce to go with the food. Food such as potatoes, onions and kidneys can also be sautéed. Cut them into slices or pieces and toss them in hot shallow fat or oil in a frying pan until golden brown and cooked.
- **To griddle** foods such as hamburgers, sausages and sliced onions, place them on a lightly oiled, pre-heated griddle (a solid metal plate). Turn them frequently during cooking. Pancakes can also be cooked this way but should only be turned only once.
- **Stir fry** vegetables, strips of fish, meat and poultry in a wok or frying pan by fast-frying them in a little fat or oil.

Health and safety

Move pans carefully in case they jar and tip fat on to the stove. Use a thick, clean, dry cloth when handling pans.

Associated techniques

There are a number of techniques associated with shallow frying which help the chef to prepare the dishes correctly.

- **Batting out** – cuts of meat are batted out using a meat hammer to give an even thickness and start breaking down the connective tissue to help cooking.
- **Coating** – covering food items prior to frying to help seal items. Breadcrumbs and flour are often used as coatings.
- **Tossing and turning** – items being shallow fried may need to be turned over to colour both sides or tossed. This is done for sauté and stir fries.
- **Browning** – colour changes caused through the cooking process by cooking at the right temperature.
- **Holding for service** – when fried foods are to be held for service they shouldn't be covered as moisture caused would turn the food soggy.

Associated products

Accompaniments and associated products include the traditional items that would be offered with specific dishes. Sauces and garnishes are normally indicated in recipes and may include jus-lié with escalopes of meat or lemon with other fried dishes.

Equipment used for deep and shallow frying

In most kitchens there will be a variety of large or small pieces of equipment used for frying, dependent upon the style of cooking and dishes served. These are fully covered in Chapter 5. Equipment specific to frying includes:

- Deep fryer, thermostatically controlled, friture or pressure fryers.
- Shallow frying pans, sauté pan and bratt pan (for large quantities)
- Specialist fryers or pans, woks, omelette, blinis, tava, griddle plate.

Quality points

To ensure the quality of finished deep- and shallow-fried dishes there are a number of things that a chef can do during the process:

- Select products that are fresh, have the correct appearance and smell and are at the appropriate temperature
- Prepare items correctly: trim, shape and size according to dish requirements as well as the coating used

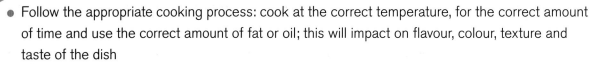

- Follow the appropriate cooking process: cook at the correct temperature, for the correct amount of time and use the correct amount of fat or oil; this will impact on flavour, colour, texture and taste of the dish
- Finish the final dish so that it is consistent, has a good appearance and appropriate portion size. Season and garnish if required and ensure the cleanliness of service equipment

Test yourself

1 Briefly describe the process for the following methods of cooking
   a Deep frying
   b Shallow frying.
2 List three types of coating that could be applied to fish before frying.
3 List five safety points a chef should consider when cooking by deep frying.
4 What are the traditional accompaniments to the following fried dishes:
   a Deep fried cod
   b Pan fried fillet of plaice?
5 List five oils that can be used for frying foods.
6 List three types of food that could be deep fried.
7 Briefly describe the term blanching in relation to deep fried potato dishes.
8 Describe how you would griddle sausages.
9 Why should you use clarified butter when deep frying?
10 List three pieces of equipment you could use when deep or shallow frying.

Deep frying recipes

Recipe 1 ## Dorset crab cake with watercress salad

Ingredients	4 portions	10 portions
Dorset white crab meat	200 g	500 g
Zest and juice of lime	½	1½
Ginger	1 cm	2½ cm
Spring onions	1	3
Small Dorset Naga chilli	½	1½
Coriander leaves	⅛ bunch	½ bunch
Soft white breadcrumbs	200 g	500 g
Eggs	1	3
Flour and beaten eggs, for coating		
Oil, for cooking		
Salt and pepper		
Dorset watercress	1 bunch	2½ bunches

 Note: Regional recipe contributed by Christophe Baffos at the Bournemouth and Poole College.

Get ready to cook

1 Wash all the vegetables and herbs.
2 Peel and finely grate the ginger, finely slice the spring onions, chop the coriander, and brunoise the chilli.
3 Pick the watercress and set aside, ready to be dressed.

Cooking

1 Pick the crab meat and place in a mixing bowl, add the zest of the lime (reserve the juice for the dressing), ginger, spring onion, chilli, coriander, half the breadcrumbs (reserve half for pané) and beaten eggs; mix thoroughly. Season to taste.

2 Divide the mix into eight cakes, flour, egg and breadcrumb them (pané à l'anglaise) and shape using a palette knife.

3 Deep fry at 175°C until golden. Probe the cakes and ensure they reach 75°C (core temperature). Drain on absorbent paper.

4 Serve hot on a bed of watercress dressed with a vinaigrette made from Dorset honey, lime juice, English mustard, salt, pepper and grape seed oil.

Recipe 2 — Fried fish in batter

Ingredients	4 portions	10 portions
White fish fillets	400 g	1½ kg
Light oil in deep fryer		
Lemons, cut into halves or wedges	2	5
Batter		
Flour	200 g	500 g
Salt, a pinch	5 g	12 g
Egg	1	2–3
Water or milk	250 ml	625 ml
Oil	2 tbsps	5 tbsps

 Note: Deep frying is suitable for cuts and fillets of white fish, such as cod and haddock. The fish must be coated with something that prevents the cooking fat or oil from penetrating into the fish. This recipe uses batter.

Get ready to cook

1 Prepare, clean, wash and thoroughly dry the fish.
2 Cut into 100 g portions.

Preparing the batter

1 Sift the flour and salt into a basin.
2 Make a well (a small hollow) in the dried ingredients and pour in the egg and the milk or water.
3 Gradually incorporate (mix in) the flour, using a wooden spoon or whisk.

4 Beat the mixture until it is smooth.
5 Mix in the oil and allow the mixture to rest for ½–1 hour before using.

Cooking

1 Pass the prepared fish through flour (cover it in flour).

2 Shake off any surplus and then pass it through the batter.

3 Taking great care, gently lower the fish, away from you, into deep fat at 175°C.

4 Allow to cook until the fish turns a golden brown.

5 Remove carefully onto kitchen paper and allow to drain well.

Serving suggestion

Serve with either quarters of lemon (pips removed) or tartare sauce. Make the tartare sauce by chopping 25 g capers, 50 g gherkins and a sprig of parsley and adding these to 250 ml of mayonnaise (see page 266).

Try something different

- Add yeast or stiffly beaten egg whites to the batter, along with chopped fresh herbs, grated ginger or garam masala.
- If a yeast batter is used, you must allow time for the yeast to ferment (bubble) and raise (lighten) the batter.
- Instead of batter, the fish could be coated with:
  - milk and flour
  - flour, beaten egg and fresh white breadcrumbs.

Recipe 3   Fish cakes

Ingredients	4 portions	10 portions
Cooked white fish and/or salmon	200 g	500 g
Potato, mashed	200 g	500 g
Eggs, beaten	1	2
Flour	25 g	60 g
Fresh white breadcrumbs	50 g	125 g

Get ready to cook

1 Prepare, clean, wash and thoroughly dry the fish, then poach it.
2 Prepare the mashed potato.
3 Beat the eggs.

Cooking

1 Combine the fish and potatoes. Taste and correct the seasoning.

2 Using a little flour, form the mixture into a long roll on a clean work surface.

3 Divide the mixture into two or four pieces per portion.

4 Mould each piece into a ball.

5 Pass the balls through flour, beaten egg and breadcrumbs.

6 Using a palette knife, flatten each shape firmly. Neaten the shapes and shake off surplus crumbs.

7 Deep fry in hot fat at 185°C for 2–3 minutes until golden brown.

8 Lift out carefully and transfer to kitchen paper to drain.

Serving suggestion

Serve the fish cakes with a suitable sauce, such as tomato or tartare.

Try something different

Bake the fish cakes in a hot oven at 250°C for 10–15 minutes. If oven baked, it is not necessary to pass them through flour, egg and breadcrumbs. They should be shaped and placed on lightly greased baking trays.

Activity

1 In groups, prepare, cook, taste, serve and assess four variations of your choice
2 Prepare one which will cater for someone on a gluten-free diet and list the adjustments you have made to the basic recipe.

Recipe 4

Deep-fried chicken

Ingredients

Chicken pieces of your choice, e.g. boneless cuts, suprêmes.

Flour

Dried spices, e.g. paprika, Chinese five spice

Light batter

Fat in deep fryer

Get ready to cook

1 Prepare the batter.

2 Mix together the flour and dried spices.

3 Heat the fat to 175°C.

Cooking

1 Coat the chicken pieces in (pass them through) the mixture of flour and spices.

2 Then pass them through the batter.

3 Deep fry them at a temperature of 175°C.

Recipe 5

Chicken Kiev

Ingredients	4 portions	10 portions
Chicken suprêmes, skin removed, 150 g	4	10
Butter	100 g	250 g
Flour, lightly seasoned with salt	25 g	65 g
Fresh, white breadcrumbs	100 g	250 g
Eggwash (beaten eggs)		

Get ready to cook

1 Season the flour.

2 Beat the eggs to make the eggwash.

 Note: The butter in a chicken Kiev can be flavoured with garlic and/or herbs.

Cooking

1 Carefully make an incision (cut) in the top of each suprême with a sharp knife.

2 Pipe 25 g of softened butter into each incision. Press down the opening to keep the butter inside.

3 Pané the chicken. This means pass it through the seasoned flour, beaten egg (eggwash) and breadcrumbs. Make sure the chicken is well coated. Pass it through the eggwash and crumbs twice if necessary.

4 Shake off any surplus crumbs. Pat the suprêmes with a palette knife to make the coating as firm as possible. Loose crumbs that come off during frying will burn and spoil the appearance and flavour of the chicken and the oil.

5 Deep fry the suprêmes at a temperature of approximately 175°C–180°C.

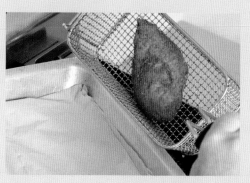

6 Fry until golden brown.

7 Remove carefully and transfer to kitchen paper to drain.

Recipe 6 Chips

Ingredients

Potatoes, scrubbed (1 kg will yield 4 to 6 portions)

Get ready to cook

1 Peel and wash the potatoes.
2 Cut into slices 1 cm thick and 5 cm long.
3 Cut the slices into chips 5 cm × 1 cm × 1 cm.
4 Wash well and dry in a cloth.
5 Preheat the oil in a deep fat fryer to 165°C.

Cooking

1 Place the chips in a frying basket and slowly and carefully immerse in moderately hot (165°C) deep fat.
2 When they are almost completely cooked, drain them and place them on kitchen paper on trays until they are needed.
3 When required, raise the temperature in the fryer to 185°C. Put the required amount of chips in a frying basket and immerse them in the deep fat.
4 Cook until crisp and golden brown.

Serving suggestion

Drain well, lightly season with salt and serve.

Recipe 7

Mushrooms fried with a polenta crust

Ingredients	4 portions	10 portions
Closed cup mushrooms	32	80
Polenta (maize meal)	75 g	187 g
Sesame seeds	3 tbsp	7½ tbsp
Eggs	2	5
Vegetable oil	2 tbsp	5 tbsp
Cream cheese	150 g	375 g
Chives	1 tsp	2½ tsp
Pepper to taste		

Get ready to cook

1 Remove the stalks from the mushrooms.
2 Trim the mushrooms, stalk side up, so that two mushrooms can be pressed together.
3 Chop the chives.

Cooking

1 Season the cream cheese with chives and black pepper.
2 Sandwich two mushrooms together with the cream cheese filling and make sure they fit snugly together.
3 Add the sesame seeds to some polenta. Pass the mushrooms through beaten egg and the polenta and sesame seed mixture.
4 Chill well.
5 Deep fry the mushrooms in hot oil until golden brown all over.
6 When cooked, drain in absorbent paper.

Serving suggestion

Serve hot with a tomato sauce.

Try something different

- You could add a little chopped chilli or paprika to the cream cheese.
- You can shallow fry the mushrooms instead of deep frying them.

Shallow frying recipes

Recipe 8 — Canal floddies

Ingredients	4 portions	10 portions
Floddies:		
Potatoes (preferably heritage potatoes from Northumberland)	350 g	875 g
Onion, medium	1	2
Sundried tomatoes	10	25
Self-raising flour	25 g	65 g
Eggs, medium free-range	1	3
Salt and pepper		
Vegetable oil	2 tbsp	5 tbsp
To serve:		
Mushy peas		
Eggs, poached	4	10

 Note: Regional recipe contributed by David Jackson, Curriculum Operations Manager, Service Industries/Catering at Gateshead College.

This is a slightly updated version of a dish from the Tyneside town of Gateshead. Traditionally these were made by the men digging the Manchester Ship Canal and fried on their shovels over a fire.

The addition of sundried tomatoes, instead of bacon, gives this dish a sweet (and modern) twist.

Get ready to cook

1 Finely chop the sun-dried tomatoes.
2 Peel the onions and potatoes.
3 Beat the eggs for the floddy mixture.

Cooking

1 Coarsely grate the potato and squeeze out any liquid and press between kitchen paper.
2 Grate the onion and mix with the potato and sun dried tomatoes.
3 Place the self-raising flour in a mixing bowl and add the beaten egg. Mix well.
4 Add the potato mixture to the flour and egg, season mix well.
5 Divide the mixture into four (one per portion) and shape into rounds.
6 Heat the oil in a frying pan and when hot add the floddies. Reduce heat a little and fry, turning until well-browned on both sides and cooked through.
7 Drain on kitchen paper.
8 Place each floddy on a plate and top with a portion of hot mushy peas and a lightly poached egg.

Recipe 9 — Pancakes with lemon

Ingredients	4 portions	10 portions
Flour	100 g	250 g
Salt	Small pinch	Pinch
Milk	¼ litre	625 ml
Egg	1	2–3
Butter, melted or a light oil	10 g	25 g
Light oil for frying		
Sugar, caster	50 g	125 g
Lemon	1	2

Note: When making a batch of pancakes, keep them flat. Pile them onto a warm plate, sprinkling a little sugar in between each. Fold them when ready for service. Lightly sprinkle them again with sugar and dress nearly overlapping on service plates.

Cooking

1 Sieve the flour and salt into a basin.
2 Make a well and add the milk and egg, gradually incorporating the flour from the side of the bowl.
3 Beat vigorously with a wooden spoon or whisk to a smooth batter. This should be thick enough to just coat the back of a spoon.
4 Mix in the melted fat.
5 Heat the pancake pan and clean it thoroughly.
6 Add sufficient oil just to thinly coat the pan. Heat this until it begins to smoke.
7 Add just enough mixture to thinly coat the pan.
8 Cook for a few seconds until brown.
9 Turn over and cook the second side for half the time.
10 Turn onto a warm plate, sprinkle with sugar, fold in half then fold again.

Serving suggestion

Serve two pancakes per portion with a quarter of lemon (remove the pips).

Try something different

If a thicker pancake is required, add another 20–60 g flour to the recipe.
   Use orange segments in place of lemon.
   Spread the pancakes lightly with warmed jam and roll them up.

| Recipe **10** | Scrambled eggs |

Ingredients	4 portions	10 portions
Eggs (medium or large)	6–8	15–20
Milk (optional)	2 tbsp	5 tbsp
Salt – use sparingly		
Butter, margarine or oil	50 g	125 g

Cooking

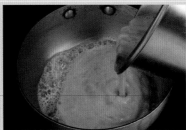
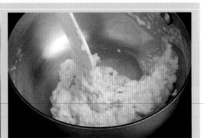

1 Break the eggs into a basin, lightly season with salt and thoroughly mix using a whisk.

2 In a thick-bottomed pan, melt half of the fat.

3 Add the eggs and start to cook over a gently heat, stirring.

4 Stir continuously with a wooden spoon until the eggs are lightly cooked.

5 Remove from the heat, taste and correct the seasoning.

6 Mix in the remaining fat.

Note: The reason for removing the eggs when they are only lightly cooked is because after the pan is removed from the stove it will still be hot and the eggs will continue cooking. Cooking scrambled eggs is a delicate task and they can easily be overcooked and spoiled.

Serving suggestion

Serve on slices of hot buttered toast or in individual egg dishes.

Activity

As a group, try the following:
- Cook two scrambled eggs following the recipe.
- Cook two scrambled eggs as quickly as possible.
- Cook two scrambled eggs using butter.
- Cook two scrambled eggs using margarine or oil.

Taste, compare and discuss the four versions.

Fried eggs

Ingredients

Eggs – allow one or two eggs per portion

Butter, margarine or oil – 25 g per egg

 Note: Only fresh, top-quality eggs should be used for frying. For the best flavour use butter or sunflower oil.

Cooking

1 Break the eggs into bowls.
2 Melt the butter, margarine or oil in a small non-stick frying pan.

3 Add the eggs carefully and gently to the pan, without breaking the yolks.
4 Cook slowly over a moderate heat and serve on a warmed plate.

Activity

As a group, try the following:

- Fry one egg following the recipe.
- Fry one egg using butter.
- Fry one egg using oil.
- Fry one egg using margarine.

Taste, compare and discuss the four versions.

Recipe 12 — Omelette

Ingredients

Eggs per portion 2–3

Small pinch of salt

Butter, margarine or oil

Cooking

1 Break the eggs into a basin and season lightly with salt.

2 Mix thoroughly with a fork or whisk until whites and yolks are thoroughly combined and no streaks of white can be seen.

3 Heat a non-stick omelette pan and wipe thoroughly clean with a dry cloth.

4 Add the butter, then turn up the heat to maximum until the butter is foaming but not brown.

5 Add the eggs and cook quickly, stirring continuously with a fork until lightly set. Remove from the heat.

6 Using the fork, carefully fold the mixture in half at a right angle to the handle of the pan.

7 Pointing the pan slightly downwards, sharply tap the pan handle with the other hand to bring the edge of the omelette up to the bottom of the pan.

8 Carefully using the fork, bring up the opposite edge of the omelette as near to the first edge as possible.

9 Take a warm plate in one hand and, holding the pan under the handle, carefully tip the folded omelette onto the plate.

10 Neaten the shape if necessary, using a clean teacloth, and serve immediately.

Try something different

There are many variations that can be made by adding other ingredients to the mixed eggs before cooking, such as:

● Chopped soft herbs – parsley, chives, chervil

● Mushrooms – sliced and cooked in butter

● Grated cheese can be added to the omelette before it is folded.

Activity

Practice is the only way to make good omelettes.

Suggest three variations. Prepare all three and taste, discuss and assess them.

Recipe 13 Shallow fried fish

Ingredients	4 portions	10 portions
White fish fillets or small whole fish	400 g	1½ kg
Flour		
Light oil	1 tbsp	2½ tbsp

Get ready to cook

Prepare, clean, wash and thoroughly dry the fish.

Cooking

1 Completely cover the fish with flour and shake off all surplus. (If you are using a non-stick pan, it is not essential to flour the fish.)

2 Heat the frying medium (usually a light oil) in the frying pan.

3 Shallow fry on the presentation side first.

7 Carefully turn and fry the other side.

Serving suggestion

When cooked and placed on the serving plates or dishes, add:

- A slice of lemon (remove the yellow and white pith and any pips first)
- A sprinkling of lemon juice.

Try something different

 Note: Do not overcrowd the pan because this will cause the temperature of the oil to drop and will affect the way the fish cooks. The fish should not be overcooked but should have an appetising light golden-brown colour.

Once the fish is cooked, carefully heat 10–25 g butter per portion in a frying pan until it turns a nutty brown colour. Pour this over the plated-up fish, sprinkle with chopped parsley and serve.

Recipe 14 Shallow-fried lamb cutlets and chops

Ingredients

Lamb cutlets or chops

Salt

Light oil or fat

Note: Both cutlets and chops are equally suitable to cook in this way.

Cooking

1 Place a thick-bottomed frying pan or a sauté pan on a hot stove.
2 Add a little light oil or fat to the pan.
3 Season the meat lightly with salt.
4 When the fat is hot, carefully place the meat in the pan. Put the edge of the meat closest to you in first and lay it away from you. This way, if any hot fat splashes it will splash away from you rather than onto you.
5 Cook on a high heat until lightly browned, then turn over and repeat.
6 Lower the heat by a half and cook for approximately 4–5 minutes in total (depending on the thickness of the meat).

Serving suggestion

Serve as for lamb cutlets or offer a suitable potato and vegetable, such as sauté potatoes (with or without onions) and leaf spinach with toasted pine nuts.

Activity

Fry a dish of cutlets or chops and serve with your idea of a suitable garnish or a potato, vegetable and/or salad. Taste, assess and discuss.

Recipe 15 Pan-fried steak

Ingredients	4 portions	10 portions
Butter or oil	50 g	125 g
Sirloin steaks (approx. 150–200 g each)	4	10
Salt and pepper		

Rare, medium or well done?

Customers may request their steak to be cooked to different degrees:

- **Very rare (or blue)** – cooked over a fierce heat for only a few seconds each side to give a good brown colour
- **Rare** – the cooked meat has a reddish tinge
- **Medium** – the cooked meat is slightly pinkish
- **Well done** – thoroughly cooked with no sign of pinkness.

Use finger pressure and the springiness of the meat, together with the amount of blood that comes from it, to check how well it is cooked: the more underdone the steak, the more springy it is and the more blood will appear on the plate.

You can also test with a temperature probe. Insert the probe into the thickest part of the meat. The internal reading should be:

- Rare 45–50°C
- Medium 55–60°C
- Well done 75–77°C.

> **Get ready to cook**
>
> Lightly season the steaks on both sides with salt and pepper.

> **Note**: This method is perfect for small to medium-sized cuts.

Cooking

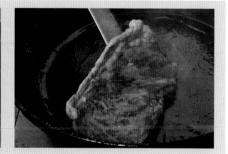

1. Heat the butter or oil in a sauté pan.
2. Fry the steaks quickly on the first side, keeping them underdone.
3. Turn the steaks over carefully.
4. Fry the other side, still keeping them underdone.
5. Dress the steaks on a serving dish.

Serving suggestion

Serve the steaks with mushrooms and tomatoes.

Recipe 16 — Egg and crumbed pork escalopes

Ingredients	4 portions	10 portions
Pork fillet or nut from the loin, 75–100 g	4	10
Flour, seasoned	25 g	60 g
Egg	1	2
Fresh white breadcrumbs	50 g	125 g
Oil for frying	60 ml	150 ml

Get ready to cook

1 Trim and remove any sinew from the meat.
2 Using a little water, bat out with a meat hammer as thinly as possible to ½ cm at least.
3 Beat the eggs to make eggwash.

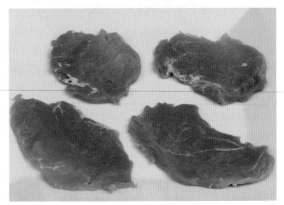

▲ Escalopes that have been batted out

Cooking

1 Each escalope needs to go through the pané process. First, pass the escalope through seasoned flour.

2 Ensure that both sides are coated in the flour.

3 Pass the escalope through the eggwash.

4 Allow the eggwash to drain off.

5 Pass the escalope through the breadcrumbs.

6 Shake off any surplus crumbs and pat each side firmly with a palette knife.

7 Shallow fry in hot fat or oil on both sides until they are golden brown and crisp.

8 Drain on kitchen paper.

Serving suggestion

Serve with a suitable sauce, for example:

- Thickened gravy (page 113) with some thinly sliced small gherkins added
- An apple purée thinned down with cream or yoghurt.

Recipe 17 — Stir fried pork fillet

Ingredients	4 portions	10 portions
Oil	2 tbsp	5 tbsp
Shallots	2	6
Garlic (optional)	1	2
Button mushrooms	200 g	400 g
Pork fillet	400 g	2 kg
Chinese five spice powder	1 pinch	2 pinches
Soy sauce	1 tbsp	2 tbsp
Honey, clear	2 tbsp	3 tbsp
White stock	2 tbsp	5 tbsp

Get ready to cook

1 Peel and finely chop the shallots.
2 Finely slice the mushrooms.
3 Cut the pork into thin strips or slices.

Cooking

1 Heat the oil in a wok or frying pan.
2 Add the shallots and sweat gently for 1 minute.
3 Add the mushrooms and cook gently until softened.

4 Increase the heat and add the pork fillet strips or slices.
5 Season lightly with salt, add the spice powder and cook for 3–4 minutes, tossing continuously.
6 Reduce the heat, add the soy sauce, honey, white stock and reduce for 2–3 minutes.
7 Taste, correct seasoning and serve.

Serving suggestion

Serve with noodles, braised rice (page 151) or stir-fried vegetables, or a combination of these.

Recipe
18

Sauté of chicken

Ingredients	4 portions	10 portions
Chicken, whole (1¼–1½ kg)	1	2½
Butter, margarine or oil	50 g	125 g
Thickened gravy	250 ml	625 ml
Parsley, fresh		

 Note: If using a whole chicken, chop up the carcass and save any trimmings to use when you are making the gravy.

If using ready cut chicken, for four portions, use two drumsticks, two thighs and two suprêmes (breasts cut in half).

 Get ready to cook

1 If you are using a whole chicken (or chickens), cut this into pieces.
2 Prepare the thickened gravy (see page 113).
3 Chop the parsley.

Cooking

1 Place the fat or oil in a sauté pan over a hot stove.
2 Season the chicken pieces lightly with salt. Place them in the pan in the following order: drumsticks, thighs, breasts (you put in the tougher pieces first as they take longer to cook).
3 Cook to a golden brown on both sides. Cover with a lid.
4 Reduce the heat and cook gently until the chicken is tender.
5 Remove the chicken pieces and drain off the fat from the sauté pan.
6 Return the pan to a moderate heat. Add the thickened gravy and bring it to the boil.
7 Taste the gravy and correct the seasoning. Pass it through a fine strainer onto the chicken.
8 Lightly sprinkle with chopped parsley and serve.

Try something different

You can make lots of variations to this basic recipe, such as adding:

- Sliced mushrooms
- Tomato concassé or tomato purée halfway through the cooking time
- Freshly chopped soft herbs, such as chives, chervil, tarragon
- Light spices, such as curry powder, five spice powder.

Activity

In groups, prepare a selection of variations of chicken sauté. Use your own ideas. Taste each other's dishes and discuss.

Recipe 19

Turkey fajita

Ingredients	4 portions	10 portions
Oil for frying	50 ml	125 ml
Onions	100 g	250 g
Garlic cloves	2	5
Turkey, diced	450 g	1⅛ kg
Green peppers	100 g	250 g
Red peppers	100 g	250 g
Cajun seasoning	½ tsp	1½ tsp
Plum tomatoes (canned)	500 g	1¼ kg
Black pepper		
Flour tortillas	4	10

Get ready to cook

1 Cut the turkey into 2 cm dice.
2 Peel and chop the garlic and shred the onion.
3 Wash the peppers and dice finely.
4 Chop the tomatoes.

Cooking

1 Heat the oil in a suitable pan. Add the onions and garlic and cook for 2 minutes.
2 Add the diced turkey, Cajun seasoning and diced peppers and fry for another 5 minutes.
3 Add the chopped tomatoes and black pepper.
4 Cook until the turkey is tender and thoroughly cooked.
5 Lay the tortillas out flat. Spoon a portion of the mixture in the centre and roll up.

Serving suggestion

Serve on a suitable plate garnished with flat parsley.

Recipe 20 Fried mixed vegetables with coconut milk

Ingredients	4 portions	10 portions
French beans	100 g	250 g
Cauliflower	75 g	185 g
Tomatoes	50 g	125 g
Carrots	50 g	125 g
Shallots	3	8
Garlic cloves	2	5
Vegetable oil	2 tbsp	5 tbsp
Mustard seeds	½ tsp	1 tsp
Curry leaves	6	10
Salt	½ tsp	1 tsp
Coconut milk	125 ml	310 ml
Chilli powder diluted with 1 tsp water	½ tsp	1 tsp
Turmeric powder diluted with 1 tsp water	¼ tsp	¾ tsp

Get ready to cook

1 Cut the French beans into 4 cm lengths.
2 Cut the cauliflower into florets.
3 Deseed and coarsely chop the tomatoes.
4 Julienne the carrots.
5 Slice the shallots lengthwise.
6 Chop the garlic.

Cooking

1 Heat the oil in a wok and fry the mustard seeds and curry leaves for 1–2 minutes. Keep stirring until the seeds pop.
2 Add shallots and garlic and fry till soft and fragrant.
3 Stir in the chilli and turmeric paste and add the tomatoes. Fry till heated through.
4 Add the coconut milk and bring to a boil. Stir in all the vegetables.
5 Cook for 4–5 minutes until the vegetables are cooked but still crisp. Season lightly with salt and simmer for another 1–2 minutes. Serve immediately.

Recipe 21 — Sauté potatoes

Ingredients

Potatoes (1 kg of old potatoes will yield 4 to 6 portions)

Oil for sautéing

Salt, pinch

Get ready to cook

Scrub the potatoes well (do not peel).

Cooking

1 Plain boil or steam the potatoes for approximately 15 minutes.
2 Cool them slightly and then peel them.
3 Cut them into 3 mm slices.
4 Toss the slices in hot shallow oil in a frying pan until nicely browned.
5 Season *lightly* with salt.

Serving suggestion

Serve sprinkled with freshly chopped parsley.

11 Regeneration of pre-prepared food

This chapter covers Unit 111, Regeneration of pre-prepared food.

By the end of this chapter you should be able to:

- List the types of regenerated foods and the foods of suitable quality for regeneration
- Describe the differences between regenerated pre-prepared foods and other food types
- Explain the purpose of regenerated pre-prepared foods in the food industry
- State the possible limitations with the use of pre-prepared foods
- Explain the potential healthy eating implications and nutritional value and content of consuming excessive amounts of regenerated pre-prepared foods

- State the correct methods for regenerating different pre-prepared foods
- Identify the purpose of regenerating pre-prepared foods
- Identify the different food types that can be regenerated
- State the suitable tools and equipment and their use when regenerating food
- List quality points relevant to selection, preparation and regeneration of pre-prepared foods
- Explain the use of any associated products used when regenerating pre-prepared foods.

Types of pre-prepared foods that can be regenerated

Pre-prepared food describes any food that has been prepared before it is needed and then held in a way to keep it safe and in best condition until it is regenerated and served. Regenerated food is pre-prepared food that has been treated in such a way that makes it safe and ready to eat. A wide range of products and meals are regenerated.

Dried (dehydrated) food

These foods have a long shelf life because the moisture that could have caused deterioration and spoilage has been removed. They are available in three basic types:

- Foods that have part or all of the moisture dried out of them. Such foods include sundried tomatoes, dried fruits, beans and peas and dried mushrooms.
- Foods that have been processed to remove their natural moisture and produce a powder-like product, for example, dried milk, stock and sauce mixes.
- A mixture of already dry ingredients to form a 'convenience mix', like scone mix, pastry mix or sponge mix.

The regeneration of dried foods will vary according to type. Dried beans are often soaked in water to re-absorb the moisture content that was taken from them. Others such as cake mixes will need the addition of a liquid ingredient such as milk, eggs or water to make them ready to use. However, some dried ingredients are used in their dry state, for example dried fruit.

▲ Dried foods

Fresh foods

An example of these would be pre-prepared and washed salad items and vegetables that have been blanched then cooled ready for finishing. Vegetables may be bought that are already peeled, trimmed and even presented in traditional cuts, such as turned potatoes. This saves considerable amounts of labour and time, though there will be an increase in the actual cost of the product. Fresh meat, fish or poultry may be bought that has already been trimmed and prepared in various ways and is ready to cook.

▲ MAP packaging

Ready-made products

Some products are simply bought 'ready-made'. These are widely used and include such items as bread, cakes, desserts, pies and other items that may be time consuming to make and would need specific equipment and skills to produce. Generally, these products would need no further processing other than perhaps heating, portioning or finishing.

 Health and safety

Ready made products such as pies, quiches, sausage rolls and desserts are food safety 'high risk' items and great care must be taken not to contaminate them with bacteria as this could cause food poisoning. For more information on food poisoning see Chapter 2.

Professional tip

Part-baked products allow for 'fresh' bread, rolls, Danish pastries and so on to be served in premises where there may not be the space, time, equipment or skills to make these items. Products can also be baked frequently and in small quantities, so hot fresh bread or pastries are available all day.

Frozen foods

The amount and choice of frozen foods available to the chef is huge and includes raw foods, ready-to-cook products, cooked items and complex desserts.

Purchased frozen items will carry full instructions about the regeneration of each particular item on the packaging. It is important to read and follow these instructions carefully. For some items such as joints of meat or a chicken, it is essential that they are fully defrosted before cooking. Not defrosting these items properly could mean they do not get hot enough when cooking and could be a possible cause of food poisoning. See Chapter 2 for more information on food poisoning. Small or thin food items like breaded fish or pizza can usually be cooked directly from frozen and this often gives the best, finished result.

There are also products that simply need defrosting before serving, like gateaux, mousses and flans; others are intended to be served frozen, such as fruit parfait or ice cream cake. Be sure to follow instructions and ask for advice from a supervisor.

Chefs may also use freezing as a way to preserve foods for later use. This could be used for raw foods such as meat and poultry, cooked items such as soups and stews or for items needing further finishing such as a beef pie with an uncooked pastry top. When freezing cooked foods, cool them as quickly as possible – a blast chiller is best for this. For all foods, wrap or package them well and label with the name of the item and when it was frozen. Place into a freezer running at −18°C or lower and keep raw and cooked foods apart. Careful defrosting will apply as above.

Health and safety

Cooked foods intended for chilling then freezing should be cooled to 8°C within 90 minutes.

Pre-prepared foods

An example of pre-prepared food would be meals made for airlines that are then re-heated on board the plane. There are many more examples, such as chains of restaurants where food is produced at a central unit and then re-heated or finished and served in the individual outlets.

This is an efficient method of food production and means that any specialist equipment and staff skills needed can all be in one place, with just finishing or re-heating equipment at the point of service.

Not all foods are suitable for pre-preparation. Items such as stews and foods served in a sauce tend to work best. Fried or grilled items and some fish and egg dishes are less successful. The food may be cooked then packaged in individual portions, or in larger units for portioning at the service point.

Health and safety

Very careful food safety procedures must be in place for cooling, storing and reheating pre-prepared foods. Follow any written instructions on packaging carefully or ask for advice from your supervisor.

Canned foods

Most canned food will not need further cooking as cooking is part of the canning process, but reheating will obviously be necessary with items such as soups and baked beans. Further cooking will be carried out where canned food is used as part of another dish or as an ingredient, for example tomatoes as part of a sauce or fruit used as a filling for a pie. Some canned foods are surrounded in the can by a liquid. The table below shows some example of liquids that are used in canned foods.

Table 11.1 Liquids used in canned foods

Liquid	Example of food type
Water	Vegetables
Brine	Ham or fish
Syrup or juice	Fruit
Oil	Fish
Sauce (sauce may be part of the item)	Baked beans, pilchards, sardines, stews

▲ Canned foods (the vegetable oil is purchased in a can but
was not processed in the can)

Professional tip

In some countries bottling is more popular than canning. The same process is used but glass jars are used
instead of cans. Some modern processes also use foil pouches instead of cans.

Pre-prepared, regenerated foods and quality

There are a number of factors that may have an impact on the quality of pre-prepared regenerated
foods.

- **Freshness** – food must be fresh, of good quality and in top condition before it is processed or
  the finished product will be inferior and possibly unacceptable.
- **Quantity** – foods may be pre-prepared in large quantities and packaged in individual portion
  sizes, multi-portion sizes or bulk catering packs.
- **Date codes** – these will vary according to the type of food. Perishable foods that need
  refrigerated storage will carry a use-by date and this must be followed by law. Foods that
  do not need refrigerated storage or are frozen will carry a best before date and it is highly
  recommended that foods are not used after this date.
- **Temperature** – always store pre-prepared foods at the recommended temperature and in the
  right environment or they will deteriorate more quickly than the best before or use-by dates
  indicate.
- **Appearance, smell and texture** – these may become changed in some pre-prepared
  foods. For example, the appearance and texture of canned salmon is very different from
  that of fresh salmon. The smell may be different too because of the canning process and
  the liquid surrounding the salmon. Dried peas may be regenerated by soaking in water then
  boiling, but these will be very different from fresh peas. With some frozen foods there are
  changes too. In delicate foods such as strawberries the structure is affected by freezing and
  the colour, appearance, texture, smell and taste will also change. With some frozen foods
  significant amounts of water run off as they defrost; this will also affect the appearance and
  texture.

▲ Canned salmon and fresh salmon

Differences between pre-prepared, regenerated food and other food types

There will be some differences between pre-prepared, regenerated foods and foods that are fresh as a result of the food going through the regeneration process. Nutritional value may be changed, as may the overall quality, appearance and taste.

Standard cooking methods and service requirements may be adapted to allow for the pre-preparation and regeneration processes, which may take place at very different times and locations. Equipment and staff skills may be selected to match the pre-preparation and the regeneration being carried out. In some cases food is completely pre-cooked and regeneration only involves portioning, heating and serving, so staff may not need to be as skilled and less equipment may be needed than for fresh foods.

Activity

1 What type of date codes would be on the following foods:
   a Fresh soup in a carton
   b Canned tuna
   c Fresh coleslaw
   d Scone mix
   e Canned baked beans
   f Chilled smoked salmon
   g Raisins?
2 List five dried foods that would be used in their dry state and not re-hydrated with water.
3 What would be the advantage of a student café area using part-baked dough products?
4 Suggest four foods where the appearance, texture or flavour is changed by processing.
5 List four food items that could be cooked directly from frozen.

The purpose of using regenerated, pre-prepared foods

Costs

Using pre-prepared and regenerated foods often reduces costs in a food operation or business because:

- Food items can be bought in bulk and when they are in season, so at their cheapest, and then preserved to use as required
- Food waste can be reduced to a minimum because only the actual amounts needed are regenerated
- Food may be regenerated and finished by semi-skilled or unskilled staff who would be cheaper to employ than trained chefs
- Regeneration of food is usually faster than whole cooking processes, so saves on the cost of long staff hours and the length of time premises need to be open
- Fewer items of expensive equipment will be needed because preparation and cooking may all be done in a central place, with specific finishing equipment where the food is regenerated.

Labour and equipment

Staff skills and equipment can be placed at a central point where the food is being pre-prepared. This reduces the costs associated with labour and equipment. Foods can often be regenerated by semi-skilled or unskilled staff.

Ensuring a consistent standard

Food served will tend to be of the same quality because it can be produced in the same place, to standard techniques and processes. This would be important in restaurant chains, for example, where the food needs to be the same in all branches.

Meeting consumer trends, demands and lifestyles

Pre-prepared foods help to meet customer demands and food trends and ensure a consistent supply of popular items all of the time. Seasonal foods can be preserved or pre-prepared when they are most plentiful and cheapest then they will be available all year round. An example of this is frozen peas.

Modern lifestyles and eating patterns often demand food to be available quickly. Pre-prepared, regenerated food allows this to happen, while maintaining a consistent standard in both hospitality outlets and for consumers at home.

Possible limitations of using regenerated, pre-prepared food

Pre-preparing then regenerating food is very successful in some cases and has had a big impact on food industries and hospitality as well as consumer markets. However, it would be unrealistic to expect that all pre-prepared products would be as good as the fresh equivalent and many foods do not return to their original state when they are regenerated.

- **Soft fruits** such as strawberries and raspberries do not withstand freezing, canning or drying well. Pre-frozen plums or strawberries might be used in a crumble or compote, but after freezing you would not serve the strawberries as traditional strawberries and cream.
- **Other fruits and vegetables** change significantly too. For example, carrots can be frozen or canned but will lose texture and be softer. Apricots can be dried but will never return to being like a fresh apricot when re-hydrated.
- **Fish** changes in texture and becomes softer and wetter.
- **Eggs, cooked rice** and many other foods will undergo a change.
- Some foods are not suitable for anything other than packaging and chilling, for example **salad leaves**.

With this in mind the types of food used for pre-preparation and regeneration are chosen carefully and the amounts of certain ingredients, how they are cooked and finished may need to be adapted without greatly increasing the cost of the finished product.

The initial cost and maintenance costs of the equipment needed for pre-preparing and regenerating food must also be considered. There can be additional costs involved in the actual production of pre-prepared food and this will depend on the processes used. Foods, cooking methods and finishing methods may need to be tested, adapted or completely changed to allow for storage and regeneration of certain foods. This can all add to the cost of producing the dish. Other costs may include suitable premises, skilled staff, specialist equipment such as blast chillers and large freezers, sealing and packaging equipment and temperature-controlled storage areas.

Before investing in the additional cost it is important to understand the market (who will be buying the food), types of hospitality outlets and the kinds of food they want for their business, as well as consumer demands for certain types and styles of food and the price they are prepared to pay for it.

Professional tip

Example of how a dish may be adapted when being pre-prepared and re-generated:

A vegetable dish that is going to be chilled may be left slightly undercooked to allow for the vegetables cooking a little more when they are reheated. The usual topping or garnish may need to be changed or added after regeneration.

Healthy eating implications and nutritional value and content of regenerated, pre-prepared foods

Pre-prepared meals have sometimes been criticised for containing larger than recommended amounts of **fat, sugar and salt**. Current health advice is to reduce intake of all of these as concerns about obesity, and heart disease grow. Because of high fat and sugar content some of these foods may also have a high calorific content too.

Some processes may also reduce the nutritional value of food – the **vitamins and minerals** that are naturally present in the food may be lost in the process or water-soluble vitamins could be lost in water surrounding food or coming from foods in defrosting. However, this does not apply to all pre-prepared foods. Some frozen vegetables such as peas and beans will actually retain more of their vitamin content than the fresh equivalent because they are frozen and packaged very quickly after harvest. The quality of some foods is changed very little by their processing, for example dried pasta and rice.

Measures have been taken by food companies to produce healthier foods with clear, easy to understand **nutritional information** on the packaging. Check the packaging for information on nutrients and allergy advice, and keep packaging so you can refer to the ingredients list if a customer has an allergy.

Because the processing of certain foods may change their composition and texture, **additives** are sometimes used to enhance the food and bring it closer to the non-processed product. **Preservatives** may also be used to extend the life of the product and prevent deterioration. Certain foods and drinks may have something added to them that is considered beneficial to health, for example, extra protein, vitamins or minerals. These are called **enhancers**.

However, there have been recent moves to reduce the number of additives and preservatives in food, partly due to public and government pressure on food processing industries. The main concerns have been about the possible short- and long-term effects that food additives may have on health and wellbeing. There are particular concerns about food additives and the effects they may have on young children who consume them.

Generally the advice is to use pre-prepared foods sensibly as part of a good balanced diet, alongside fresh foods.

With pre-prepared meals it may be more difficult for the consumer to 'measure' the types of food they are eating. The '5 a day' portions of fruit and vegetables and the advice to eat more wholegrain foods to promote good health is generally understood, but it is difficult to know just how much is in a pre-prepared meal, though information is available on packaged foods. Also, the balance of nutrients may be difficult to monitor. For example, if someone chooses a portion of grilled white fish it will be high in protein with very little fat and no carbohydrate. If they choose breadcrumbed, deep fried goujons of white fish the dish is likely to be high in fat and carbohydrate.

For more information on nutrients see Chapter 4.

KEY WORDS

Canning – suitable food is placed in the can, sealed and heated under pressure to very high temperatures to kill any micro-organisms that may be present in the food. The cans are then cooled and labelled.

Adapted – change made so it is more suitable.

Calorific content – the number of calories in a particular item.

Additive – something added to food to improve or preserve it.

Preservative – something added to make food last longer.

Enhancer – something added to food that is considered to be beneficial to health, for example extra protein, vitamins or minerals.

Deterioration – losing quality and breaking down.

Activity ···

1 Suggest three ways that the nutritional value of food could be changed by preserving and regenerating it.
2 What is a food additive and what are the reasons for putting these into food?
3 List three foods that may look and taste different after they have been processed to make them last longer.
4 List three nutrients/items considered bad for health that some processed foods may have too much of.

Regenerating pre-prepared foods

Purpose

Pre-prepared foods are used for their convenience, efficiency, ease of use and sometimes as a cost-saving measure. They need to be regenerated to make them edible and bring them to a similar state as freshly cooked products.

It is important that these foods are regenerated correctly to retain or enhance flavours and to ensure the best quality and appearance. Follow instructions on the product or given to you by a supervisor or chef with care. This will make sure that the procedure is completed safely, to the required food safety standards and that the quality of food remains consistent.

Methods

How the regeneration is done depends on the type of food and how it has been processed. Sometimes pre-prepared foods may be mixed or used with a wide variety of other ingredients in the regeneration and finishing process. For example, fresh vegetables could be added to or served with a pre-prepared meat dish, cheese could top a pasta dish and sauces could be added and a variety of garnishes used.

There are four methods of regenerating pre-prepared foods:

● **Re-heating** – bringing food to the required temperature for serving and to make it safe to eat. This must be done carefully and according to instructions to ensure the best quality. Food must be reheated to 75°C+ right in the centre and held at this temperature for at least 2 minutes (in Scotland the regulations state 82°C for reheating). Re-heating should be done quickly to prevent bacteria multiplying and spores forming. (For more information on reheating food see Chapter 2.)
● **Rehydrating** – replacing the water taken from dried food when it was in its natural state. For example, rice is dried which means it can be stored for a long time without it deteriorating and without refrigeration. To make it suitable for eating the moisture must be put back by a process such as boiling. The rice is re-hydrated and cooked at the same time.
● **Cooking** – taking food from its raw state to cooked by one or more of the cooking methods available to make it safe to eat and taste better. Cooking can also tenderise food where necessary and to add flavours, colour and textures.

- **Defrosting (thawing)** – taking food that has been frozen to the required temperature for eating, cooking or re-heating. This is best done in a special defrosting cabinet or for meat, fish and poultry at the bottom of a fridge in a deep tray and covered with cling film. Other items such as cooked pies and cakes could be defrosted at the higher levels in the fridge but must be covered and kept well away from raw items.

Table 11.2 How to regenerate foods

Fresh foods – prepared or packaged ready for use	
Foods	**How to regenerate the food**
Salads Cooked meat and fish Fruit items Pre-prepared raw foods	Follow instructions on the packaging Many of these items are 'ready to eat', so handle carefully and protect from contamination. Cook as appropriate.

Dried (dehydrated) foods	
Moisture has been removed so that they will keep for longer. The foods need to be rehydrated.	
Foods	**How to regenerate the food**
Dried fruit	Usually eaten in the dried form. Soak before use if the recipe tells you to.
Rice Dried pasta Dried pulses	These items need to be rehydrated and cooked to the required degree. Use enough water to do both.
Stock or sauce mixes Soup or stuffing mixes	Follow instructions on the packaging. Mix with water, stock or milk, then cook.
Bread, scone, pastry or cake mixes	Follow instructions on the packaging. Mix with water, stock, milk and/or eggs, then cook.
Dried milk	Mix with water according to the instructions on the packaging. The regenerated milk can be used in recipes in the same way as fresh milk.

Frozen foods	
Some will need to be defrosted before use. Generally, larger or more solid items will need defrosting. Smaller, less dense items will not. *Do not start to cook food while it is defrosting; wait until there are no ice crystals left at all.*	
Foods	**How to regenerate the food**
Frozen meat, poultry or raw fish	These probably need to be defrosted (check instructions on packaging).
Small items (e.g. breaded fish, burgers, pizza)	Because these items are small or thin, heat will penetrate quickly, so the food will defrost and cook in the same process. Follow instructions on the packaging, including the correct temperature and cooking time.
Uncooked pastry goods (e.g. pies, pasties) and dough products	Many can be cooked from frozen – follow instructions on packaging.
Frozen vegetables	Most of these can be cooked from frozen. For large quantities, defrost before cooking.
Stews, soups, sauces or stocks Large pies	For large quantities, defrost fully before cooking or reheating. There is a risk of contamination if defrosting is not completed. Small quantities, and small pies, can be cooked from frozen.

(continued)

Table 11.2 (continued)

Chilled, pre-prepared foods

Store ready-to-eat food below 5°C until needed.
For other ready-made food, follow cooking instructions on the packaging or ask a chef/supervisor.

Foods	How to regenerate the food
Pre-cooked food (individual meals or multi-portion food)	Reheat thoroughly. Make sure the safe core temperature is reached (see above) and maintained for at least two minutes. If holding for service, do not let the temperature fall below 63°C.
Chilled desserts	Store or display below 5°C until needed.

Canned food

This has been cooked during the canning process, but it may need further cooking when used in a dish.

Foods	How to regenerate the food
Canned food	The texture will already be like a cooked food, so be careful not to overcook. Tomatoes going into a sauce will be fine, but asparagus is more delicate. Foods like baked beans or soup just need reheating. Heat thoroughly. Hold above 63°C until served. Make sure canned salmon or kidney beans are separated from the surrounding liquid before use.
Food from a can that has been opened	Once the can has been opened, treat the food like fresh food, i.e. keep it below 5°C or above 63°C. To refrigerate, remove it from the can. Place in a clean bowl, cover, label and date.

Part-baked products

Food	How to regenerate the food
Bread loaves/rolls Croissants and Danish pastries Brioche	Remove from vacuum packaging and place on baking trays. Finish (e.g. glaze with egg, sprinkle with seeds) as required. Bake according to instructions on the packaging, including the correct temperature and cooking time. Once baked, treat it like fresh bread.
Frozen part-baked items	Most items can be cooked from frozen.

Equipment

A variety of large and small equipment will be used in regenerating pre-prepared foods. These may be traditional pieces of kitchen equipment such as deep fryers and salamanders, or specially designed items such as special regenerating ovens. Service equipment and tools may again be traditional or specially designed for the specific regenerated food. All equipment must be kept clean, hygienic and well maintained.

Quality

As much care with quality must be given to pre-prepared and regenerated food as you would give to traditionally cooked dishes.

- Only regenerate good quality products that have been stored properly, at the correct temperatures and are within their best before or use-by dates. Do not use any items where the consistency is wrong (for example, too wet or too dry), where they smell or taste unpleasant or look in poor/inferior condition.
- Always observe the correct temperatures when cooking, reheating, hot holding and chill holding for each food type. Do not take food out of chilled storage and into the warm kitchen too soon.
- Cook or reheat food as instructed using the required methods, equipment and techniques to achieve the required colour, flavour and texture and appearance.
- Consideration must also be given to extra and accompanying items. Sauces may be part of the dish and would be regenerated together with the main food items, for example as with a stew or curry. In other dishes the sauce or accompaniments may be served separately and could be in separate packaging such as a vacuum pack or plastic tub or bag. Follow instructions with care. Garnishes may need to be adapted so they still enhance the dish but withstand the processing; it is more likely that fresh garnishes would be added at the re-generation point.
- Take care with the garnishing and display so the food is presented is at its best. Keep garnishes and finishes neat, appropriate and consistent. Presentation and serving equipment must be in good condition, completely clean, the right size and appropriate.

Pre-preparation and regeneration of poached eggs

An example of how pre-preparation and regeneration is used in everyday situations in a kitchen would be where poached eggs form part of a menu item. Pre-preparation speeds up service and makes it more efficient.

Pre-preparation

See the recipe in Chapter 7 for additional photos of this process.

1 Prepare a pan of water, add some vinegar (1 tablespoon per litre of water) and bring it to the boil. Once it has boiled reduce the heat of the water to just below boiling point.
2 Break the eggs one at a time into a cup or small bowl and gently slide the egg into the water.

3 Cook until just lightly set (3–3½ minutes).

4 Remove the eggs very carefully with a perforated spoon into a bowl of iced water (this will stop the eggs cooking any further and cool them quickly). Trim the edges of the whites if necessary.

Reconstitution

1 Prepare a pan of water to just below boiling point.

2 Add the egg when needed using a perforated spoon and reheat for 1–1½ minutes.

3 Remove from the pan carefully with the spoon and drain well (eggs could be placed on a clean cloth or kitchen paper to dry them fully).

4 Serve as required.

KEY WORDS

Reheat – to bring food that has been cooked, cooled and then chilled or frozen back to the required serving temperature

Rehydrate – to replace the water content that was previously removed from a food such as dried rice or pasta

Cook – to apply heat to food in order to make it safe to eat, tenderise it and add the required colour, texture and flavour

Defrost – to allow frozen food to return to refrigerator temperature

Test yourself

1 Why must the reheating of chilled meals be done exactly to instructions?

2 If using dry mixes for cakes and scones why should you keep the packaging or written information?

3 Why might it be an advantage for a busy shopping centre restaurant to use some pre-prepared products? What are five products they could use?

4 What makes the following types of food last longer than the fresh equivalent?
   a Dried pasta
   b Frozen cheesecake
   c Canned salmon
   d Dried apricots.

5 If you defrosted some chickens ready for roasting but thought they had an unpleasant smell what would you do?

6 What would be three disadvantages of eating pre-prepared, regenerated food all the time?

7 Why do canned foods not need thorough cooking before you use them?

8 What are three canned items you would serve hot?

9 What are three canned items you would serve cold?

10 Which of these frozen items would you defrost before cooking?

   a Whole chicken

   b Pizza

   c Plaice goujons

   d Whole salmon

   e Leg of lamb

   f Small spring rolls

   g Two portions of soup

   h Large deep lasagne.

11 What are four points you would observe to ensure the quality of regenerated food?

12 What are three cost savings that could be made by using pre-prepared, regenerated food and what are two possible additional costs?

12 Cold food

This chapter covers Unit 112, Cold food preparation.

By the end of this chapter you should be able to:

- State the meal occasions when cold food may be presented
- List the types of food used in cold food preparation
- State the quality points when preparing cold food
- Explain the term hors d'oeuvre
- State examples of salads for cold food preparation
- State types of sandwiches for cold food preparation
- Explain why the presentation of cold foods is important
- Explain how the different styles of service will affect the presentation of cold food
- Identify suitable equipment to present cold food
- List the techniques used to present cold food
- State the quality points when presenting cold food
- State the amount of time cold products can be left ambient.

Preparing cold food

Cold foods are popular and versatile dishes. Well-planned organisation is essential to ensure adequate preparation of cold foods, so that they are assembled with a good workflow and are ready on time. Cold food can be prepared in advance, allowing a large number of people to be served in a short space of time.

Before, during and after being assembled, the foods must be kept in a cool place or refrigerator to minimise the risk of food contamination and growth of bacteria. High standards of personal, food and equipment hygiene must be maintained with all cold work.

Meal occasions when cold food may be presented

Cold foods are served at breakfast, lunch, afternoon tea, high tea and supper. They can be served on their own or with a variety of hot dishes.

Breakfast

Continental breakfast includes croissants, brioche, fresh bread and preserves. It may also include yogurt, plated fresh fruit, cheeses and cold meats (ham, salami).

Snacks

These are foods that are available throughout the day. Examples of typical snack foods are nut selections, dried fruit selections, energy biscuits and fresh fruit.

Lunch

A cold buffet lunch will often include a variety of sandwiches, baguettes, paninis, cold meats, smoked fish, terrines and salads. A variety of cold sweets, sometimes gateaux, and often a cheese board will also be available.

For table service the range of cold starters includes terrines, salads, fish and shellfish cocktails.

Afternoon tea

Afternoon tea is a British tradition. A variety of sandwiches, scones, served with clotted cream, jams, tea, and pastries (for example fruit tartlets, éclairs and fondant fancies) are served.

High tea

High tea often includes items in afternoon tea, but may also feature some more substantial items, such as open sandwiches, cold chicken drumsticks and wraps.

Dinner

Dinner menus may offer cold items as a starter. Some establishments, especially resort hotels and cruise ships, may offer a cold buffet in the evening but this will very often include some hot items.

Supper

Supper menus are usually offered late in the evening. Supper may be offered in some hotels after the normal dinner service, when guests may be offered a selection of cold meat and salads, cold desserts and fresh fruit. Depending on the weather, a hot soup may also be on offer in addition to the cold food. Cold soups such as gazpacho may be served at lunch or dinner, especially in the summer.

Special occasions

Very often in hotels and restaurants chefs are required to plan a special buffet, this may include a theme, for example an opening night for a new film or an awards evening. Here the chef can demonstrate his or her full creativity.

Types of food used

Cold main courses include a variety of food types:
- **Fruit** - For example melon, grapefruit, avocado and orange.
- **Vegetables** - For example potatoes; onions (peeled and finely chopped; sometimes blanched); mushrooms (cooked or left raw); cauliflower (cut into florets; cooked or left raw); carrots (peeled and cut into fine strips or grated); celery (shredded into crescents or diced); cabbage (diced); beetroot (peeled, chopped, sliced or grated); courgettes (peeled, cut into fine slices and served raw in salads); spinach (shredded and used raw in salads).
- **Meats** - A variety of meat can be served cold: ham, beef, pork, salami, chicken, turkey and pâtés, terrines and pies.

> **Professional tip**
> When serving cold meat it is advisable to cook the meat, allow it to cool and serve immediately, this helps the eating quality. Cold meats left in the refrigerator for long periods affect the eating quality and the taste.

- **Fish** – There is a range of types of fish available that can be served cold, including smoked (for example salmon, mackerel or trout), tinned (for example, sardines and tuna), pickled (for example, herring), precooked and fresh (for example prawns and salmon), or frozen (for example, crab or prawns – defrost thoroughly before use).

> **Professional tip**
>
> Serving suggestions for fish:
> - Fresh salmon can be neatly dressed and garnished with lettuce leaves, cucumber slices and quarters of tomato, accompanied by mayonnaise
> - Canned fish can be served simply with lettuce leaves
> - Accompany prawns with mayonnaise and brown bread and butter, or with shells removed and served with shredded lettuce, thin slices of cucumber and/or tomato and mayonnaise of vinaigrette.

- **Salad items** – These include lettuce (for example, friseé, oakleaf, rosso, raddicio, little gem, lollo), cucumber (peeled or unpeeled and cut into thin slices), tomatoes (skins on or peeled, and cut into slices or segments), cress, radishes and peppers (green, orange, red or yellow; cut into fine strips).

> **Professional tip**
>
> To peel a tomato, plunge it into boiling water for ten seconds, then remove and cool under cold running water. Peel.

- **Dairy products** – For example cheese (often served on a cheese board with biscuits or fresh bread and sticks of celery); and eggs (hard-boiled, pickled or Scotch eggs and a variety of quiches can, with self-service salad, provide an appetising and healthy meal).
- **Bread** – A good selection of breads or/and rolls (such as white, brown, wholemeal, wholegrain and speciality) are often served with cold meals.

Quality points when preparing cold food

- **Freshness** – Foods should be bought frequently, stored correctly (usually in refrigerators below 5°C) and checked carefully to ensure that they are in good condition (with no blemishes) and within the use-by date.
- **Smell** – The smell should always be fresh and appetising.
- **Preparation** – Dishes should always be prepared according to recipes and specifications, cut into even-sized portions and trimmed if necessary, with minimum waste.
- **Portions** – Portion sizes will vary according to the type of establishment and the types of customers you are serving. For example, office workers generally require smaller portions than workers who are involved in manual work.
- **Appearance** – Dishes should be neatly dressed and simply garnished.

Hors d'oeuvres

In establishments where lunch and dinner is offered, menus will often include cold hors d'oeuvres, which are served as an appetiser before a main meal. Hors d'oeuvres open the meal and should create a good impression.

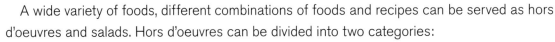

A wide variety of foods, different combinations of foods and recipes can be served as hors d'oeuvres and salads. Hors d'oeuvres can be divided into two categories:

- Single cold food items (for example, smoked salmon, pâté or melon)
- A selection of well-seasoned cold dishes.

Hors d'oeuvre may be served for luncheon, dinner or supper. The wide choice of dishes, their colour appeal and versatility make many items and combinations of items suitable for snacks and salads at any time of day.

Salads

Salads may be made from a wide variety of foods – raw or cooked. They may be served as an accompaniment to hot and cold foods or as dishes in their own right. They can be served for lunch, tea, high tea, dinner, supper and snack meals. Salads can be divided in two types:

- Simple, using one ingredient (for example, tomato, cucumber, green salad, potato salad)
- Mixed or composite, using more than one ingredient (for example, coleslaw, Russian, mixed, Waldorf).

A rice or pasta salad can be a simple salad if it is simply seasoned; it becomes a composite salad when mixed with other ingredients such as diced peppers, sweetcorn, peas, tomatoes or diced cucumber.

Accompaniments (dressings and sauces)

Accompaniments to salads include dressings and cold sauces. There are two basic sauces used with cold food, both of which have many variations. These are:

- Vinaigrette (recipe 6)
- Mayonnaise (recipe 7)

Commercial mayonnaises and vinaigrettes are available in many brands. If you decide to use one of these, always taste it to check that you like it before using it.

▲ Some salads may form part of a composite hors d'oeuvre

> **Professional tip**
> Always finish salads at the last minute, especially when using vinaigrette, so that they remain crisp and fresh.

Sandwiches

Sandwiches are a quick, timesaving snack and are available from many food outlets. The traditional sandwich is made by spreading butter or a butter substitute on two slices of bread, placing a filling on one slice and covering it with the other. The crust may or may not be removed and the sandwich then cut into two or four pieces.

Types of bread

There is a wide variety of breads available (for example, white, brown, wholemeal, granary, seeded) and many bakers will bake bread according to your specification (for instance, tomato, basil, rosemary, walnut and olive) and will slice it ready for use.

Fillings

There is an almost endless variety of

▲ Sandwiches

sandwich fillings that can be used – single food items, such as ham, cheese, or roast beef can be used; alternatively a mix of food items can be used, such as ham and tomato, egg and cress, and chicken and lettuce.

Types of sandwiches

There are many different types of sandwiches available:

- Toasted sandwich
- Club sandwich
- Bookmaker sandwich
- Double- or triple-decker
- Open sandwiches.

Instructions for making these types of sandwich are in the Recipes section later in this chapter: in hotels, dainty, finger-sized sandwiches sprinkled with cress are offered for afternoon teas.

Cold canapés

Canapés are served at a variety of functions, before a formal dinner or a buffet reception and may be offered as an accompaniment to drinks.

Canapés are small items no larger than a fifty pence piece and can be eaten with one bite.

Bases for canapés can be made from a variety of breads (including rye and French breads), pastry (short and puff) and brioche, or with no base at all such as a cherry tomato, scooped out and filled with meat or cream cheese.

▲ A selection of canapés prepared for a function

Examples of canapés include:

- Rye bread topped with a slice of lobster, asparagus tip garnished with fresh herbs
- Rye bread with slices of smoked duck garnished with mango
- Small cooked new potatoes, scooped out and filled with sour cream and chives

- Small choux pastry éclairs filled with liver pâté
- Brioche croutes with apricot chutney and gorgonzola
- Small choux buns filled with prawns in cocktail sauce.

Preparing cold canapés involves a range of skills to make them easy to eat, flavoursome and appetizing. Garnishes need to be cut neatly, and canapés can be cut in a range of creative shapes, including round, rectangular, triangular, square, or boat-shapes.

Canapés are presented in a range of styles on specially designed plates (rounds, squares or rectangles; white and black); they can also be presented on slates or mirrors.

Presenting of cold food

It is important that cold food is presented well so that it is attractive and appealing to customers.

Styles of service

There is a full range of service styles available, which helps to make the food attractive and presentable.

- **Plate service** – Usually food served in restaurants is plated in the kitchen and served on the plate to the customer.
- **Silver service** – food is sent into the restaurant on silver or stainless steel flats, vegetable dishes or other types of service equipment and it is served from these containers by the waiter or waitress using a spoon and fork and placed onto the customer's plate. Very few restaurants today use silver service.
- **Function banquets** – At a formal lunch or dinner the cold food is plated. Where the function is a buffet the food is displayed on a service table.

▲ New ways of presentation show the creative and innovative skills of the chef

- **Finger buffet** – items are generally passed around by food servers on plates. It is important that the food served in a finger buffet is prepared so that items are easily eaten with the fingers.
- **Fork buffet** – food offered should be easily eaten with a fork. The food needs to be prepared for ease of service. It has become fashionable to offer bowl food in a buffet, this is food which can be easily eaten from a china bowl, either with a fork or a spoon.
- **Take away** – food is individually priced in take away containers and does not need to be eaten in the establishment serving it. This is very popular for people who wish to have a working lunch.

Equipment used to present cold food

The type of equipment a chef uses will depend on the style of service. Food may be served on plates or platters, or in bowls or service dishes. It is usually served straight from the display cabinet. If it is to be displayed for a long time, then a chilled display cabinet is required. For example, in a salad bar in a restaurant all the salads would be held in a chilled display cabinet.

Sliver and stainless steel salvers are used to present cold food on a cold buffet table. Many establishments today serve food on a range of plain white plates of varying shapes and sizes.

▲ Plain white plates for serving cold food

For take away service there is a variety of attractive containers now available in the market; all food must be clearly labelled and dated, and if possible, nutritional content included.

Presentation techniques for cold food

The following points are very important when preparing the ingredients; a chef must be able to master these skills as they will greatly enhance the quality of the dishes.

- **Peeling** – some vegetables need to be peeled; this must be done carefully so as not to remove too much of the flesh. For example, when peeling a courgette it is important to carefully remove the skin enough to expose the green surface; if peeling too deep then the courgette will be white.
- **Cutting and chopping** – careful cutting and chopping enhances the presentation, texture and mouth feel and flavour of the dish. Finely chopped herbs in a dish will greatly enhance the flavour; if they are roughly chopped they will not contribute so well.
- **Carving and portioning meats** – doing this correctly is an important skill and makes sure the correct portion control is achieved to avoid wastage. Good carving enhances the presentation of a dish; in some cases, skilled carving is done in a restaurant in front of customers.
- **Slicing** – sliced foods include smoked salmon, tomatoes and cucumber. Cucumber sliced too thickly can be very difficult to eat; thinly sliced cucumber looks better and is easier to eat.
- **Shredding** – many vegetables are shredded, including white cabbage when used to make coleslaw and red cabbage for pickling or to use raw in a salad. Lettuces are also finely shredded for shellfish cocktails. Finely shredded vegetables provide good texture and are easy to eat. Rough cut shredded vegetables are difficult to eat and do not blend with other ingredients very well.
- **Portioning** – each customer's portion should be the same size and have the same proportions. Correct portioning also helps with planning and costing.
- **Accompaniments and dressings** – Accompaniments and dressings enhance cold food preparation, they add flavour, moisture and a contrasting texture, and improve the overall eating quality.

- A good vinaigrette will improve many salad items. A number of different herbs may be added to the vinaigrette; different spices are used to make the cold dishes more interesting.
  - Mayonnaise is used as an accompaniment or as a dressing.
  - Crème fraîche may be used in place of yogurt.
  - In some salads soured cream is used.

- **Garnishing and presentation**– this makes dishes more attractive and appealing. Cold dishes are garnished in a number of ways: using a range of mixed leaves, artistically cut lemon, lime, tomato, radish, spring onion. Garnishing should include a balance of colour, flavour, and texture.

- **Seasoning** – cold food can be seasoned by using fresh herbs and spices; avoid using salt for health reasons.

▲ Garnishing of cold dishes: an example

> **Professional tip**
> Use a variety of fresh herbs to enhance the flavour of traditional salads and cold dishes, like basil, tarragon, coriander, rosemary, chives, parsley.

Food safety and quality for cold food presentation

- At all times maintain the highest standard of food safety when preparing and serving cold food. Separate the raw and cooked items to avoid cross-contamination.
- All equipment and utensils must be kept clean and in good condition to prevent contamination of food.
- Food for cold presentation must be of the best quality and if cooked must be prepared and cooked adequately following the recipe and temperature requirements precisely. Do not reheat any cooked food once it has been on display, as this is a dangerous practice. Allow to cool and serve.
- All food items must be stored in a clean tidy refrigerator, labelled, covered and dated. Remove the covering at the last minute before service. Ideally serve straight from the refrigerator to avoid any possible contamination. Counters, utensils and serving dishes must be scrupulously clean.
- Remember it is a legal requirement under the Food Safety Act that ambient food is served within 4 hours. Food not served after this time may be unsafe and therefore should be thrown away and must not be offered to customers or staff.

> **Professional tip**
> Remember, the quality of the food is assessed by the customer by colour, texture, flavour and the portion size.

Test yourself

1 Name three meal occasions where cold food items can be served.
2 What are the differences between an open, a closed and a club sandwich?
3 Name two simple salads.
4 Name two compound salads.
5 Give four examples of cold hors d'oeuvres that could appear on a menu.
6 When presenting cold dishes, apart from presentation and garnish what else needs to be considered?
7 What is the appropriate presentation for cold food on a:
   a Finger buffet
   b Canapé reception.
8 Name the types of service equipment that can be used to present food.
9 What is the maximum time a cold buffet can be left for presentation at a room temperature?

Cold food recipes

Recipe 1 — Toasted sandwiches

Toasted sandwiches can be made in two ways.

1 Add the filling between the two slices of hot, freshly buttered toast.
2 Use an item of equipment called a sandwich toaster. Put the filling between two slices of bread and toast the whole sandwich in the sandwich toaster. Some toasters will seal the sandwich, remove the crusts and cut the sandwich in half.

Recipe 2 — Club sandwiches

1 Butter three slices of hot toast.

2 On the first slice, place slices of grilled, crispy streaky bacon.

3 Place slices of tomato and lettuce on the bacon.

4 Put the second slice of toast on top of this and spread mayonnaise on it. Layer sliced cooked chicken breast over the top.

5 Add slices of hard-boiled egg.

6 Finally, put the third slice of toast on top. Then press down carefully on the sandwich, make it as compact as possible, and secure it with cocktail sticks.

7 Cut it in halves or quarters. Serve with potato crisps.

Try something different

Use three or four slices of bread, toasted or untoasted, to make other double-decker and triple-decker sandwiches.

Recipe 3

Bookmaker sandwich

Place an underdone thin sirloin steak between two slices of toast made from a bloomer loaf.

 Note: This kind of steak is known as a minute steak because it only needs a minute over a fierce heat to cook.

Recipe 4

Open sandwiches

To prepare open sandwiches, butter a slice of any type of bread and top this with a variety of foods, such as:

- Smoked salmon, lettuce, potted shrimps, slice of lemon
- Cold roast beef, sliced tomato, gherkin fan
- Shredded lettuce, slices of hard-boiled egg, cucumber slices and mayonnaise
- Pickled herring, slices of hard-boiled egg, sprinkled with chopped gherkins, capers and parsley.

Recipe 5 — Soused herring or mackerel

Ingredients	4 portions	10 portions
Herrings or mackerel	2	5
Salt and pepper		
Button onions	25 g	60 g
Carrots, peeled and fluted	25 g	60 g
Bay leaf	½	1 ½
Peppercorns	6	12
Thyme	1 sprig	2 sprigs
Vinegar	60 ml	150 ml

Get ready to cook

1 Clean, scale and fillet the fish.
2 Peel and wash the onion and carrots, and cut into neat, thin rings.

Cooking

1 Wash the fish fillets well and season with salt and pepper.
2 Roll up with the skin outside.
3 Place in an earthenware dish.
4 Blanch the onion and carrots for 2–3 minutes.
5 Add to the fish with the remainder of the ingredients.
6 Cover with greaseproof paper or aluminium foil and cook in a moderate oven for 15–20 minutes.
7 Allow to cool.
8 Place in a dish with the onion and carrot.

Serving suggestion

Garnish with picked parsley, dill or chives.

 Note: this dish is also known as pickled herring.

Recipe 6 · Vinaigrette

Ingredients	4–6 portions
Olive oil	3–6 tbsp
Vinegar	1–2 tbsp
French mustard	1 tsp
Salt	1 tsp

Preparing the dish

1 Combine vinegar with the mustard and salt.

2 Slowly whisk in the oil.

Try something different

You could use:

- English in place of French mustard
- chopped fresh herbs, chives, parsley, tarragon, and so on
- different oils, such as sesame oil
- different vinegars, or lemon juice instead of vinegar.

▲ Vinaigrette video,
http://bit.ly/XYuqis

Activity

Suggest two more variations to a basic vinaigrette.

Recipe 7 · Mayonnaise

Ingredients	8 portions
Egg yolks, pasteurised (recommended)	3
Vinegar or lemon juice	2 tsp
Small pinch of salt	
English or continental mustard	½ tsp
A mild-flavoured oil such as corn oil or the lightest olive oil	250 ml
Water, boiling	1 tsp

Note: Because of the risk of salmonella food poisoning, it is strongly recommended that pasteurised egg yolks are used.

Preparing the dish

1 Place yolks, vinegar, salt and mustard in the bowl of a food mixer.

2 Whisk until thoroughly mixed.

3 Continue to whisk vigorously and start to add the oil – this needs to be done slowly.

4 Keep whisking until all the oil has been added.

5 Whisk in the boiling water.

6 Taste and correct seasoning if necessary.

Try something different

Add:

- fresh chopped herbs
- garlic juice – peel a
  clove garlic and press
  it using a garlic press
- thick tomato juice.

Note: If the mayonnaise becomes too thick while you are making it, whisk in a little of water or vinegar.

Mayonnaise may separate, turn or curdle for several reasons:
- you have added the oil too quickly
- the oil is too cold
- you have not whisked enough
- the egg yolks were stale and weak.

To reconstitute (bring it back together) either:
- Take a basin, pour 1 teaspoon of boiling water and gradually but vigorously whisk in the curdled sauce a little at a time
- In a clean basin, whisk a fresh egg yolk with ½ teaspoon of cold water then gradually whisk in the curdled sauce.

Activity

1 Suggest three further variations.
2 Deliberately curdle some mayonnaise and reconstitute it.

Salad recipes

Recipe 8 Potato salad

Ingredients	4 portions	10 portions
Potatoes	200 g	500 g
Vinaigrette	1 tbsp	2½ tbsp
Mayonnaise, natural yoghurt or crème fraîche	125 ml	300 ml
Onion or chive (optional)	10 g	25 g
Parsley or mixed fresh herbs	½ tsp	1 ½ tsp
Salt		

Get ready to cook

1 Wash and peel the potatoes (or cook in skins and then peel).
2 Cook potatoes by boiling or steaming.
3 Cut potatoes into ½–1 cm dice or slices.
4 If desired, blanch the onion by placing in boiling water for 2–3 minutes, cooling and draining. (This will reduce its harshness.) Then chop it up.
5 Chop the herbs.
6 Prepare the vinaigrette (see Recipe 6).

Preparing the dish

1 Put the potatoes into a bowl and sprinkle on the vinaigrette.
2 Mix in the mayonnaise, onion and chive.
3 Finally, chop and mix in the parsley or other herbs and season to taste.

Try something different

At the end, add chopped mint or chopped hard-boiled egg.

Recipe 9 Vegetable salad

Ingredients	4 portions	10 portions
Carrots	100 g	250 g
French beans	50 g	125 g
Turnip	50 g	125 g
Peas	50 g	125 g
Vinaigrette	1 tbsp	2–3 tbsp
Mayonnaise or natural yoghurt	125 ml	300 ml
Salt		

Get ready to cook

1 Peel and wash the carrots and turnips, and cut into neat dice (macédoine).
2 Top and tail the beans and cut into ½ cm pieces.
3 Prepare the vinaigrette (see Recipe 6).

Preparing the dish

1 Cook the carrots, beans and turnips separately in lightly salted water, then refresh and drain well.
2 Cook, drain and refresh the peas. Drain well.
3 Mix all the vegetables in a basin with the vinaigrette and then add and mix in the mayonnaise or yoghurt.
4 Taste and correct the seasoning if necessary.

Try something different

Potato can be used in place of turnip.

A little of any or a mixture of the following can be chopped and added: chives, parsley, chervil, tarragon.

Activity

Suggest two or three more ingredients that could be added.

Recipe 10 Beetroot salad

Ingredients

Beetroot (quantity as required)

Vinaigrette, if desired

 Get ready to cook

Wash the beetroot.

Prepare the vinaigrette (see Recipe 6).

Preparing the dish

1 Cook the beetroot in their skin in a steamer or gently simmering water until tender.
2 Cool and test by rubbing the skin between your fingers and thumb. When cooked, the skin should peel (rub) off easily.
3 Cut into ½ cm dice and either serve plain or lightly sprinkled with vinaigrette.

Try something different

Sprinkle with chopped onion, or chive and parsley, or other fresh herbs.

Recipe 11 Tomato salad

Ingredients	4 portions	10 portions
Tomatoes	200 g	500 g
Lettuce leaves		
Vinaigrette	10 g	25 g
Onions (sliced) or chives (optional)		
Finely chopped parsley and/or fresh mixed herbs		

 Get ready to cook

1 Wash and dry the tomatoes.
2 Remove the stem eyes.
3 Leave the skins on, or peel by plunging them into boiling water for ten seconds, then removing them and cooling them under cold running water.
4 Slice the onion and, if desired, blanch it in boiling water.

 Note: The amount of lettuce required will depend on type and size.

Preparing the dish

1 Slice the tomatoes.
2 Arrange them neatly on washed, well-drained lettuce leaves.
3 Sprinkle on the vinaigrette and the onion.
4 Chop the parsley or other herbs and sprinkle these on.

Recipe 12 Coleslaw

Ingredients	4 portions	10 portions
Cabbage, white or Chinese	200 g	500 g
Carrot	50 g	125 g
Onion (optional)	25 g	60 g
Mayonnaise or natural yoghurt	125 ml	300 ml
Salt		

Get ready to cook

1 Trim off the outer cabbage leaves.
2 Wash and peel the carrot.
3 Finely shred the onion, and blanch and refresh it to remove the harsh taste (optional).

Preparing the dish

1 Cut the cabbage into quarters and cut out the hard centre stalk.
2 Wash the cabbage, finely shred it and drain it well.

3 Cut the carrot into fine strips (known as julienne – for large quantities this can be done in a food processor).
4 Mix the vegetables together.

5 Stir in the mayonnaise.
6 Taste and season very lightly with salt, only if necessary.

Activity

Prepare batches of coleslaw:

1 without the onion
2 with the onion
3 with the onion blanched.

In a group, taste and assess the different coleslaws and note down your findings.

Recipe 13 Rice salad

Ingredients	4 portions	10 portions
Tomatoes	100 g	250 g
Long grain rice, cooked	50 g	125 g
Vinaigrette	1 tbsp	2 ½ tbsp
Salt		

Get ready to cook

1 Cook the rice.

2 Cook the peas.

3 Skin the tomatoes.

4 Prepare the vinaigrette (see Recipe 6).

Preparing the dish

1 Cut the tomatoes into quarters, remove the seeds and cut into ½ cm dice.

2 Mix the tomatoes with the rice, peas and vinaigrette.

3 Taste and correct the seasoning.

Recipe 14 Green salad

- There are a large number of salad leaves available, including different varieties of lettuce. You can use whichever you choose, or a mixture of several.

- Green salad is a mixture of salad leaves, well washed and dried, served on a plate or in a bowl with vinaigrette served separately.

- Tossed green salad is the same as green salad but with the vinaigrette added. It is tossed in a salad bowl using two salad servers, to coat the leaves in the dressing.

- Tossed green salad with herbs is a tossed salad with chopped fresh herbs mixed in.

Recipe 15 Warm Asian bean salad with satay dressing

Ingredients	4 portions	10 portions
Butternut squash, peeled, deseeded and cut into 2 cm dice	250 g	625 g
Broad beans, cooked and skinned	240 g	600 g
Clear honey	1 tbsp	2 tbsp
Lime, grated zest and juice	½	2
Peanut satay	80 g	200 g
Coriander, chopped	6	15
Radishes, thinly sliced	4	10
Roasted cashew nuts, roughly chopped	50 g	125 g

Get ready to cook

1 Peel and deseed the butternut squash and cut into 2 cm dice.
2 Cook and shell the broad beans.
3 Wash and slice the radishes.
4 Roughly chop the spring onions.
5 Roast and chop the cashew nuts.

Note: Satay is peanut sauce. You can buy this ready-made or you can make it yourself. To make it, add the following ingredients to a food processor and blend until smooth:
● 4 tbsp peanut butter
● 2 tbsp sesame oil
● 1 tbsp soy sauce
● 1 tbsp honey
● 1 tbsp milk or water
● 1 garlic clove, peeled and crushed/chopped
● ½ lime, juice only

Preparing the dish

1 Blanch the butternut squash in boiling water for 3–4 minutes and drain.
2 Place the butternut squash in a large bowl with the cooked broad beans.
3 Prepare the dressing by mixing together the honey, lime juice and peanut satay.
4 Roughly chop the coriander and add this, along with the chopped spring onions, sliced radish and cashew nuts, to the squash and broad beans.
5 Mix in half the dressing.

Serving suggestion

Serve on plates, on a bed of mixed salad leaves. Drizzle over the remainder of the dressing and serve.

Recipe
16
Asian rice salad

Ingredients	4 portions	10 portions
Flat-leaf parsley, chopped	2 tbsp	5 tbsp
Coriander, chopped	2 tbsp	5 tbsp
Mint, chopped	1 tbsp	2 ½ tbsp
Garlic, finely chopped	1 clove	4 cloves
Ginger, finely chopped	2 cm	5 cm
Reduced salt soy sauce	2 ½ tbsp	6 tbsp
Lime juice	1 tbsp	2 ½ tbsp
Honey	1 tbsp	2 ½ tbsp
Sunflower oil	4 tbsp	10 tbsp
Basmati rice, cooked	400 g	1 kg
Courgettes	1	3
Peas, lightly cooked	125 g	300 g
Spring onions	2	5

Get ready to cook

1 Lightly cook the peas.
2 Cook the rice lightly in salted water. Drain and cool.
3 Very finely dice the courgette and finely slice the spring onion, cutting on the slant – for this salad the pieces must be small.
4 Peel and finely chop the garlic and ginger.
5 Roughly chop the herbs.

Preparing the dish

1 Blitz the herbs, garlic, ginger, soy sauce, lime juice and honey in a food processor.
2 Slowly add the oil to create a glossy mixture.
3 To the rice add the courgettes, peas and spring onions and combine.
4 Stir through the dressing.

Recipe 17 — Pesto pasta salad

Ingredients	4 portions	10 portions
Green pesto	70 g	200 g
Lemon juice	1 tbsp	3 tbsp
Reduced-fat mayonnaise	2 ½ tbsp	6 tbsp
Penne pasta	400 g	1 kg
Extra virgin olive oil	1 tbsp	2 tbsp
Cooked chicken breasts	1 – 1 ½	3
Parsley, chopped	1 tbsp	5 tbsp

Preparing the dish

1 Mix the pesto, lemon juice and mayonnaise together and stir into the pasta.

2 Cut the chicken into thin slices and combine with the pasta.

3 Chop the parsley and stir through the pasta.

Try something different

If you leave out the chicken and mayonnaise this can be served as a simple pasta salad with pesto.

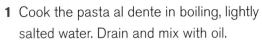

Get ready to cook

1 Cook the pasta al dente in boiling, lightly salted water. Drain and mix with oil.

2 Cook the chicken breasts by poaching, steaming, shallow frying or roasting. Remove the skin.

3 Slice the remaining onion, spring onions and chilli.

Recipe 18 — Green bean salad

Ingredients	4 portions	10 portions
Green beans	200 g	500 g
Vinaigrette	1 tbsp	2 ½ tbsp
Onion, if required	15 g	40 g
Chives		
Salt		

Preparing the dish

1 Combine all ingredients.

2 Taste and season as necessary.

Try something different

- This recipe can also be made using any type of dried bean. Many dried beans are available ready cooked in cans.

- Make a three-bean salad using three different types of dried bean, such as red kidney, black-eyed, flageolet.

Get ready to cook

1 Cook the green beans.

2 Chop and blanch the onions.

3 Prepare the vinaigrette (see Recipe 6).

Recipe 19 Greek salad

Ingredients	4 portions	10 portions
Large tomatoes – preferably vine tomatoes	2	6
Cucumber, sliced	½	1
Feta cheese, diced	150 g	400 g
Olive oil	60 ml	150 ml
Lemon juice	2 tbsp	6 tbsp
Salt and black pepper		
Oregano, to garnish	1 level tbsp	3 level tbsp
Pitted black olives, to garnish	6	15

Get ready to cook

1 Wash the tomatoes and cut them in half lengthwise. Cut out the core, and cut each half into four wedges.
2 Wash and slice the cucumber.
3 Dice the feta cheese.

 Note: If you are not keen on the idea of eating olives, just try them and see what you think. They go particularly well with the other flavour and texture of this salad.

Preparing the dish

1 Put the tomatoes into a large salad bowl and add the cucumber and feta cheese.
2 Spoon over the olive oil and lemon juice.
3 Season lightly with salt and black pepper. Go easy on the salt, as feta cheese is already salty!
4 Toss gently to mix.

Serving suggestions

Sprinkle the salad with fresh oregano and decorate with olives.

Recipe 20 **Garden salad**

Ingredients	4 portions	10 portions
Medium lettuce, crispy variety like iceberg or cos, torn into pieces	½	1
Carrot, cut into fine julienne	1	2
Red cabbage, chopped finely	125 g	350 g
Radish, thinly sliced	2	8
Onions, thinly sliced	1	3
Red pepper, thinly sliced	1	2
Celery, thinly sliced	1 stick	3 sticks
Frozen peas, cooked	250 g	500 g

Get ready to cook

Bring the peas to the boil and cook until just tender. Drain and refresh.

Preparing the dish

1 Wash and dry the lettuce and then tear into pieces.
2 Cut the carrots into julienne and finely slice the rest of the vegetables.
3 Combine the ingredients in large bowl with the peas.

Serving suggestions

Drizzle with a salad dressing of your own choice, such as vinaigrette, or serve plain.

Try something different

- This works well with bean sprouts for added crunch.
- Add flakes of canned tuna to make an interesting tuna salad.
- Add beans such as chickpeas or butter beans for a different texture.
- It also works well with 300g (125 g) of feta cheese.

Activity

Prepare six salads and present them in three or four different ways.

Glossary

Accident an unplanned incident may cause injury.

Adapted change made so it is more suitable.

Additive something added to food to improve or preserve it.

Allergy a substance that the body has an adverse reaction to, where the immune system reacts to certain types of food.

Antioxidant molecules that help prevent cancer cells forming in the body.

Assembly point the place where people should stand when they have been evacuated from a building.

Balanced diet a balanced diet contains sufficient amounts of fibre and the various nutrients (carbohydrates, fats, proteins, vitamins, and minerals) to ensure good health. Food should also provide the appropriate amount of energy and adequate amounts of water.

Best before date for non-perishable foods that do not need refrigeration. It is best practice not to use after this date.

Blanquette a white stew; the sauce is made by thickening the cooking liquor at the end of the cooking process.

Calorific content the number of calories in a particular item.

Canning suitable food is placed in the can, sealed and heated under pressure to very high temperatures to kill any micro-organisms that may be present in the food. The cans are then cooled and labelled.

Catering the provision of food and drink.

Chef's skullcap a close-fitting hat.

Cholesterol a substance produced by the body which can clog the arteries to the heart. Not all cholesterol is bad; some types of cholesterol are important for the nervous system and other body functions.

Circuit breaker a safety device that breaks the flow of electricity in emergency or in case of electrical overload.

Cleaning schedule a planned programme of cleaning areas and equipment.

Colleagues the people you work with.

Commercial sector providing hospitality and catering is the main purpose of the organisation.

Commitment determined and keen to do something.

Compensation a payment that may be made because of accident or injury.

Condensation moisture and water droplets produced by steam.

Contact dermatitis occurs in some people when their skin reacts to certain chemicals or foods they work with. It can be controlled by avoiding direct contact between the substances or food and the skin, for example by wearing gloves.

Contamination anything in food that should not be there. Contaminated food could cause harm or may just be unpleasant.

Contract of employment a formal agreement document between employer and employee.

Control measure something put in place to make a hazard as safe as possible.

Cook to apply heat to food in order to make it safe to eat, tenderise it and add the required colour, texture and flavour.

Corrosive action that breaks a material down, such as rusting.

COSHH Control of Substances Hazardous to Health; this is legislation to ensure safe use of chemicals.

Courteous considerate and polite.

Critical Control Point a point at which something could go wrong and a control measure could be put in place to keep the hazard under control.

Cross-contamination when contaminants are moved from one place to another, for example, bacteria from raw food being transferred to cooked food.

Cultural ethnic or social beliefs and customs.

Customer focused everything is planned and carried out with the customer in mind.

Danger zone the temperature range where bacterial multiplication could take place: 5°C–63°C.

Debris rubbish, waste and unwanted items.

Defrost to allow frozen food to return to refrigerator temperature.

Dependable responsible and loyal.

Dermatitis a skin problem causing inflammation of the skin, making it red, scaly and itchy.

Deterioration losing quality and breaking down.

Diabetes a medical condition where the body cannot regulate the glucose levels in the body.

Disinfection bringing any pathogenic bacteria present to a safe level.

Due diligence proving that you have completed the necessary procedures to ensure food safety.

EHO/EHP Environmental Health Officer (now often called Environmental Health Practitioner). This person is employed by the local authority to enforce health and safety (and food safety) standards in their area, but also to offer help, advice and training on these matters.

Ejection something being thrown out at high speed.

E-learning learning using online resources.

Electric shock when a current of electricity passes through the body.

Electronic communication includes a wide range of computer and mobile phone systems. Some electronic systems are designed specifically for hospitality businesses.

Enhancer something added to food that is considered to be beneficial to health, for example extra protein, vitamins or minerals.

Environmental your surroundings or location.

Evacuate leave the building.

Evacuation route the route designated for leaving the building quickly.

Exceed go further than expected.

Extraction (kitchen) removal of stale air, steam and condensation.

FIFO first in-first out, referring to using older food stocks before new deliveries.

Food safety putting measures in place to ensure food is safe to eat and will not cause illness.

Food spoilage food deteriorating, usually detected by taste, smell, appearance, texture, colour and so on.

Fricassée a white stew; the sauce is thickened as part of the cooking process.

Fuel gels flammable gels often used to heat food service equipment.

Harassment behaviour, including bullying, that makes someone feel threatened or uncomfortable.

Hazard something with the potential to cause harm.

Hazard analysis identifying all the possible hazards and putting in measures to prevent them causing harm.

High-risk areas areas that could be sources of contamination, for example raw meat preparation areas.

Hospitality to be hospitable, to look after people by providing services such as food, drink and accommodation.

Immune system a system of the body that fights against disease.

Impact being hit by something or colliding with it.

Improvement notice a business is given a set amount of time to improve on certain issues highlighted.

Intolerance the body reacts to certain types of food. This does not involve the immune system, and therefore produces less dramatic symptoms.

Intoxication being under the influence of alcohol or other substance.

Irritant can cause a reaction or irritation of the skin.

Jargon terms, abbreviations or descriptions used by a particular group.

Legal requirement something that must be done by law.

Low-risk areas where clean processes are carried out.

Management staff staff who monitor and develop overall quality standards, making sure that all staff deliver to the required standard expected by customers. Managers are also responsible for compliance with legislative requirements. Senior managers are also responsible for budgeting, finance and planning for the future.

Mandatory something that you must do or must use.

Manual handling lifting of heavy or awkward items.

Mirepoix a mixture of roughly cut onions and carrots, a sprig of thyme and a bay leaf, used as a base for certain dishes, e.g. stews.

Navarin a brown lamb stew; the sauce is thickened as part of the cooking process.

Negligent not taking care or ignoring something.

Noise often unwanted sound that can be loud.

Nutrient a chemical providing nourishment and purpose in the diet.

NVQ National Vocational Qualification. Qualifications that are delivered and assessed in the workplace and assessed by observation in the workplace and by a portfolio.

Obesity a medical condition in which excess body fat has accumulated to the extent that it may have an adverse effect on health, leading to reduced life expectancy and/or increased health problems.

Obstacle a hazard or something in the way.

Occupational work related.

Occupational health care of employees' health while at work.

Operational procedure the standards set by an employer for the way things must be done.

Operational staff staff who work in practical areas.

Oxidising reacts in the presence of oxygen.

PAT Portable Appliance Testing. This usually involves a qualified electrician testing the electrical equipment in an area such as a kitchen to ensure it is safe to use.

Pathogenic bacteria micro-organisms that could multiply in food and cause food poisoning.

Personal hygiene keeping yourself clean and hygienic to avoid contaminating food.

Pest a creature that could enter food premises, cause damage and contaminate food

PPE Personal Protective Equipment (and clothing). This is equipment or clothing to protect you from hazards at work. In a kitchen it may include a full chef's uniform but also items such as disposable gloves, masks and safety shoes.

Preservative something added to make food last longer.

Prioritising putting the most important tasks first.

Productivity the amount of work that can be completed in a certain time.

Prohibition something you must not do, not use or an area you must not go into.

Prohibition notice a business is unsafe to operate and can be closed down.

Pronunciation the way you say words and speak.

Public service sector the provision of hospitality is not the main purpose of the company. Examples include schools and hospitals.

Reheat to bring food that has been cooked, cooled and then chilled or frozen back to the required serving temperature.

Rehydrate to replace the water content that was previously removed from a food such as dried rice or pasta.

Reliable trustworthy and consistent.

Report recording something, often in writing. An incident or accident would need to be reported.

Revenue money received (income).

Risk the likelihood of someone being harmed by a hazard.

Risk assessment identifying hazards and risks in a workplace.

Safety shoes strong, enclosed shoes with reinforced toecaps to protect the feet from heavy or sharp objects and hot liquids.

Sanitise cleaning and disinfecting together with one product.

Septic cuts, burns and so on infected with pathogenic bacteria. They are often wet with a white or yellow appearance.

Spore a state some bacteria can achieve to survive high temperatures and disinfection.

Status someone's seniority or position.

Supervisory staff staff who oversee and supervise the work of the operational staff and are concerned with day-to-day issues and problems that may occur.

Time management planning your work so you use the available time well.

Toque a traditional tall chef's hat.

Toxic poisonous and harmful.

Toxin a poison produced by some bacteria.

Use-by date these are on perishable foods that need refrigeration, and the date must be observed by law.

Velouté a basic white sauce made using stock and a blond roux.

Voice projection making your voice carry a little further so you can be heard by more people.

VRQ Vocational Related Qualification. Full-time courses delivered in college and assessed by written and practical assessment.

Workflow efficient and logical methods of work.

Workplace the location where most of your work is completed; it could also include a different site, off-site functions or work vehicles.

Index

A page number in **bold** indicates a recipe.

Practical Cookery for the Level 1 Diploma

Practical Cookery for the Level 1 Diploma

Practical Cookery for the Level 1 Diploma